THE INDIVIDUAL EMPLOYMENT RIGHTS PRIMER

THE INDIVIDUAL EMPLOYMENT RIGHTS PRIMER

Kurt H. Decker

Baywood Publishing Company, Inc.
AMITYVILLE, NEW YORK

Copyright © 1991, Baywood Publishing Company, Inc., Amityville, New York. All rights reserved. No part of this book may be reproduced in any form, by mimeograph or any other means, without permission in writing from the publisher. Printed in the United States of America.

Library of Congress Catalog Number:91-21508
ISBN Number: 0-89503-089-6 (paper)

© 1991 Baywood Publishing Company, Inc.

Library of Congress Cataloging-in-Publication-Data

Main entry under title:
Decker, Kurt H.
   The individual employment rights primer / Kurt H. Decker.
    p. cm.
   Includes index.
   ISBN 0-89503-089-6 (pbk.)
   1. Employee rights--United States. 2. Labor laws and legislation--United States. 3. Privacy, Right of—United States. I. Title.
KF3457.D434   1991
344. 73'01—dc20
[347.3041]   91-21508
                                                                     CIP

Dedication

For Hilary, Christian, Allison, and
all who pursue fairness, understanding,
and cooperation in the workplace.

Preface

One of the most rapidly evolving areas of law involves individual employment rights. Individual employment rights has no clearly defined boundary. It encompasses a multitude of employment statutes and court decisions. It finds its support in constitutional law and has developed as part of specialized employment law areas involving record keeping and disclosure, labor relations, health and safety, labor standards, fair employment practices, etc.

This book consolidates these fragmented individual employment rights into a centralized reference source. It is designed to meet four needs. First, it brings together into one source the broad spectrum of individual employment rights that is contained in federal and state statutes, court decisions, administrative agency findings, and arbitration awards.

Second, individual employment rights are examined in general and specialized terms. This is necessary to obtain an overall understanding of the legal issues that may potentially arise.

Third, this book is intended to be theoretical as well as practical. It is meant to be used by the researcher, practitioner, or student as a beginning point in understanding this area.

Fourth, this book can be used as a supplementary text for students using M. Rothstein, A. Knapp and L. Liebman, *Employment Law: Cases and Materials*, 2d Ed., Mineola, New York (Foundation Press, 1991) or M. Finkin, A. Goldman and C. Summers, *Legal Protection for the Individual Employee*, Saint Paul, Minn., (West Publishing Company 1989).

Chapter 1 discusses the developing law of individual employment rights. Chapters 2 through 7 cover specific individual employment rights that arise during hiring, at the workplace, and outside the workplace by examining issues present in: 1) initial employment contacts; 2) employment data verification; 3) records; 4) medical concerns; 5) information collection; 6) personal workplace concerns; and 7) those outside the workplace. Chapter 8 reviews litigation concerns.

Kurt H. Decker

Acknowledgments

Little in life is a solitary undertaking. Much is a culmination of other people's thoughts and efforts. In preparing this text, many individuals either provided opportunities or shared their knowledge. Among these were Professor Paul H. Sanders for instilling the recognition for conflict resolution's importance in employment law, Dr. Harry Kershen for his assistance in recognizing the importance of individual employment rights for a new Journal, Dr. Edwin M. Wagner for encouraging the sharing of knowledge through teaching, Professor Robert N. Covington for cultivating my interest in employment law, Arbitrator John M. Skonier who over the years always offered his friendship and encouragement to continue research, writing, and teaching, and Ronald L. Williams, Esquire for his thoughts and friendship. Above all, this project would not have been undertaken without the foresight of Stuart Cohen, President of Baywood Publishing Company, Inc.

Finally, I am appreciative of those individuals at Baywood and Stevens & Lee who labored over this text's physical preparation. Among these individuals were Marcie L. Silfies, who maintained all the communications with Baywood and for the *Journal of Individual Employment Rights*, Bobbi Olszewski, Evelyn M. Stepp, Lauren K. Lorah, Jolene R. Kaufman, Niki Bartnicki, Catherine A. Bestwick, Nancy D. A. Cawley, Bonnie J. DeCarlo, Donna L. Guidara, Donna L. Heiden, Joan M. Lease, Alecia M. Lilley, Stephanie Manning, Kathleen O'Connor, Judie L. Riddell, Karen Shuker, and Linda A. Zielinski.

Contents

Chapter 1
The Developing Law of Individual
Employment Rights 1
    The Employment Relationship 2
    The At-Will Employment Relationship 2
    Employment Privacy 5
    Exercising Individual Employment Rights 7
    Employee Concerns 9
    Employer Concerns 11
    Legislative Action 12
    Judicial Responses 14
    Employment Information Collection 16
    Employment Information Maintenance and
        Internal Use 18
    Employment Information Access 19
    Employment Information Disclosure to Third Parties . . . 20
    Employee Lifestyles At and Outside the Workplace 21
    Avoiding Individual Employment Rights' Litigation . . . 22

Chapter 2
Hiring Guidelines 27
    Initial Employment Contacts 28
        Advertisements 29
        Applications 30
        Interviews 34

Employment Data Verification	40
Credit Checks	40
Arrest Records	42
Criminal Convictions	44
Fingerprinting	47
Photographs	48
Immigration Requirements	49
Reference Checks	51
Employment Testing	54
Medical Screening	54
Genetic Screening	56
Blood Testing	59
Skill Testing	59
Polygraph Examinations	64
Honesty Testing	67
Handwriting Analysis	70
Negligent Hiring	71

Chapter 3
Employment Records ... 73
    Employment Records ... 73
    Medical Records ... 79

Chapter 4
Medical Concerns ... 85
    Physical Examinations ... 85
    Health and Safety Complaints ... 86
    Smoking ... 88
    Employee Assistance Programs ... 91
    Alcohol and Drug Abuse ... 92
    Human Immunodeficiency Virus (HIV) ... 106
    Sterilization ... 118

Chapter 5
Information Collection Procedures ... 121
    Searches ... 121
    Monitoring ... 128
    Surveillance ... 132
        Union Meeting Surveillance ... 133
        Workplace Surveillance ... 134
        Employee Manipulation ... 136

CONTENTS / xv

    Camera Surveillance 137
    Electronic Surveillance 137
    Literature Solicitation and Distribution 138

Chapter 6
Employee Concerns at the Workplace 141
    Jury or Witness Duty 141
    Voting Time 142
    Whistleblowing 143
    Dress and Grooming Codes 143
    Spousal Policies 145
    Nepotism 150
    Third Party Representation 152
    Performance Evaluations 157
    Name Changes 161
    Identification Tags 161
    Religious Accommodation 162
    Privacy Misconduct 162
    Language Requirements 164
    Sexual Harassment 164
    Video Display Terminals 167

Chapter 7
Outside the Workplace 171
    Personal Associations 172
        Basic Associations 172
        Bankruptcy/Debtors 174
        Unions 175
    Lifestyle Regulation 176
    Loyalty 179
    Conflicts of Interest 182
    Off-Duty Misconduct 184
        Non-Criminal Misconduct 184
        Criminal Misconduct 186
    Residency Requirements 188

Chapter 8
Individual Employment Rights Litigation 191
    Personal Right Violations (Torts) 192
        Invasion of Privacy 192
        Defamation 193

False Imprisonment 198
Intentional Infliction of Emotional Distress 199
Negligent Maintenance or Disclosure of
  Employment Records 200
Fraudulent Misrepresentation 201
Intentional Interference with Contractual
  Relations 202
Public Policy 202
Contract Violations 203
  Employment Contracts 204
  Restrictive Covenants 206
  Employment Handbooks and Policies 210
  Collective Bargaining Agreements 213

Index 219
About the Author 223

1

The Developing Law of Individual Employment Rights

Employment law is a maze of common-law doctrines, statutes, contract-established rules, judicial pronouncements, and administrative agency findings. Symmetry and clearly discernible legal patterns are not often recognizable. Even within a narrow area, employment law can vary considerably, depending whether an administrative agency or a court is involved. Statutes and court decisions reflect this shifting conflict balance between employee and employer making employment law one of the most political of legal areas.

Employment laws provide a mechanism to deal with conflict. Conflict involves not only wages, hours, and employment conditions, but also power contests within and between various groups and personalities within and outside organizations. This may include confrontations between employees, union officials, governmental agencies, and employers. Employment law is concerned with "rules of the game" where law and economics constantly confront ethical and moral problems for resolution.

Individual employment rights consist of the at-will employment relationship and employee privacy interests. At-will employment allows termination of employment by either an employee or employer at any time for no reason.

Employee privacy has varied meanings. It encompasses a broad spectrum of individual employment rights relating to the intrusiveness and fairness of information collection, maintenance, use, and disclosure along with employee lifestyle regulation at and outside the workplace. These interests arise prior to, during, and after the employment relationship is terminated.

This text reviews individual employment rights for all those interested in this developing area of the law. Along with examining at-will employment and employee privacy, guidance is offered to limit employer liability arising out of the individual employment relationship when dealing with these workplace situations.

THE EMPLOYMENT RELATIONSHIP

Employee and employer relationships are the basis of our economic structure affecting most people over the greater part of their lives. People increasingly depend on others to offer them the means to produce their daily income. Employment loss can be a considerable hardship having disastrous consequences. This relationship has become fundamental to society. Outside of marriage, no other relationship preoccupies daily affairs so completely.

Through multi-faceted human resource functions, wage and benefit programs, and government regulation, the employment relationship has become complex. Correspondingly, this relationship generates large quantities of information and records.

By entering into an employment relationship, little employee choice exists in providing sensitive, often detailed information. This information may reveal the employee's innermost beliefs, interests, and actions. It may cause incorrect evaluations by those who lack decision-making authority affecting the employee's standing and reputation at and outside the workplace. Through this, the employee may experience restricted opportunities to develop and maintain political, economic, and social relationships.

THE AT-WILL EMPLOYMENT RELATIONSHIP

Historically, the employment relationship has limited an employee's ability to challenge an employer's unfair, adverse, or damaging practices. It generally denies any right to the employee who is arbitrarily treated without a union or a contract. Absent a statutory or contractual restriction, an employee or employer can generally terminate the employment relationship at any time, for any or no reason, with or without notice, making it at-will.

Employee and employer rights within the United States trace their beginnings to England's Statute or Labourers. The Statute of

Labourers was enacted in response to the extreme labor shortage that resulted from the Black Death in the mid-14th century. It provided that a "general hiring" of labor for an unfixed term was presumed to be for a year and that a "master" could not "put away his servant" except for "reasonable cause." After its repeal, English courts continued to apply the statute's spirit by presuming that a "general hiring" was intended to serve as an employment contract for one year. If the employment continued for longer than one year, it could be terminated only at the end of an additional year.

The American at-will employment doctrine has been viewed both as a departure from and as part of this English heritage. Early American courts adopted the English approach. In the 1880s, however, American courts developed their own version of at-will employment.

In 1887, H. G. Wood's treatise on the master-servant relationship articulated what seemingly became America's at-will employment doctrine. H. Wood, in the treatise *Master and Servant* 134 (3d ed. 1886), wrote that:

> With us the rule is inflexible that a general or indefinite hiring is prima facie a hiring at will, and if the servant seeks to make it out a yearly hiring, the burden is upon him to establish it by proof. A hiring at so much a day, week, month, or year, no time being specified, is an indefinite hiring, and no presumption attaches that it was for a day even, but only at the rate fixed for whatever time the party may serve.

Although Wood's "Rule" has been challenged and in certain instances negated, it has become the primary basis for what remains of at-will employment in this country.

American courts probably adopted Wood's Rule to facilitate economic development during the industrial revolution of the 1800s by promoting the prevalent ideology of *laissez faire* and freedom of contract. Within this framework, Wood's Rule seemed equitable. It provided the employer the flexibility to control the workplace through the unchallengeable power to terminate the employment relationship at will. In turn, the employee retained the freedom to resign if more favorable employment presented itself or if working conditions became intolerable. The at-will employment relationship has been codified in several jurisdictions.

Congress and various state legislatures have prohibited, in certain instances, the summary termination of an at-will employee. Courts have found that an employer may terminate an employee for any reason except when statutorily prohibited. The primary federal statutes limiting an employer's right to terminate an at-will employee are the National Labor Relations Act (NLRA) and the Civil Rights Act of 1964 (Title VII). The NLRA prohibits termination for exercising the right to organize and select an employee representative. Title VII prohibits any termination based upon discrimination involving race, color, religion, sex, or national origin. Other federal legislation restricting employee terminations are the:

1. Age Discrimination in Employment Act of 1967 (ADEA);
2. Occupational Safety and Health Act of 1970 (OSHA);
3. Vietnam Era Veterans Readjustment Assistance Act;
4. Fair Labor Standard Act (FLSA);
5. The Vocational Rehabilitation Act of 1973;
6. The Employee Retirement Income Security Act of 1974 (ERISA);
7. Energy Reorganization Act of 1974;
8. Clean Air Act;
9. Federal Water Pollution Control Act;
10. Railroad Safety Act;
11. Consumer Credit Protection Act; and
12. Judiciary and Judicial Procedure Act.
13. Americans with Disabilities Act of 1990

State statutes contain similar limitations.

The principal goals of this federal and state legislation have been to:

1. Promote unionization as a countervailing force against employer power and control;
2. Establish a minimum level of employee economic entitlement;
3. Combat discrimination against specific groups in hiring and terminations;
4. Protect employee health and safety; and
5. Guarantee a minimum level of security for retirement and for the survivors of wage earners.

Until recently, courts consistently upheld the legality of arbitrary terminations and denied damage claims even where the termination reasons were based upon false information, mistake, malice, or where the employer did not follow its own published disciplinary and appeal procedures. Courts and legislatures are now creating exceptions to this *laissez faire* relationship of at-will employment by permitting employees to contest certain employer actions. These exceptions may arise out of public policy considerations employer documents, or rest on the assumption that an implied covenant of good faith and fair dealing exists in every employment relationship whether oral or written.

EMPLOYMENT PRIVACY *Law Review-article*

The concept of privacy within the United State is generally traced to an article by Samuel D. Warren and Louis D. Brandeis. [Warren and Brandeis, *The Right to Privacy,* 4 Harv. L. Rev. 193 (1890).] Prior to 1890, no American cause of action for damages could be brought for a privacy invasion. Warren and Brandeis maintained that even though no prior case law explicitly supported a privacy right's existence, a reasoned development of common law principles and society's changing circumstances supported it. Their basic assumption was that the law recognizes novel causes of action. They noted the need for this innovation due to the newly developed methods of invading private and domestic life through photography and newspapers.

Employee privacy is a growing concern. Since George Orwell raised the spector of "Big Brother" with his book *1984,* computer technology, court decisions, government intrusion, and the employer's right to know more about the individuals they employ have eroded the employee's sense that his/her life is a private matter.

Next to at-will employment, privacy is the most rapidly evolving individual employment rights area. Privacy concerns the nature and extent of an employee's "right to be let alone" or to be free from "unwarranted intrusions."

From the moment an individual first walks through an employer's entrance, privacy rights are relinquished. As an employment condition, employees must disclose personal facts about their background and continually submit to employer scrutiny that may or may not be performance related. The employee may confront a physical examination, polygraph examination, psychological evaluation, or even an antibody test for Human Immunodeficiency Virus (HIV). Physical intrusion may also occur through locker searches or frisking as employees leave the workplace, even though no reasonable suspicion of theft exists.

Privacy interests are implicated where an employer conducts routine surveillance and monitoring. Employers have been known to operate video cameras in employee restrooms. Some employers have installed computers to monitor performance of video display terminal operators.

Employment privacy concerns extend to employer efforts to collect personal information that is not job-related. Employers have a legitimate need to know certain things about their employees, including their abilities, honesty, and prior employment histories. Some employers want to know much more. They assert mistakenly, that everything about an employee is relevant to employment and that it is necessary to examine the "whole person" to determine whether employment suitability exists. The employer wants to know if the employee smokes marijuana at home, is a homosexual, she/male, or socializes with the "wrong" kind of people.

When employers disclose employment information to third parties other employee privacy interests are implicated. These disclosures are primarily made to prospective employers as job references. The employer may disclose an employee's confidential medical records to those who have no legitimate need to view them or may disclose negative private facts out of spite or revenge. This may cause embarrassment by subjecting the employee to ridicule from friends and acquaintances. It may injure the employee's reputation and limit future employment prospects.

Today, legislatures and courts are increasingly concerned about individual employment rights. While employers may have legitimate business interests that sometimes require infringing on employee privacy, there are compelling reasons to limit the employer's trespass on employee privacy where no legitimate business reason exists.

Employment privacy interests exist in the:

1. Employee's person, property, or private conversations;
2. Employee's private life or beliefs;
3. Use of irrelevant, inaccurate, or incomplete facts to make employment decisions; and
4. Disclosure of employment information to third parties.

The can be summarized into the five main employment privacy themes of:

1. Speech—what is said about someone;
2. Beliefs—what one thinks;
3. Information—what is collected, maintained, used, and disclosed;
4. Association—with whom one shares similar interests; and
5. Lifestyle—how one lives.

It is these privacy interests that recur throughout employment as they relate to hiring, the workplace, and life outside the workplace.

Individuals are generally comfortable in relating the more intimate aspects of their lives to a friend. They are secure with the friend's use of what is learned. The friend is trusted to continue respect for them, despite what may be known as a consequence of a request for assistance or guidance.

An important difference between an individual's relationship with family and friends and their relationship with employers, is that employers treat them as continuing performance evaluation objects. Among family and friends the individual's life is perceived to be conducted "in private" and involving "private relations." They believe themselves safe from scrutiny and secure. This is not true of the employment relationship.

Within the employment relationship there are two basic privacies. One concerns "informational privacy" or the interest in controlling employment information collection maintenance, use, and disclosure. The other relates to "behavioral privacy" or the interest in participating in activities free from employer regulation or surveillance at and outside the workplace.

"Privacy" and "confidentiality" are similar but yet distinct. Employment information "privacy" concerns what should be collected, how much should be maintained, and what should be disclosed. Through "confidentiality," the employer represents to those from whom it collects information that unauthorized uses or disclosures will not be made through procedures that ensure this information's security. Confidentiality requires security controls in oral and written communications as well as in manual and computerized records.

EXERCISING INDIVIDUAL EMPLOYMENT RIGHTS

In entering into the employment relationship, the employee must often relinquish considerable autonomy. Most employees do not bargain for their employment position. They adhere to the employer's unilateral terms. If they do not follow these employment terms, they may not be employed.

If employed by a large employer, the employee must conform with the employer's expectations, rules, and procedures that define specific rights and responsibilities. Many employees are wholly dependent upon their employers for their economic well-being.

Based on the anticipated continuance of this relationship, the employee creates various social and financial commitments. These may include marriage, children, home, automobile, etc. This establishes a social or financial reliance in others that is also dependent upon the employee's relationship with the employer.

Absent statutory restrictions, an employer can generally collect, maintain, use, and disclose employment information along with influencing an employee's lifestyles. Likewise, where an at-will employment relationship exists, an employer can generally terminate an employee who objects to the employer's collection, maintenance, use, and disclosure of information along with how the employee's lifestyle is regulated at and outside the workplace. The employee can accept, protest by confronting possible termination, or voluntarily terminate employment. For the employee, none of these options are desirable because of the potential economic hardship they may cause.

Concerns over individual employment rights exist while hiring, at the workplace, and outside the workplace. All involve the collection, maintenance, use, and disclosure of employment information along with employee lifestyle regulation outside the workplace.

Hiring privacy alone can affect an employee through advertisements, applications, interviews, credit checks, arrest records, criminal convictions, fingerprints, photographs, immigration requirements, reference checks, medical screening, genetic screening, blood testing, skill testing, polygraph examinations, honesty testing, handwriting analysis, negligent hiring, etc. The workplace creates questions over employment records, medical records, health and safety, smoking, employee assistance programs, alcohol and drug abuse, human immunodeficiency virus (HIV), sterilization, searches, monitoring, union meeting surveillance, workplace surveillance, employee manipulation, camera surveillance, electronic surveillance, literature solicitation and distribution, jury or witness duty, voting time, whistleblowing, dress codes and grooming, spousal policies, nepotism, third party representation, performance evaluations, name changes, identification tags, religious accommodation, privacy misconduct, language requirements, etc. On the other hand, individual employment rights may be impacted outside the workplace through employee personal associations involving employee bankruptcy/debtors and unions, lifestyle regulation, loyalty, conflicts of interest, off-duty misconduct involving noncriminal or criminal activities, residency requirements, etc. It is in these areas that individual employment rights become increasingly significant and susceptible to employer breaches for which employees today are inclined to seek redress for damages through a variety of litigation theories.

The emphasis of this text is on individual employment rights as legislatures and courts interpret them. It should be noted that those who are confronted with these questions, should not limit consideration to a particular state's statutory or case law. What occurs in one jurisdiction may be different from what has happened elsewhere. This is especially true where the state's highest court has not dispositively decided these issues. Even in states that do not clearly address individual employment rights, later recognition may occur, given more compelling facts or a different legal theory. The available federal law should also be consulted.

These discussions are intended to provide practical approaches for dealing with individual employment rights. They also encourage employer procedures and policies that comport with the statutory and judicial pronouncements as this employment law area develops. Throughout this text, the collection, maintenance, use, and disclosure of employment information along with regulating an employee's lifestyle at and outside the workplace will be examined as each affects a particular individual employment right.

EMPLOYEE CONCERNS

Employment is generally a close relationship between employee and employer that anticipates a hopeful continuation over an indefinite time period. Through this, many situations arise where individual employment rights may become significant.

Concerns arise whether or not an employment relationship is created over individual employment rights. They are present at hiring, during employment, and after employment terminates. Involved are employment information:

1. Collection for hiring decisions;
2. Storage, retention, and maintenance;
3. Internal use in making decisions after hiring; and
4. Disclosure to third parties.

Accompanying these employment information interests is employee lifestyle regulation at and outside the workplace.

Collection normally begins with an application form requesting employment, educational, financial, medical, and criminal histories.

During employment, other records are created. These may include performance evaluations, promotion reports, discipline notices, payroll data, government reports, fringe benefit records, pension information, and health insurance data. This employment information may be maintained in a recordkeeping system that is either manual or computerized.

Information provided to create and maintain the employment relationship may potentially harm an employee. The employee disclosed this information for a specific employment purpose only. Years later, other persons, prospective employers, credit agencies, governmental agencies, etc., may be granted access to this information. This may occur absent the employee's knowledge or consent. It is here that safeguarding individual employment rights takes on particular significance.

The employment relationship produces a need for reliance upon written information for decision making. Little, if any, employee control exists in what employment information is collected, maintained, used, or disclosed. This is usually unilaterally employer administered. The search of an employee's desk, personal files, or locker presents other concerns.

Employment information is often maintained long after the original collection purpose expires. Records are written memories not subject to forgetfulness. No promise of destruction exists and a risk for their potential misuse is constantly present. Normally, it is the employer who decides what information must be disclosed and when it must be provided. Economic circumstances compel the employee's submission to the employer's information requests. Rarely can an employee verify this information's accuracy, contents, and use or participate in deciding when, where, and to whom it is disclosed.

The employee can only surmise and guess regarding what employment information exists. There may be official as well as unofficial employment records. Identifying errors and finding their source may be difficult. The employee does not know whether those with which a confidential relationship is thought to exist may have disclosed information to others without knowledge or prior consent. Through the collection, maintenance, use, and disclosure of employment information, the employee loses control over personnel information in the employer's possession. Overshadowing these concerns is the manner in which an employer regulates the employee's lifestyles at and outside the workplace.

EMPLOYER CONCERNS

Recordkeeping, disclosure, and statutes along with their accompanying case law, have made individual employment rights a significant employer concern. Employers find themselves with conflicting requirements that restrict their operations. For example, while record-keeping requirements mandate information collection, privacy statutes restrict that process. Similarly, while privacy requirements seek to protect employment information, disclosure statutes require access.

Increased governmental regulation of the employment relationship has expanded employer record-keeping obligations. Employers are subject to federal statutes that impose explicit and implicit record-keeping requirements. The Occupational Safety and Health Act of 1970 (OSHA) and the Civil Rights Act of 1964 (Title VII) have the greatest impact. OSHA requires employers to conduct employee medical surveillance and maintain records concerning employee occupational health. Title VII requires an annual statement of the employer's workforce's racial, ethnic, and sex composition. This results in extensive and detailed employer governmental record-keeping for which employee information must be collected.

Despite these statutory requirements, employers must themselves collect, maintain, use, and disclose employment information to effectively operate their businesses. Information from employees is necessary to make decisions for hiring, promotion, training, security, compensation and benefits, retirement, disciplinary actions, termination, and other job opportunities. It is here that individual employment rights must be balanced with the employer's need to make legitimate business decisions.

As additional statutes are enacted, employers must become more cautious in their collection, maintenance, use, and disclosure of employment information. Unaccustomed to outside scrutiny, employers are surprised to discover that certain employment information must be disclosed. Unions also request and obtain employment information. To deal with this, employers must know what federal and state statutes specify about employment information disclosure to avoid and limit their potential liability. Disclosure should not violate individual employment rights. Employer familiarity with these requirements is critical to protect individual employment rights, operate their businesses effectively, and maintain good relations with other organizations.

LEGISLATIVE ACTION

No comprehensive nationwide statutory protection of individual employment rights currently exists. However, federal and state statutes impose certain restrictions. Actions by state legislatures have been more innovative and far reaching than similar federal responses. Constitutional protections for personal privacy have traditionally been safeguards against governmental rather than private intrusions. That distinction, however, has disappeared in states whose constitutions protect against both. States have recognized the need to balance privacy interests against other societal values.

The Freedom of Information Act (FOIA) allows the public to "have all the information that the security of the Nation permits." It also exempted certain confidential information from public disclosure; i.e., "personnel and medical files and similar files the disclosure of which would constitute a clearly unwarranted invasion of personal privacy."

In 1974, the United States Congress debated legislation increasing the protection of governmental information maintained on individuals. A Senate bill provided for a Federal Privacy Board to oversee the collection, maintenance, and disclosure of information. The House bill focused on federal agency standards for data collection and maintenance. These two bills were combined without a formal conference committee meeting and report into the Privacy Act of 1974.

Under the Privacy Act, an individual has input over what government information is maintained, as well as how and by whom it is used. The individual may request the correction, amendment, or deletion of information, and may take legal action if the request is denied.

The Privacy Act defines an "individual" as "a citizen of the United States or an alien lawfully admitted for permanent residence." This has been construed to exclude foreign nationals, nonresident aliens, and corporations. The "records" protected include anything containing "name, or the identifying number, symbol, or other identifying particular assigned to the individual." Subject to twelve exceptions, records may not be released unless pursuant to a written request by, or with the individual's prior consent.

Other federal statutes and executive orders also affect individual employment rights. These include the:

1. Fair Credit Reporting Act;
2. National Labor Relations Act (NLRA);
3. Civil Rights Act of 1964 (Title VII);

THE DEVELOPING LAW / 13

4. Age Discrimination in Employment Act of 1967 (ADEA);
5. Vocational Rehabilitation Act of 1973;
6. Americans with Disabilities Act of 1990 (ADA);
7. Civil Rights Statutes (Sections 1981, 1983, 1985, and 1986);
8. Executive Order 11246 (Affirmative Action);
9. Occupational Safety and Health Act of 1970 (OSHA);
10. Omnibus Crime Control and Safe Streets Act;
11. Bankruptcy Act;
12. Executive Order 12546 (Drug Testing);
13. Hatch Act;
14. Whistleblowing Protection;
15. Immigration Reform and Control Act; and
16. Employee Polygraph Protection Act.

"Mini-Privacy Acts" were enacted by various states in the 1970s to address the need for protection of individual employment rights. In acknowledging the right to "be let alone," these statutes regulate the collection, maintenance, use, and disclosure of information about individuals by state and local agencies. Like the Federal Privacy Act of 1974, these state statutes generally:

1. Give an individual the opportunity to know what information government collects, maintains, and discloses;
2. Permit an individual to correct or amend inaccurate government records; and
3. Regulate the collection, maintenance, use, and disclosure of information by government.

Other state responses to individual employment rights involve:

1. Disclosure of credit information;
2. Little "Hatch Acts";
3. Whistleblowing;
4. Employee access to personnel files;
5. Regulating medical files;
6. Disallowing employers from asking a prospective employee or an employee about arrests and convictions;
7. Fingerprinting;
8. Employment references;
9. Prohibiting polygraph examinations in employment;
10. Psychological matters;
11. Highly communicable diseases;
12. Sickle cell anemia;

13. Smoking;
14. Voting; and
15. Wrongful termination limitations.

JUDICIAL RESPONSES

Judicial protection of individual employment rights is generally premised on constitutional, tort, or contract litigation theories. In their constitutions, the federal government and some states provide a limited right to personal privacy or a right to be free from intrusion into one's private affairs. These rights differ between the federal constitution and what each state constitution may provide.

Information contained in personnel files involving performance evaluations, test scores, salary histories, and medical information, which if disclosed by an employer, could result in an invasion of privacy. There are indications that as individual employment rights develop, this cause of action will take on greater importance.

Defamation consists of the publication of an untrue statement that holds a person up to ridicule, hatred, contempt, or opprobrium. In the employment relationship, defamation may arise when an employer communicates false or derogatory employee information. Negative performance evaluations or reasons for termination may create liability. [See *Biggins v. Hanson*, 252 Cal. App.2d 16, 59 Cal. Rptr. 897 (1967).] Employers are protected by a qualified privilege to defame. This absolves employers of liability when the communication is made in good faith, in response to a legitimate inquiry, and within the employment relationship's normal information distribution channels to an employee that has a right to know the information.

False imprisonment protects the individual's interest in freedom from restraint of movement. It occurs in the employment context when an employer or its agent restrains an employee. This is usually to search or interrogate the employee regarding employer property theft. [See *Faniel v. Chesapeake and Potomac Telephone Co.*, 404 A.2d 147 (D.C. App. 1979).]

Conduct intruding upon individual employment rights must rise to the level of outrageous conduct for intentional infliction of emotional distress to arise. This litigation action redresses the most extreme employer conduct. It may arise where an employee is terminated for refusing to discontinue a social relationship with another employee outside the workplace where no adverse employee job performance results or it negatively affects the employer's business. [See *Patton v.*

[Handwritten note at top: K. Mart case — customer accused employee of theft, security strip searched down to underwear — customer present — fired employee.]

J. C. Penney Co., Inc., 75 Or. App. 638, 707 P.2d 1256 (Or. App. 1985), aff'd, rev'd in part, 301 Or. 117, 719 P. 2d 894 (1986).]

The tort of negligent maintenance of employment records is also recognized. A duty exists to act carefully in maintaining employment records or in providing employment references. Employees have recovered damages against employers who negligently disclosed to third parties inaccurate employment information. [See *Quinones v. United States*, 492 F.2d 1269 (3d Cir. 1974).] Fraudulent misrepresentation may exist where an employer induces an employee to act or to refrain from acting. The employer could misrepresent reasons for collecting, maintaining, using, or disclosing employment information. [See *Mueller v. Union Pacific Railroad*, 220 Neb. 742, 371 N.E.2d 732 (1985).]

Intentional interference with contractual relations may arise where the employer interferes with a prospective contractual relationship. Individual employment rights are affected by the employer's interference in matters where no right exists. This could occur where an employer writes another employer that an employee should not be hired. [See *Gordon v. Lancaster Osteopathic Hosp. Ass'n*, 340 Pa. Super. 253, 489 A.2d 1363 (1985).]

With at-will employment's continued modification, public policy violations may also protect individual employment rights. Causes of action have been permitted for:

1. Violating a clear statutorily declared policy—[See *Perks v. Firestone Tire and Rubber Co.*, 611 F.2d 1393 (3d Cir. 1979) (polygraph examination prohibition)];
2. Reporting unlawful or improper employer conduct. [See *Palmateer v. International Harvester Co.*, 85 Ill.2d 124, 421 N.E.2d 876 (1981) (criminal activities)], and
3. Refusing to accede to improper employer demands. [*Monge v. Beebe Rubber Co.*, 114 N.H. 130, 316 A.2d 549 (1974) (sexual harassment).]

Contractual commitments may form another basis to protect individual employment rights. These may arise out of:

1. Oral and written employment contracts;
2. Restrictive covenants;
3. Employment handbooks and policies; and
4. Collective bargaining agreements.

EMPLOYMENT INFORMATION COLLECTION

Increasingly, employment information collection must be conducted with government agencies, record-keeping organizations, and employers as partners. Concerns arise in:

1. The initial collection;
2. Ensuring accurate collection;
3. Restricting use to the collection purpose; and
4. To what extent disclosure occurs.

When applying for employment, an individual provides personal information to assist the employer in making the hiring decision. This information may be supplemented and verified by testing, interviews, medical screening, references, and credit reviews along with a background investigation. Should hiring occur, this information is expanded to accommodate records for wages, benefits, performance evaluations, promotions, attendance, etc.

Absent hiring, information is still created about applicants and employees. Because of this information's extent, entities unrelated to the employment relationship often consider it a valuable resource. This may include governmental agencies. Confidentiality in information use and disclosure is of legitimate concern to the applicant and employee. Correspondingly, the employer's inquiries about applicants and employees should not become intrusive.

The first employment information collection record established by employers is the application form. It collects basic employment information. Employers not only collect information directly from an employee, but also from third parties. It is not uncommon to request reports from credit agencies whose information is frequently based upon interviews with friends, neighbors, and relatives.

Sophisticated employer information collection processes have been developed that may intrude upon individual employment rights. Psychological testing, polygraph examinations, and electronic storage of personal data are among these. Collection methods should not violate individual employment rights. Information that is irrelevant, confidential, or likely to be used unfairly in decisions should not be collected.

The polygraph examination is intended to be a truth-verification collection device. It consists of: 1) a corrugated rubber tube that is attached to the subject's chest to measure the respiratory rate; 2) an inflated rubber cuff attached to the arm that measures blood pressure and pulse rate; and 3) two electrodes attached to the hand that measure the flow of electric current (galvanic skin response) as the rate of perspiration increases. The polygraph's intrusive nature and accuracy have been disputed. For employees, it affronts their mental and physical dignity. Its use is regulated or prohibited by various federal and state statutes.

The personality test is a broad review of an employee's personal life measuring emotional adjustment, social relations, motivation, and interests. It attempts to ascertain the innermost thoughts on family life, religion, racial attitudes, national origin, politics, atheism, ideology, sex, etc. Obtaining employment information through these attitudinal responses can be considered a mental "search" for private facts.

There are two types of personality tests. The inventory test provides an objective measure of the subject's interest in certain types of activities or of particular personality traits. It is used to predict job performance. The Minnesota Multiphasic Personality Inventory (MMPI) is a familiar example of this test. A personality test is projective. It requires the subject to observe several ink blot types and describe what is seen. The Rorschach ink blot test typifies this.

Other employment information collection tests include fingerprinting, blood tests, physical examinations, and work area surveillance. These can be distinguished from polygraph and personality tests. They have generally been considered valid collection methods because their scope of inquiry is not as broad. They are related more to collecting evidence than to compulsory extraction of incriminating facts. Fingerprinting is only a means of verifying the required information and involves no additional intrusion. A routine physical examination or blood test is likewise not an offensive prying. Photographing employees in work areas can be a reasonable employer method to improve efficiency when recording what is already public.

Employment information should be collected through methods of accepted reliability that seek to discover only employment-related facts. In providing this information, the employee should be able to preserve dignity, prevent personal embarrassment, and foreclose economic harm. Responsibility in providing employment information, however, must be balanced with the employer's need for efficient decision making.

Employees should not be required to disclose private thoughts by submitting to collection methods producing anxiety and humiliation reminiscent of a criminal interrogation. Employer background investigations should not interview individuals without employee knowledge. Requiring that the employee at least know of the investigation would not be burdensome. Statutory or court protection should safeguard employees from collection processes that are overly inquisitorial and that obtain information unrelated to decision making.

EMPLOYMENT INFORMATION MAINTENANCE AND INTERNAL USE

After collecting employment information, internal employer use begins. This involves information disclosure and the decisions based on that information. Decision making utilizing employment information concerns:

1. Selection and placement;
2. Developmental decisions of transfer, promotion, demotion, and training;
3. Discipline;
4. Administration of employee benefits; and
5. Separation by involuntary or voluntary termination.

Disclosure of employment information may involve the human resources department, the payroll department, or supervisory personnel. This is necessary for certain employer decision making. Specific employer decision making includes what person is hired, terminated, placed, transferred, promoted, demoted, trained, or disciplined along with what compensation and benefits are to be paid.

Every employer decision maker does not need to review or have access to all of this employment information. It is unnecessary for a supervisor preparing a performance evaluation to review an employee's medical and financial history. Likewise, a payroll clerk should not review an employee's performance evaluations. This employment information is not essential for the particular decision they are making.

Employees have a legitimate interest in restricting information use to the purpose for which the employer originally collected it. The employee normally has no right to prevent these disclosures. Usually, the employee is not aware that they might occur. Concern has been expressed for the employee's interest in employment information collection along with its improper use and disclosure.

Improper internal use can be minimized by requiring disclosures only for a "routine use" to designated personnel having a "need to know." "Routine uses" for employment information should be established. Each routine use would be evaluated according to whether it corresponds with the purpose for which the information was collected and the decision for which it is applicable. A performance evaluation's routine use would include decisions about promotions, wages, or discipline. It would not be used for fringe benefit decisions. Routine uses for medical information would include decisions about hiring and employee medical and life insurance plans. It would not be used for employee wage rate decisions.

Employment information access should only be granted by the employer on a "need to know." Limiting access based on a "need to know" does not hinder an employer's operational efficiency. It minimizes employment information misuse and protects the employee.

EMPLOYMENT INFORMATION ACCESS

The employee lives in several sociological "roles." These roles may involve family, marriage, work, church, politics, and social relationships. In each role, the employee's response to daily situations may, or perhaps must, be different depending upon what needs or requirements exist.

The employee has an interest in maintaining privacy to live in these different roles without having performance in one role placed in conflict with another absent permission. By allowing the employee to "edit oneself," the employee can adjust internal needs for solitude, companionship, intimacy, and general social intercourse with anonymity and responsible participation in society.

The employee should have access to this employment information. This personal information was generally first in the employee's exclusive possession. It may reveal personal details affecting potential security, dignity, and reputation. This personal information was generally obtained by the employer through the employee's economic need.

Computer technology enables the employer to administer large volumes of employment information. Through this, employers can transfer and assemble employment information almost anywhere within microseconds. Storage capabilities prolong employment information longevity making improper disclosure and misuse almost as permanent as the information itself.

To safeguard individual employment rights, employers should regularly purge their records of unnecessary and out-dated employment information. Likewise, employees should be granted access to employment information for correction and supplementation.

The employee's ability to present "oneself" in different "roles" depends upon society's accessibility to information. However, the employee should not be permitted to perpetrate fraud on an employer. Fraud could occur through the employee's failure to disclose discreditable personal information that would affect the employee's job performance or harm the employer's business. This would be similar to a seller's product defect concealment.

Fraud may arise where an employer is induced to enter a transaction it would not enter had the truth been known. To the extent that an employee conceals personal information to mislead, the justification for according protection to this information is no better than that for permitting fraud in the sale of goods. The employee should be required to disclose all information that is directly related to job performance.

Access to employment information should be granted the employee to make corrections or additions. This affords an employee knowledge of what information is maintained to assure accuracy regarding what could be disclosed to others. It would be the employee's responsibility to exercise this. This access would minimize employment decisions made from inaccurate, incomplete, or irrelevant facts.

EMPLOYMENT INFORMATION DISCLOSURE TO THIRD PARTIES

Employment information internal use is a necessary function. It relates to employee wage rates, promotions, reassignments, and work performance. Disclosures to third parties are ordinarily discretionary. They primarily affect the employee's life outside rather than at the workplace. Frequently, they involve employment references for a new job or disclosures to credit agencies. A negative disclosure's adverse effect may continue for years. Mandatory employer disclosures to third parties include responses to subpoenas and reports required by government regulations.

While employer policy and practice has been to provide some confidentiality to employment information, whatever confidentiality exists is generally the result of employer voluntary action. Only limited statutory controls exist to preserve employment information confidentiality. Employment information disclosure to third parties involves the unpredictability or uncertainty of the employer's goodwill and personal value system in handling these matters.

The employee's ability to disclose knowledge and information about oneself, is the lynchpin of individual employment rights. This corresponds with the employee's opportunities to limit or monitor employer information disclosures about oneself. Random employment information disclosures absent an employee's knowledge or consent should be curtailed to limit potential employer liability.

EMPLOYEE LIFESTYLES AT AND OUTSIDE THE WORKPLACE

Generally, an employee's private activities at and outside the workplace are not open to employer scrutiny or regulation. These activities outside the workplace are usually within the employee's exclusive purview. The employment relationship does not make the employer guardian of the employee's every personal action. Yet, in certain areas directly affecting the employer's business affairs, the employer may attempt to regulate the employee's lifestyles. This may result in employee disciplinary actions up to and including termination where employee lifestyle actions adversely affect the employer's business.

Lifestyle regulation at the workplace may concern dress and grooming standards, spousal employment, consumption of alcohol, smoking, and drug use. Outside the workplace limits on an employee's lifestyle may be placed on who the employee may have contact with socially, other employment opportunities that may directly conflict with the employer's business, and what type of image the employee maintains in the community.

Where employee lifestyle regulation at and outside the workplace occurs, it should be reasonable and directly related to the employee's position. Regulation should occur only where the employee's lifestyle will have a definitive adverse result on the employer's business affairs. Each limit on an employee's lifestyle at and outside the workplace should be evaluated on its own merits.

Employee lifestyle regulation at and outside the workplace should be readily discernible and obvious to a third party as being in the employer's business interest. It should be harmful in that the employer will sustain financial loss absent the regulation. Mere speculation regarding impact on the employer's affairs should not suffice to permit a constraint placed on the employee's lifestyle at or outside the workplace.

AVOIDING INDIVIDUAL EMPLOYMENT RIGHTS' LITIGATION

Given the increasing sympathy shown to employees by the courts, employers should act as if their disciplinary decisions are reviewable under the most restrictive standards. Even if the employer is operating in a nonunion setting, every employment action should be treated as if it were subject to labor arbitration under a collective bargaining agreement; that is, an employer should be prepared to meet a just cause standard to defend its actions.

Most collective bargaining agreements in the private and public sectors require a cause or just cause standard to sustain adverse employment actions. If this standard is not explicitly specified in a collective bargaining agreement, many arbitrators imply a just cause limitation. In the absence of precise definitions, *cause* or *just cause* may be considered any combination of:

1. The "law of the shop" regarding a particular employment action; that is, the employer's response to that action developed over a given time period;
2. A consistent pattern of rule and regulation enforcement, along with making these known to all employees;
3. Case histories of other similar employment actions;
4. Known practices of severe discipline for certain offenses because of the product manufactured, service rendered, or safety considerations;
5. Offenses calling for immediate suspension and those not requiring termination;
6. Workplace and outside-the-workplace offenses, along with differences in their treatment;
7. General arbitral authority derived from awards, articles, etc.;
8. The arbitrator's own sense of equity and subjective judgment regarding the significance, seriousness, and weight to be given the incident, the employee's record, or the circumstances causing the employment action;
9. The severity of the incident's facts;
10. Attempts made to rehabilitate the employee by the employer;

11. Progressive discipline steps that may or may not have been taken;
12. The discipline penalty imposed as it relates to the incident's facts;
13. Whether a second chance is warranted from the employee's prior record; and
14. Whether the employee is unreclaimable as indicated by his/her prior record or the incident's facts.

Before a discipline or termination decision is made, it should be reviewed by an additional management level. This may be a human resource officer or a specific employer official responsible for reviewing all proposed discipline or terminations. In the more difficult disciplinary situations, legal counsel should be consulted. The following documents should be considered:

1. Performance evaluations;
2. Warning notices;
3. Personnel policies or work rules;
4. Witness statements;
5. Witness interview notes; and
6. Other relevant documents including complaints, written statements from the employee, other employees, accident reports, work records, overtime records, timecards, safety inspections, etc.

After these documents are reviewed, the following should be evaluated:

1. Is the employee a long-service employee?;
2. Is the employee's record of promotions and salary increases inconsistent with past unsatisfactory work performance?;
3. Were the employee's salary increases labeled "merit" or something else?;
4. Has the employee received any commendations or awards?;
5. Is the discipline or termination consistent with treatment given other employees in similar incidents?;
6. Does the written record support the decision?;
7. Does the articulated reason for the decision comply with the employer's personnel policies, work rules, and with the evidence?;
8. Is there a credibility dispute and how do the employer's witnesses compare to the employee's?;

9. Does the employee's explanation raise any mitigating circumstances or compelling sympathies?;
10. Should an action less severe than termination be imposed?;
11. Did the employer's decision maker—
    - Have firsthand knowledge of the facts?,
    - Review the written record before making the decision?,
    - Talk to the witnesses?, and
    - Present the image of a believable witness?;
12. Can the employer prove the facts that allegedly exist:;
13. After the discipline or termination decision has been made, it is important that—
    - The employer explain the reasons for the employer's action at an interview,
    - The explanation need not be in writing, but should be candid, consistent with the evidence, and consistent with any explanation the employer intends to use, and
    - The interview should be carefully documented and a suitable employer witness should be present at the interview to verify the conversation;
14. The reason for the discipline or termination should be discussed openly and frankly with the employee in that:
    - There should be an attempt to persuade the employee that the reason is legitimate and consistent with the employer's past practice in similar cases,
    - The employee should be advised what will be told prospective employers,
    - If the termination reasons are reduced to writing, they should be thorough and accurately stated, and
    - To avoid possible invasion of privacy, defamation, or intentional infliction of emotional distress claims, the employer should generally not disclose the reasons for the discipline or termination to other employees or third parties;
15. Centralized control of the discipline and termination process permits the employer to determine its best witness if the case is litigated:
    - This may be a member of the human resources staff who has knowledge of the relevant facts concerning the employee's work performance and the work performance of similarly situated employees,
    - This should allow the employer's presentation of its case to be more coherent and easier to follow,

- A jury may be less inclined to view the litigation as a conflict between one individual against an impersonal organization with a member of the human resources staff as the employer's main witness,
- The jury might be persuaded to view the case as a test of that official's credibility and fairness as opposed to the employee's, and
- If the employer does decide to have the human resources staff monitor all discipline and termination decisions, that individual should be mature, responsible, articulate, and able to convey the impression of being fair and sympathetic toward employees and their problems. [See American Hospital Association, *The Wrongful Discharge of Employees in the Health Care Industry* 52-55 (1987.]

No employer desires engaging in litigation if it can be avoided. Even when an employer prevails, it may suffer damage from poor publicity. Lawsuits, whether justified or not, generate poor public relations for employers. Employers can lessen their exposure to involvement in these cases. The following suggestions may aid in minimizing employer liability.

1. The employer should follow clear-cut, well-publicized and consistent procedures for all disciplinary actions.
2. Put the grounds for termination in writing and distribute this information to all employees.
3. Document every termination action. Keep precise records of conferences, warnings, probationary notices, remedial efforts, and other steps that precede termination. The employer should be able to document that a termination was for *cause* to prevent lawsuits, contest unemployment compensation claims, defend union challenges, or successfully litigate discrimination charges.
4. Refine performance evaluations to give honest appraisals of each employee's weak and strong points.
5. Watch for signs of an employee's work problems. Job-related stress or discontent over working conditions may turn a once satisfactory performer into a termination possibility. Try to reclaim such an employee before termination becomes necessary.
6. Provide advance warning that an employee has taken a course possibly leading to termination unless changes occur in his/her performance.

7. Involve two or more persons in the termination process. This practice can minimize suits that allege malice or personality conflicts between a terminated employer and a supervisor.
8. Review severance pay policies. If a terminated employee considers a severance payment fair, he/she may be less likely to initiate litigation. Any extra money expended usually amounts to only a fraction of what a court might award.
9. Develop a severance package that includes continuance, for a limited time, of health and life insurance benefits. These courtesies may preclude any charges of vindictiveness and may help to mollify any injured feelings.
10. Terminate only when no other choice exists, and terminate only with care and compassion. An exit interview should be conducted away from other employees to avoid embarrassment. The reason(s) for termination should be explained clearly and the nature of any reference to be given should be described.

2

Hiring Guidelines

Today, the employment relationship has become complex through increased human resource functions, benefit programs, and government regulation. Correspondingly, the information about individuals that employment creates has also grown.

When seeking employment, an individual must disclose considerable personal information and allow the employer to verify it. Hiring procedures create vast employment information resources through physical examinations, psychological tests, extensive interviews, and background investigations. After hiring, this information will be expanded through attendance records, compensation data, medical reviews, benefit reports, performance evaluations, disciplinary notices, etc.

This information base creates countless possibilities for individual employment right intrusions. For the employee, intrusions may occur knowingly or unknowingly. Generally, the employee lacks sufficient knowledge regarding this information's extent. Others outside the employment relationship may also consider this a valuable resource. These may include prospective employers, credit agencies, government agencies, etc.

To protect individual employment rights and limit employer liability, an overall hiring procedure should be developed that considers advertisements, applications, and interviews. The overall hiring procedure should ensure that only relevant or job-related information necessary for employment decisions is collected, maintained, and used.

Likewise, this information's sensitivity should be preserved through confidentiality procedures in effect prior to, during, and after employment termination. This should be done to minimize employee claims that may arise out of federal or state FEP statutory violations as well as those arising from other legal complications. In developing an overall hiring procedure, the following should be considered in preserving individual employment rights:

1. Determine who should be the interviewer;
2. Determine who should review records;
3. Obtain information from verifiable sources;
4. Obtain information by acceptable methods;
5. Obtain information only from reliable consumer reporting agencies and regularly reevaluate the selection;
6. Maintain information confidentiality;
7. Exercise caution in reference checking;
8. Inform applicants what information will be maintained;
9. Inform applicants of the uses to be made of collected information;
10. Adopt procedures to assure the information's accuracy, timeliness, and completeness;
11. Permit review, copying, correction, or amendment of this information;
12. Limit internal use;
13. Limit external disclosures, including disclosures made without authorization, to specific inquiries or requests to verify information; and
14. Provide for a regular internal compliance review of hiring procedures.

INITIAL EMPLOYMENT CONTACTS

Individual employment rights problems arise immediately after initial employer contacts occur. The individual must determine what and how much information should be revealed. Most employees only reveal the information necessary to obtain employment and not jeopardize their opportunities. All information disclosed may be subject to employer verification. These initial employment choices and limitations arise through newspaper advertisements, employment applications, and interviews.

Advertisements

Through newspaper advertisements, many individuals make their first employer contact. Depending upon the advertisement, the individual may inquire further or may refrain from making an inquiry. When someone does not apply for employment because they believe that it would be futile, individual employment rights are affected.

Advertisements specifying sex, race, religion, age, national origin, handicap, or relating to these areas may invite challenges to the hiring process. Employers are prohibited from using help-wanted advertisements under "male" and "female" headings unless sex is a *bona fide* occupational qualification. The constitutionality of statutes prohibiting help-wanted advertisement designation by sex has been upheld. [*Pittsburgh Press Co. v. Pittsburgh Comm'n on Human Relations*, 413 U.S. 376 (1973).]

Generally, advertisements are not employment offers because neither the advertiser nor the reader understands that employment can be finalized without further negotiations. Advertisements are requests to consider, examine, and negotiate. Despite this, an advertisement may have legal consequences. Advertisements containing specified terms may bind the employer. Where an employer advertised: "WE WANT enthusiastic, ambitious men to represent us locally. Professional training program w/450 monthly guarantee if qualified..." a binding commitment resulted. When the employee's commissions fell below the guaranteed $450 per month, the employee was entitled to the difference. [*Willis v. Allied Insulation Co., Inc.*, 174 So.2d 858 (La. 1965).] However, where an employee claimed that the employer's advertisement of a "career opportunity" was binding, this was not considered an offer. [*Horizon Corp. v. Weinberg*, 23 Ariz. App. 215, 531 P.2d 1153 (1975).]

Preparing an effective employment advertisement is more involved than it appears. Several preliminary considerations can ensure an advertisement's success by:

1. Checking the job description and job specifications to be sure they are correct;
2. Conducting a job analysis if there is doubt about a job description's or job specification's accuracy;
3. Writing the advertisement so that it can be easily read, omitting technical language; and

4. Selling the job to prospective applicants by writing advertisements to be appealing in structure and content, considering—
   - Printing style,
   - Borders,
   - Layout, and
   - Factual statements that highlight the job's major features. [D. Myers, *Human Resources Management: Principles and Practice* 288-90 (1986).]

To minimize employer litigation risks, the following should be considered:

1. Advertisements specifying sex, race, religion, age, national origin, handicap, or relating to these areas may invite employee challenges under federal and state FEP statutes;
2. Employers are prohibited from using help-wanted advertisements under "male" and "female" headings unless sex is a *bona fide* occupational qualification;
3. Advertisements should be worded to avoid creating contractual commitments by not suggested—
   - Long-term employment,
   - Guaranteed job security,
   - Guaranteed wages or salary, and
   - Career security;
4. To ensure consistency, the employer should centralize responsibility for advertisement development, writing, and placement with one group, namely the human resources staff, to minimize individual employment right problems.

Applications

Applications form the primary records about applicants, current employees, and former employees. They are used for blue-collar as well as white-collar employees. Applications generally request name and address, along with employment and educational histories. Some applications require a signed statement authorizing employer background information verification. Reference letters may be requested or they may be obtained absent the employee's knowledge. Detailed medical information is usually not requested; however, it may indicate that a pre-employment physical is an employment condition. Some request written consent for this physical examination.

HIRING GUIDELINES / 31

Background investigations may be done by the employer or by an outside organization. Outside organizations may retain a copy of this report for their files. This background investigation may be limited to verifying employment and education information disclosed on the application. However, it may involve credit checks, criminal record verifications, military record reviews, etc., along with inquiries of neighbors, friends, and other employees. These inquiries may involve the applicant's political activity, lifestyle, beliefs, opinions, character, family relationships, sexual preferences, etc.

Through these inquiries, applications can cause considerable individual employment rights problems. Initial employer decisions may be made solely based on these. This may eliminate certain applicants from consideration before they can demonstrate or have their qualifications for a particular position evaluated.

Applications generally impact individual employment rights, through federal and state fair employment practice (FEP) statutes. These relate to race, color, sex, national origin, handicap, and age. FEP statutes provide remedies for certain individual employment right violations. Depending upon the circumstances, tort litigation theories involving invasion of privacy, defamation, intentional infliction of emotional distress, negligent maintenance of disclosure of employment records, or public policy may be relevant. Contractual theories should also be consulted.

Applications should always be analyzed on the assumption that in subsequent litigation the employer will be required to defend: 1) the use of the information requested; or 2) to explain why the information was collected but not used. Problem questions on applications affecting individual employment rights involve:

1. Religion;
2. Sex discrimination;
3. Height/weight;
4. Marital status;
5. Education;
6. Arrest;
7. Convictions;
8. Military discharges;
9. Citizenship;
10. Credit status; and
11. Relatives.

Requesting one's clergy as a reference is the same as asking an applicant's religion. Sex discrimination may arise through inquiries regarding minor children and who will care for them during working hours. No employer has ever been able to justify that being married, widowed, divorced, or single has any legitimate relation to job performance. This information has traditionally been used to discriminate against women. Height and weight job requirements may also affect individual employment rights, particularly for police and fire services. It was once thought that tall police officers were more visible, less often attacked, and more authoritative. This has been proven untrue. Height requirements generally eliminate women and certain national origin groups. Height requirements for physically active jobs or those where safety is involved, however, may be job-related.

High school or college training inquiries must be necessary for the job in question. More education cannot be required than is a verifiable job requirement.

Statistics indicate that minorities are arrested more often for crimes of which they are ultimately found not guilty. Because of this, a strong job relation must exist to withstand discrimination claims.

Convictions, likewise, cannot be used to arbitrarily deny employment. They only can be used where the conviction is job-related. A recent conviction for theft might bar the applicant for a bank teller's position. Where convictions are inquired into, the employer should state on the application that conviction is not an absolute employment bar.

A legitimate business reason must exist to hire only those with honorable military discharges. This may be minority status discrimination because statistics show that minority groups receive a higher percentage of less-than-honorable discharges than non-minority groups.

Denying employment to legal aliens without a legitimate business necessity is national origin discrimination. The type of employment must be considered; i.e., citizenship alone cannot be the basis for disqualification.

Financial ability can also pose problems. Inquiries concerning home rental or ownership status, car ownership, bank accounts, bankruptcy, etc. that reveal an applicant's credit rating or history may affect statutorily protected interests or result in discrimination.

Inquiries regarding preference for relatives and friends working for an employer may indicate an intent to exclude minorities. It indicates not only that minorities are excluded but an intent to maintain this by hiring relatives and friends of white employees who also are white.

Information needed to provide employee benefits applies only to employees already hired. Questions about age, marital status, children, next of kin and whom to notify in the event of an emergency can be asked after the employee is hired. Retention of applications can also affect individual employment rights. FEP statutes require that these be retained for certain periods. Applicants, employees, and former employees are covered by this. The federal Civil Rights Act of 1964 (Title VII) requires a six-month retention while the Age Discrimination in Employment Act (ADEA) requires one year. Often these are retained much longer where they become part of an employee's personal file.

This retention imposes on-going employer concerns for safeguarding individual employment rights. Fair employment practice problems can still result along with claims for invasion of privacy, defamation, intentional infliction of emotional distress, negligent maintenance or disclosure of employment records, public policy, and contractual enforcement.

Initially, the employer must determine what information is needed to determine which applicant is best suited for a position. This may involve inquiries into education, professional licenses or certifications, previous work experience, special skills, talents, fluency in a foreign language, etc. The employer's special needs for the position may warrant that certain additional information be elicited.

After determining what job-related and general background information should be collected from the applicant, the remainder of the application should be drafted to preserve applicant privacy and limit employer liability by:

1. Informing the applicant that the employment is at-will;
2. Providing an applicant's acknowledgment that any information falsification or omission may result in termination;
3. Requiring the applicant's representation that the information provided is complete and accurate,
4. Including a release protecting the employer and those persons the employer contacts regarding references;
5. Inquiring only whether the applicant has any job-related physical condition or limitations that would disqualify him/her from performing the job; however, this may require that the applicant's physical condition be examined to determine if reasonable accommodations under federal and state FEP statutes could be made for the applicant to perform the job; and
6. Not inquiring regarding the applicant's filing for and/or receiving of benefits related to work-related illnesses or injuries, because this may be considered retaliation for these benefits' receipt.

The following should be considered regarding individual employment rights and applications:

1. Collecting only information that is relevant to specific employment decisions;
2. Telling applicants, employees, and former employees what use will be made of the collected information;
3. Letting applicants know what kinds of information will be maintained;
4. Adopting reasonable procedures to ensure that application information is accurate, timely, and complete; and
5. Limiting application disclosure internally and externally.

Interviews

Individual employment rights that are present in applications also exist in employment interviews. Unlike the application's written inquiry, the employment interview is primarily oral although a written record may be created. Information solicited by the application was initially responsible for determining who should be interviewed along with any pre-employment test's results. Interviews may be conducted with the prospective employee present, by telephone, or a combination telephone and in-person interview.

After the initial employment interview, others may be conducted prior to the final hiring decision. Depending upon the position recruited, these interviews may involve various authority groups within the employer's organization. At each interview, individual employment rights may be affected because each employer decision-making level attempts to refine the information initially requested to determine final selection by obtaining additional information to set the applicants apart.

Individual employment rights present in the interview process are primarily protected by federal and state fair employment practice (FEP) statutes. These FEP statutes apply not only to recruitment and hiring, but also to employee transfer and promotion. Depending upon the circumstances and the inquiry's scope, claims may also be asserted for invasion of privacy, defamation, intentional infliction of emotional distress, negligent maintenance or disclosure of employment records, public policy, or contractual enforcement.

Inquiries regarding race, sex, national origin, marital status, and religion should be avoided. Other areas that should not be considered include:

1. Former name;
2. Parents' names;
3. Place of birth;
4. Second language unless the job requires use of a second language;
5. Arrest record unless it can be proven that there is a legitimate business necessity for that requirement;
6. Who will take care of the children while the applicant works unless both sexes are asked and there is no unfair impact on one sex or the other;
7. Name of religion or clergy;
8. Religious clubs or organizations;
9. Date of birth;
10. Age;
11. Educational background unless it is job related; and
12. Physical disabilities unless it would affect job performance.

If this information is needed for legitimate business purposes, it can be obtained after hiring. Collection for insurance purposes would be one of these. This minimizes certain hiring concerns; however, maintaining and using this information after hiring may affect other interests by causing others to discriminate.

To maximize the benefits that can be derived from interviews, and to prevent statements during an interview that may lead to liability, the employer should use:

1. Well-informed and well-prepared interviewers who:
   - Become well-informed sufficiently prior to the interview by reviewing applications, resumes, and other pertinent information;
   - Know what further job-related information should be obtained from the applicant during the interview;
   - Know what information to convey about the employer; and
   - Know what information to convey about the particular job for which the applicant has applied.
2. Interviewers who are not only knowledgeable about the employer's advantages and benefits, but are aware that certain statements should not be made to *sell* applicants on the employer involving:
   - Overemphasizing the employer's virtues to avoid creating enforceable employee rights against the employer if the employee is later terminated;

- Becoming specific and promising definite employment terms and conditions greater than or different from the employer's oral or written policies, to avoid binding commitments; and
- Asking questions that could be considered discriminatory or an employee privacy intrusion; that is, only job-related inquiries should be used. [See American Hospital Association, *The Wrongful Discharge of Employees in the Health Care Industry* 20-21 (1987).]

The following are examples of impermissible interview inquiries and their acceptable counterparts:

Age

UNACCEPTABLE
1. What is your age?;
2. When were you born?; and
3. Dates of attendance or completion of elementary or high school.

ACCEPTABLE
1. Statement that hire is subject to verification that applicant meets legal age requirements?;
2. If hired can you show proof of age?;
3. Are you over eighteen years of age?; and
4. If under eighteen, can you, after employment, provide a work permit?

Arrest, Criminal Record

UNACCEPTABLE
1. Arrest record; and
2. Have you ever been arrested?

ACCEPTABLE
1. Have you ever been convicted of a felony, or, within two years, a misdemeanor which resulted in imprisonment? This question should be accompanied by a statement that a conviction will not necessarily disqualify the applicant from the job requested.

Birthplace, Citizenship

UNACCEPTABLE
1. Birthplace of applicant, applicant's spouse, or relatives; and
2. Are you a U.S. citizen?

ACCEPTABLE
1. Can you, prior to employment, submit verification of your legal right to work in the United States?;
2. Statement that this proof may be required at employment; and
3. Requirements that the applicant produce naturalization, first papers, or alien card prior to employment.

Bonding

UNACCEPTABLE
1. Questions regarding refusal or cancellation of bonding.

ACCEPTABLE
1. Statement that bonding is a condition of hire based on the position.

Military Service

UNACCEPTABLE
1. General questions regarding military service that pertain to date, type of discharge, etc., and
2. Questions regarding service in a foreign military.

ACCEPTABLE
1. Questions regarding relevant skills acquired during applicant's United States military service.

Name

UNACCEPTABLE
1. Maiden name.

ACCEPTABLE
1. Have you ever used another name?; and
2. Is any additional information regarding a name change, assumed name use, or nickname necessary to check on your work or education record? If yes, please explain.

National Origin

UNACCEPTABLE
1. Questions regarding nationality, lineage, ancestry, national origin, descent, or parentage of applicant, applicant's parents, or spouse;
2. What is your mother tongue?;
3. Language commonly used by applicant; and

4. How applicant acquired ability to read, write, or speak a foreign language.

ACCEPTABLE
1. Language applicant reads, speaks, or writes for job-related purposes.

Notice in Case of Emergency

UNACCEPTABLE
1. Name and address of relative to be notified in case of accident or emergency.

ACCEPTABLE
2. Name and address of person to be notified in case of accident or emergency.

Organizations/Activities

UNACCEPTABLE
1. List all organizations, clubs, societies, and lodges to which you belong.

ACCEPTABLE
1. List job-related organizations, clubs, professional societies, or other associations to which you belong. Omit those indicating or referring to your race, religious creed, color, national origin, ancestry, sex, or age.

Physical Condition/Handicap

UNACCEPTABLE
1. Questions regarding applicant's general condition, state of health, or illness;
2. Questions regarding receipt of worker's compensation; and
3. Do you have any physical disabilities or handicaps?

ACCEPTABLE
1. Statement by employer that the offer may be made contingent on applicant passing a job-related physical examination; and
2. Do you have any physical condition or handicap that may limit your ability to perform the job requested? If yes, what can be done to accommodate your limitation?

Race, Color

UNACCEPTABLE
1. Questions regarding applicant's race or color;

2. Questions regarding applicant's complexion or color of skin, eyes, or hair;
3. Requirement that applicant affix a photograph to application;
4. Requesting applicant, his/her option, to submit a photograph; and
5. Requiring a photograph after interview but before employment.

ACCEPTABLE
1. Statement that photograph may be required after employment.

Reference

UNACCEPTABLE
1. Questions of applicant's former employers or acquaintances which elicit information specifying the applicant's race, color, religious creed, national original ancestry, physical handicap, medical condition, marital status, age, or sex.

ACCEPTABLE
1. By whom were you referred for a position?; and
2. Names of persons willing to provide professional and/or character references for the applicant.

Religion

UNACCEPTABLE
1. Reference regarding applicant's religion,
2. Religious days observed, and
3. Does your religion prevent you from working weekends or holidays?

ACCEPTABLE
1. Statement by employer of regular days, hours, or shifts to be worked.

Sex, Marital Status, Family

UNACCEPTABLE
1. Questions indicating applicant's sex;
2. Questions indicating applicant's marital status;
3. Number and/or ages of children or dependents;
4. Questions regarding pregnancy, childbearing, or birth control;
5. Name(s) of spouse or children of applicant; and
6. Questions regarding child care.

ACCEPTABLE
1. Name and address of parent or guardian if applicant is a minor;

2. Statement of employer policy regarding work assignment of related employees; and
3. Do you have any relatives already employed? If so, give names and positions held.

EMPLOYMENT DATA VERIFICATION

Upon submitting an application, the employer may use various procedures to verify employment information. This may occur with or without the applicant's consent or knowledge. Subsequent verification may result from information obtained at employment interviews.

Data verification affects individual employment rights by collecting other information than the employee disclosed. This information may be irrelevant and not job-related. It may result in denying employment and may affect employment interests even where hiring occurs. This information may be maintained, used, and disclosed to limit subsequent employment opportunities. Verification may occur by checking credit, arrest records, criminal convictions, fingerprints, photographs, immigration requirements, and references.

Credit Checks

One of the most serious individual employment right violations is also the most common; i.e., the accumulation and disclosure of personal and often intimate information by credit bureaus. Often an employer will desire additional information about an individual than what was learned from applications, interviews, or references. These employer needs may be fulfilled by credit information.

Credit is essential for many employees. Banks, savings and loan associations, credit unions, and retailers are the usual credit grantors. Recorded information is essential to establish and maintain credit relationships. A credit bureau's records can disclose much about an individual's beliefs, associations, and lifestyle. Expenditures may reveal information about possessions, lodging, eating habits, travel, and associates. In addition to employment history, an employer may request a credit bureau to obtain information regarding reasons for leaving employment, whether a prior employer would rehire the individual, and records concerning education, including grades and class rank.

Individuals applying for credit consent to certain privacy intrusions. The more credit an individual requires, the more likely information will be disclosed, no matter how irrelevant. The individual's only concern at the time is obtaining the credit. Later, when the disclosed information's import can be assessed, the credit process has already been completed and the disclosed information has been recorded.

Federal and state statutes place certain restrictions on credit information use for employment purposes. Consumer credit reports are generally any oral, written, or other information communication by a credit reporting agency concerning an individual's credit eligibility, standing, or capacity. These may be used by employers in evaluating applicants or employees for promotion, reassignment, or retention.

Employers requesting these must certify the purpose for which they will be used and that they will not be used for another. Should an applicant be denied employment either wholly or partly because of a consumer credit report, the employer must so advise the applicant and furnish the consumer credit reporting agency's name and address. Consumer investigative reports provide information regarding character, general reputation, personal characteristics, or mode of living. This information is obtained through interviews with neighbors, friends, associates, or other personal acquaintances. Some states have enacted statutes regulating investigative consumer reports. Restrictions on investigative report use are similar to those contained in the Federal Fair Credit Report Act (FCRA).

Where an investigative consumer report is sought for employment purposes other than promotion or reassignment, some states require that an employer must notify the individual that the investigation has been requested. This written notification must explain that an investigative consumer report regarding character, general reputation, personal characteristics, and lifestyle will be made. It must also include the consumer reporting agency's name.

Non-job-related investigative reports may violate federal and state fair employment practice (FEP) statutes. A requirement that applicants and employees have a good credit record may have to be justified by business necessity.

Census figures and other statistics show that many more non-whites than whites are below the poverty level. It has been concluded under the federal Civil Rights Act of 1964 (Title VII) that an employer's good credit record requirement for job applicants had a disproportionate impact on nonwhites. [*EEOC Decision No. 74-02*, 6 Fair Empl. Prac. Cas. (BNA) 830 (1973).] Likewise, a bank's good credit record requirement had an adverse impact when statistics revealed that 35.4 percent of the nonwhite persons in the local geographic area were below the poverty level compared to 10.3 percent of the area's whites. [*EEOC Decision No. 72-0427*, 4 Fair Empl. Prac. Cas. (BNA) 304 (1971).] A general applicant background investigation that included inquiries into financial history violated Title VII where it disqualified a disproportionate number of minority applicants and was not job-related. [*U.S. v. Chicago*, 549 F.2d 415 (7th Cir. 1977).] Business necessity may be a defense. It was used to justify a bank's credit checks on successful job applicants where they were done on blacks and whites alike. For employment of tellers, a legitimate job-related business purpose was served. [*EEOC v. American National Bank*, 21 Fair Empl. Prac. Cas. (BNA) 1595 (E.D. Va. 1979).]

Credit investigations should be limited to job related information and be used only for applicants to positions involving access to highly confidential or classified information. Refusal of employment on these reports may be insufficient to withstand challenges of noncompliance with federal and state FEP statutes. Employers may be liable for an investigative firm's illegal acts where those acts are beyond the contract's scope.

Apart from liability imposed for wrongful nondisclosure, most fair credit reporting statutes, including the FCRA, prohibit an employee from suing an employer for defamation or invasion of privacy. Only a few states allow invasion of privacy claims. Maine does not immunize employers from invasion of privacy suits. California prohibits invasion of privacy actions arising out of consumer credit reports, but permits them for consumer investigative reports.

Employees may have potential legal claims against their employers where they discover that the employer obtained information from a credit agency that it was not legally permitted to request from employees directly. Applicants who are denied employment based on non-job-related information or information believed or known to be false, may be able to litigate claims based on a wrongful refusal to employ.

Arrest Records

Most employers believe that arrest history is critical or at least relevant to employment. Because of this, arrest information raises various concerns over individual employment rights. An arrest indicates only that a law enforcement officer believed that probable cause to arrest existed for some offense. It does not reflect that the person actually committed the offense. Someone may have been arrested for an apple's theft. Further investigation may reveal that the apple had been given to the individual. Yet, the arrest remains on the individual's record absent the reason why a conviction was not pursued. It's mere presence raises an unfounded suspicion about the individual.

Constitutional standards specify that convictions, not arrests, establish guilt. Denial of employment or employment opportunity curtailment because of an unproved charge, a charge that has been dismissed, or one for which innocence has been established, is fundamentally unfair. Individual employment rights are affected when this information is collected, used, maintained, or disclosed. It tends to impact associational and lifestyle interests. Some states expressly prohibit employment decisions based on arrest records.

Refusing employment or terminating employees because of arrest records is unlawful without evidence that the requirement is necessary to the employer's business operation. This excludes a disproportionate number of minority applicants or employees because they are more likely to be arrested.

Even when a legitimate pre-employment inquiry is made regarding arrest records, an applicant's rejection based solely on an arrest record may violate federal and state fair employment practice (FEP) statutes. Employment decisions that are based on an applicant's or employee's falsification or incomplete answer to an arrest record inquiry are not permitted. These questions have a chilling effect on minority applicants. They may solicit more false or incomplete answers by minority group members who suffer a disproportionate number of arrests making them disproportionately vulnerable to discipline for the falsification.

A practice of terminating employees for arrest record information falsification on job application forms did not violate the federal Civil Rights Act of 1964 (Title VII). The application set forth that a false statement would be cause for termination. The employee's claim that this was race discrimination against blacks because they are arrested in proportionately greater numbers than whites was rejected. The employee was not terminated for an arrest record, but for falsifying the application. To establish a prima facie case of disparate impact, the employee would have to show that blacks were excluded for falsifying arrest records at a higher rate than whites. [*Jimerson v. Kisco Co.,* 404 F. Supp. 338 (D. Mo. 1975), *aff'd,* 542 F.2d 1008 (8th Cir. 1976).]

Criminal Convictions

Criminal conviction records present different individual employment rights concerns than arrests. A conviction is a societal judgment regarding an individual's actions. Unlike arrests, a conviction record is complete; i.e., guilt and accountability have been finalized.

Federal and state statutes sometimes require certain employers to review conviction records for employment. Banks are required by the Federal Deposit Insurance Corporation (FDIC) to check every applicant for convictions involving crimes of dishonesty or breach of trust. Similarly, the Department of Transportation requires trucking companies to ascertain whether drivers have been convicted of reckless driving. The Bureau of Narcotics and Dangerous Drugs requires drug manufacturers to check conviction records.

Uneasiness exists for employers regarding conviction information collection, maintenance, use, and disclosure. Even though an employer may take employment actions based on criminal convictions where it correlates to the offense's nature, gravity, and time elapsed since the conviction to job-relatedness, concerns still remain over subsequent use that impact associational and lifestyle interests.

Under the federal Civil Rights Act of 1964 (Title VII), conviction cannot automatically deny employment, because of an adverse impact against blacks and other minorities, unless it is justified by business necessity. A policy of automatically terminating employees convicted of crimes discriminated against blacks because they are convicted at rates significantly in excess of their percentage in the general population. [*EEOC Decision No. 80-28*, 26 Fair Empl. Prac. Cas. (BNA) 1812 (1980).] Automatically excluding applicants with criminal convictions may be national origin discrimination in the southwest United States where the Spanish-surnamed population has a disproportionate conviction percentage than whites.

Employers must consider all the job-related circumstances of a conviction before determining that employment would be inconsistent with its safe and efficient business operation. These circumstances include:

1. The time, nature, and number of convictions;
2. The facts surrounding each offense;
3. The job-relatedness of each conviction;
4. The length of time between a conviction and the employment decision;

HIRING GUIDELINES / 45

5. The applicant's employment history before and after the conviction; and
6. The applicant's efforts at rehabilitation.

The employer must also demonstrate that the particular criminal conviction would prevent performance of the job in an acceptable businesslike manner.

The relationship between a conviction and the job cannot be too remote to justify disqualification. Remoteness existed where an employer:

1. Refused to hire a black as a mechanic because of a gambling conviction. (*EEOC Decision No. 71-2682,* 4 Fair Empl. Prac. Cas. (BNA) 25 (1971)];
2. Terminated a black utility operator in a manufacturing plant who was convicted of unlawful delivery of marijuana. [*EEOC Decision No. 80-18,* 26 Fair Empl. Prac. Cas. 1802 (1980)]; and
3. Failed to hire a black crane operator because of an armed robbery conviction. [*EEOC Decision No. 80-20,* 26 Fair Empl. Prac. Cas. (BNA) 1805 (1980).]

Job-relatedness was established where an employer:

1. Terminated a hotel's bellman for theft convictions and receiving stolen goods. [*Richardson v. Hotel Corp. of America,* 332 F.Supp. 519 (E.D. La. 1971), *aff'd,* 468 F.2d 951 (5th Cir. 1971)];
2. Refused to hire a black applicant for a custodial job because of a felony robbery conviction where the job required possession of a master set of keys. [*EEOC Decision No. 76-50,* CCH EEOC Dec. ¶6636 (1975)];
3. Refused to employ persons convicted of violent crimes where violent altercations occurred among employees during work hours on employer property. [*EEOC Decision No. 76-84,* CCH EEOC Dec. ¶6662 (1976)];
4. Terminated a black public auditorium utility worker because of a criminal record for rape, assault and battery, drunkenness, and a firearms offense. [*EEOC Decision No. 78-35,* 26 Fair Empl. Prac. Cas. (BNA) 1755 (1978)];
5. Terminated a black apartment manager who had unsupervised access to apartments and rent receipts, because of three convictions for theft-related offenses. [*EEOC Decision No. 79-40,* CCH EEOC Dec. ¶6778 (1979).]

Rehabilitation, a good work record, and the remoteness in time of the conviction can be used to overcome conviction job disqualifications. The business necessity defense was not effective where an employer:

1. Rejected a black bus driver applicant based on a burglary conviction because six years had passed since the conviction and the applicant's subsequent work history and rehabilitation efforts were good through recommendations from previous employers, community leaders, and parole and police officers. [*EEOC Decision No. 78-10*, CCH EEOC Dec. ¶6715 (1977)];
2. Failed to hire a black photographer who would have been required to handle money, because of a forgery conviction, where six years had elapsed between the conviction and the application for the job and the applicant had cooperated with authorities at the time of the conviction, had been steadily employed following his conviction, and had continued his education. [*EEOC Decision No. 80-16*, 26 Fair Empl. Prac. Cas. (BNA) 1799 (1980)];
3. Refused to hire a black crane operator/welder because of a six-year-old murder conviction where the applicant had worked for the employer for sixteen years before the conviction without disciplinary or violent incidents and where the violent crime was inconsistent with the applicant's established behavior. [*EEOC Decision No. 80-17*, 26 Fair Empl. Prac. Cas. (BNA) 1800 (1980)]; and
4. Failed to hire a black for a truck driver or dockman job because of a thirteen-year-old conviction for driving on a revoked license and two drunkenness convictions where the most recent conviction occurred four years before the job application. [*EEOC Decision no. 76-53*, CCH EEOC Dec. ¶6638 (1975).]

Job-relatedness considerations can outweigh evidence of the individual's rehabilitation, good work record, or the remoteness in time of the conviction. Business necessity prevailed where an employer:

1. Terminated a black truck driver because of a drunk driving conviction, even though the offense occurred on off-duty time in the employee's private vehicle and the driver had an otherwise clean criminal and work record. [*EEOC Decision No. 79-13*, CCH EEOC Dec. ¶6744 (1978)];
2. Terminated a black delivery person for a drug manufacturer because of larceny, receiving stolen property, and illegal weapons

offense convictions, even though the employee's work record was good. [*EEOC Decision No. 79-47,* CCH EEOC ¶6782 (1979)];
3. Refused to hire a black as a kitchen helper because of eleven convictions, six of which were theft-related, and the most recent of which was only six months before the job rejection, despite that the applicant had made consistent efforts to find work since his prison release. [*EEOC Decision No. 79-61,* CCH EEOC Dec. ¶6795 (1979)]; and
4. Failed to hire a black applicant as a bill collector involving entry to customers' homes because of a murder conviction, even though the applicant had worked satisfactorily for the employer for four years before the conviction and the crime was not consistent with the employee's established behavior before or after the murder. [*EEOC Decision No. 79-5,* CCH EEOC Dec. ¶6736 (1978).]

Employment policies calling for applicant or employee termination for falsely responding to employer conviction record inquiries are subject to Title VII challenge. However, it must be established that minority group members either lie about conviction records more often than others or that they are disproportionately excluded from employment because of this falsification. Despite this, an employer must still use due care in selecting and retaining only competent and careful employees. Liability for a negligent hiring may be alleged against an employer where an employee with a criminal conviction adversely affects or injures another during the employment relationship.

Fingerprinting

Fingerprinting is often used during the initial hiring process to verify information. As a collection method, it presents individual employment rights problems involving maintenance, use, and disclosure of these records that could also subsequently affect the employee's lifestyle.

Fingerprinting has generally been considered a valid collection method related more to verifying information than to compulsory incriminating fact extraction. Despite its primary use in verifying information, some states regulate fingerprinting to limit privacy abuses. California prohibits an employer from requiring that an applicant or employee be photographed or fingerprinted for the purpose of furnishing information to a third party as a condition precedent to securing or retaining employment where this information could be used to the applicant's or employee's detriment.

Even though fingerprinting has not previously encountered severe individual employment right challenges, it is possible that the future may alter this. Because of the continued regulation of lie detectors and other truth eliciting devices, fingerprinting may be used as an alternative in certain situations. Consider a theft situation involving a locked drawer. To ascertain responsibility, the employer could use fingerprinting to investigate the theft.

Depending upon the circumstances, this could lead to employee claims. If police were used, fourth amendment search and fifth amendment self-incrimination rights might be present through state action involvement. Should the employer's actions become sufficiently outrageous, tort actions could arise for:

1. Invasion of privacy;
2. Defamation where an employee is accused of the theft and this is published throughout the workplace;
3. False imprisonment where the employee is restrictively confined to obtain the fingerprints;
4. False arrest and malicious prosecution where the theft claim against the employee is ungrounded;
5. Intentional infliction of emotional distress where the employer's conduct in procuring the fingerprints is sufficiently outrageous; and
6. Public policy.

Contractual claims could also be asserted, where applicable, for employer violations of search procedures under collective bargaining agreements and handbooks.

Photographs

The mere taking of someone's photograph without consent has not ordinarily been considered a privacy invasion. Most individuals do not object to having their photograph taken. It is not until the photograph is published that they become offended. This may occur for some purpose that is offensive or for commercial use.

Employers have been permitted to photograph employees over their objections when a legitimate business purpose existed. This might be to improve safety or to identify employees who are violating employer rules.

Photographing employees during the initial hiring process, however, has raised objections. These have been primarily protected under the federal and state fair employment practice (FEP) statutes. The Equal Employment Opportunity Commission's (EEOC's) Rules and Regulations have consistently cautioned against unnecessary identification tools in personnel actions. Should an employer require a photograph, this may not be *per se* discrimination; however, as a potential method to practice discrimination, the EEOC may consider this negatively. Prohibited inquiry information not readily available from an application can be determined from a photograph; i.e., race, sex, national origin, and age.

The requirement that an applicant affix a photograph to an application at any time prior to hiring or at their option has been considered illegal in many states. California prohibits an employer from requiring that an applicant or employee be photographed or fingerprinted for the purpose of furnishing information to a third party as a condition precedent to securing or retaining employment where this could be used to the applicant's or employee's detriment.

Immigration Requirements

The Immigration Reform and Control Act of 1986 creates an additional recordkeeping requirement for employers in curtailing illegal immigration into the United States. It is a major policy effort to remove the incentive for illegal immigration by eliminating job opportunities. The Act requires every employer to ask applicants for specific written verification establishing that they can be employed. Civil and criminal penalties are provided for employers who knowingly hire or recruit an alien.

Every employer must verify the identity and eligibility for employment of every person that is hired. One of the following may be used to establish the identity and the authorization to work of an employment applicant:

1. A United States passport;
2. A United States citizenship certificate;
3. A naturalization certificate;
4. An unexpired foreign passport, if the passport has an appropriate, unexpired endorsement of the Attorney General authorizing the individual's employment in the United States; or
5. A resident alien card or other alien registration card that contains a photograph or other personal identifying information that is evidence of authorization for employment in the United States.

Where an applicant cannot produce one of the dual purpose documents, the employer must ask for two documents that provide separate evidence of identification and of work authorization. A document that establishes only evidence of employment authorization is:

1. A Social Security Card;
2. A certificate of birth in the United States or establishing United States nationality at birth; and
3. Other documents approved by the Attorney General in forthcoming regulations.

Documents establishing the individual's identity are:

1. A driver's license or similar document issued for identification purposes by a state containing a photograph or other personal identifying information; or
2. For persons under sixteen years of age of in states that do not provide identification cards other than a driver's license, other documentation approved by the attorney general in forthcoming regulations.

The employer must attest on a form that it has verified that an applicant is not an illegal alien. The employee must also attest on the same form that he/she is either a citizen of the United States, an alien lawfully admitted for permanent residence, or an alien who is authorized to work. The form must then be retained for three years after hiring or for one year after employment termination, whichever is longer.

The Act prohibits employers from discriminating against applicants through their national origin. It is an "unfair immigration-related employment practice" to discriminate against any individual in hiring, recruitment, termination because of that individual's national origin or citizenship status.

This information should not be collected until the applicant pool has been sufficiently narrowed prior to hiring. Otherwise, the potential for individual employment right problems exist by disclosing age, national origin, or other discriminatory data. Once collected, it should be maintained separate from the employee's personnel file to prevent disclosures that could have a discriminatory impact. This will minimize individual employment right challenges arising out of federal or state fair employment practice (FEP) statutes.

Reference Checks

Confronted with federal and state fair employment practice (FEP) statute limits on the information that can be collected from an applicant, many employers use verbal or written employment references to expand these data. This information is often collected or disclosed absent the employee's knowledge. It often involves former employers who may be solicited without the employee's knowledge or consent.

Some states statutorily regulate employee references. California makes it a misdemeanor for an employer to make misrepresentations that prevent or attempt to prevent a former employee from obtaining other employment. The employer also commits a misdemeanor if it permits one of its employees to make a misrepresentation or if it fails to take reasonable steps to prevent the misrepresentation. Employers may furnish a truthful statement concerning the reason for a former employee's termination or voluntary termination. If this statement is not in response to a request or should it be accompanied by marks or symbols that convey information contrary to the statement, it is prima facie evidence of a misrepresentation. The employer can be liable for treble damages in a civil action.

A negative employer reference can be questioned under federal or state FEP statutes when the former employee claims that it was issued because of the employee's membership in a protected group. This may occur where an untruthful negative reference is given about a black employee because of racial animosity toward blacks. When an employer responds truthfully to a prospective employer's request, the employer may not retaliate for an employee having filed a claim under certain statutes.

Where the employer discloses to a large number of people true but embarrassing private facts about an employee, public disclosure of private facts may also offer relief. Revealing information from an employee's personnel file about health, family, or job performance in a news article might impose this liability. This occurred even without broad public announcement of private facts where a supervisor disclosed to employees that he had sexual relations with another employee. However, the employee had waived her cause of action by her own disclosure to others. [*Cummings v. Walsh Construction Co.*, 561 F.Supp. 872 (S.D. Ga. 1983).]

Defamation may impose employer responsibility. This affects the employee's privacy interest in reputation. It encompasses any false and unprivileged communication, either oral or written, that injures the employee. If the communication is made with malice, the employer may be subject to punitive damages.

Employees who claim that an employer's reason for termination was false may assert that the employer "defamed" them where this is repeated in a reference to a prospective employer. However, employers have a legitimate need to exchange information about former and prospective employees without fear of litigation. A *qualified privilege* for employment references has been recognized.

Employers who issue references are generally protected where the reference was made in good faith, without any malice, or a reckless disregard for truth. This qualified privilege may be lost if the reference includes information that was extraneous to job performance or if the circumstances indicate it was motivated by personal animosity. The doctrine of qualified immunity protected federal officials from liability for remarking to a prospective employer that a former employee had used excessive leave and had trouble with other employees. [*Jefferson v. Ashley,* 643 F. Supp. 227 (D. Or. 1986).]

A former hospital employee claimed that he had been defamed by the hospital's statement to a prospective employer that he had been terminated "for cause." The employer maintained that stating it had acted with "cause" could not be defamatory. However, the statement's defamatory meaning had to be tested against the average reader's understanding because "for cause" could be interpreted as implying incompetence. [*Carney v. Memorial Hospital,* 64 N.Y.2d 770, 485 N.Y.S.2d 984 (1985).]

A viable defamation claim was stated against an employer who had stated only that its employee, a lawyer, had "suddenly resigned." The employer argued that the phrase "suddenly resigned" was incapable of any defamatory meaning. This phrase suggested to a prospective employer "that the party who resigned did so under a veil of suspicion or scandal. [*Klages v. Sperry Corp.,* 118 L.R.R.M. (BNA) 2463 (E.D. Pa. 1984).]

The "name, rank and serial number" approach to employment references may not absolve an employer from liability. This occurred where an employer adopted a policy of refusing to discuss former employees with prospective employers. Although the employer explained to the four employees that it was terminating them for "gross insubordination," the employer did not "publish" that statement to any other person or directly to any prospective employer. When the employees sought other employment, they encountered questions from prospective employers about their prior employment. The employees "republished" the employer's stated "grounds" for termination. Because the republication should have been *reasonably foreseeable* to the former employer and the claim of "gross insubordination" was not substantially true, the employees received a nearly one million dollar jury award of compensatory and punitive damages. [*Lewis v. Equitable Life Assurance Soc'y,* 361 N.W. 2d 875 (Minn. App. 1985).]

Intentional interference with contractual relations may also impose employer liability. Relief may be available if a prospective employer decides not to hire an employee based on false statements or inappropriate facts disclosed to the former employer. Generally, this requires:

1. A valid contractual relationship or business expectancy;
2. Knowledge of the relationship or expectancy by the former employer;
3. Intentional interference, inducing, or causing a breach or termination of the relationship or expectancy; and
4. Resultant damage.

Allowing an employee to litigate the truth of an employer personal action is *de facto* recognition of a "just cause" termination standard. Given the potential for liability an employer should devote care and caution to any employment reference request. Supervisors and managers should be thoroughly briefed on the precise policy and approach selected. References should never be given by telephone unless adequate verification by a return telephone call of the caller's identity has been obtained. If a telephone reference is given, a written record of the dates and details should be maintained for the employer's protection.

Where a policy of not furnishing references has been adopted, supervisors or clerical employees should be briefed on a standardized explanation. It should be made clear that the employer's no-reference policy is a neutral measure applicable to all and not just to a specific person.

If references are given concerning former employees, the employer should act on the assumption that the reference and the underlying personnel action will someday be subject to scrutiny. A reference should be limited to a fact statement that the employer is prepared to defend.

EMPLOYMENT TESTING

Testing has long been an employment selection device. They are attractive to employers for further identifying those who are the most qualified for a particular job. However, many employers test for more than skill or ability to do the job. They test areas that are at best arguably related to predicting job performance but often concern moral and medical standards. Often this testing probes individual employment rights present in or related to beliefs, speech, associations, and lifestyles.

Outside of testing for job performance, employers are increasingly evaluating employees through medical screening, genetic screening, blood testing, polygraph examinations, honesty testing, and handwriting analysis. For individual employment rights, all testing raises significant concerns.

Testing impacts all aspects of information collection, maintenance, use, and disclosure. The results of any test has the potential of affecting employee lifestyles outside the workplace should inaccurate data be collected, maintained, used, or disclosed. Diminished employment opportunity, financial expectations, or social relationships may result.

Medical Screening

It is often difficult to determine what caused employment rejection. The individual may know the information that they disclosed to the employer, but they may not know what other information was collected to make the hiring decision. During the hiring process, medical questionnaires or physical examinations may be completed. This may result in employment denial because of uncertain medical conditions involving obesity, color blindness, arthritis, hypertension, allergies, and varicose veins.

For individual employment rights, this raises concerns over information collection, maintenance, use, and disclosure. Because this information may be collected without the employee's knowledge or its results may not be disclosed, the employee loses control over this decision-making information. This prohibits the employee from presenting an adequate rebuttal to counter medical findings. Once collected, this information presents an ongoing problem regarding the potential for subsequent disclosures. This may occur when the employee applies for another position. If collected, the employee should be entitled to copies of all medical screening information to also evaluate the effect it has on current and future employment opportunities.

The unfairness of an unfavorable employment decision based on medical screening often continues beyond exclusion from one job. Once refused, it may be difficult to obtain similar or other employment. Medical screening programs consist of several tests and procedures. Certain findings will result in automatic exclusion. Employers are reluctant to divulge what these are. Urine and blood tests could be used to screen out pregnant females or to identify various maladies, ailments, or diseases for which the employer does not wish to risk exposure. Medical screening may be used instead of reducing workplace hazards.

Health *history records* should be considered separately from *health condition records*. A health history reveals the employee's past medical condition. This history may disclose past incidents of alcoholism or other sensitive items that the employee desires to remain confidential. It is more sensitive regarding privacy because it often documents prior conditions that may be embarrassing that are not part of the employee's present ability to be employed. Medical condition concerns the employee's present health condition.

Increasingly, employers may be subject to litigation over medical screening information. Depending upon whether private or public sector employees are involved, constitutional, statutory, or other litigation theories may be applicable. Where three long-time sales employees of a pharmaceutical company were required to complete a biographical summary that included information about business experience, education, family, home ownership, physical data, activities, and aims invasion of privacy was raised. The medical history section asked about serious illnesses, operations, accidents, nervous disorders, smoking, and drinking habits. The employees considered this information personal and irrelevant. They either refused to answer these questions or did so incompletely. The employees were thereafter terminated. No invasion of privacy occurred because the employees did not complete the questionnaire. Had the questionnaire been completed and had more intensive questions been asked, at-will employment's public policy exception may have been relevant. [*Cort v. Bristol Myers Co.*, 385 Mass. 300, 431 N.E.2d 908 (1982).]

A sex discrimination claim related to invasion of privacy was partly successful. Where a female applied for a job she was required to complete a medical history form. One section marked "Women" asked about menstruation, pap smears, etc. The female did not complete this section and her physician, who performed the pre-employment physical examination, wrote "healthy female." When she was denied employment for failing to complete this medical questionnaire, she filed a complaint under the state's fair employment practices (FEP) statute. She contended that the form was discriminatory by requiring urogenital health of only females and not males. This was found to be discriminatory and rejected the employer's defenses that the questions were necessary to detect specific health problems. [*Wroblewski v. Lexington Gardens, Inc.*, 188 Conn. 44, 448 A.2d 801 (1982).] It is possible that federal and state FEP statutes may provide relief to medical screening intrusions where appropriate facts exist.

Under collective bargaining agreements, arbitrators require that employers demonstrate that medical information be job-related for current employees. [See *Bondtex Corp.*, 68 Lab. Arb. (BNA) 476 (1977) (Coburn, Arb.).] Employees are not required to release all medical records to the employer as a prerequisite to a physical examination. [*Western Airlines*, 74 Lab. Arb. (BNA) 923 (1980) (Richman, Arb.).] Random physical examinations absent specific cause are not permitted. [*Conchemco, Inc.*, 55 Lab. Arb. (BNA) 54 (1970) (Ray, Arb.).]

A disturbing aspect is that most individuals confronted with medical screening inquiries acquiesce to employer demands and provide this information. With the increasing use of medical screening, there is a likelihood that applicants or employees may refuse information disclosure based on religious, ethical, medical, privacy, or other reasons. Limited constitutional, statutory, or other litigation relief exists. Unless the medical screening violates a specific statute, regulation, or collective bargaining agreement little recourse may exist but to suffer employment denial.

Genetic Screening

Recent scientific data suggest that there may be a correlation between inherited genetic traits and occupational disease caused by exposure to workplace hazards. [See M. Rothstein, *Medical Screening of Workers* 69 (1984).] Genetic traits are inheritable and all children of a person with a certain genetic trait may be subject to employment denial on the same basis. Substantial portions of a racial or ethnic group could be disqualified. Denying employment because of genetic factors may disproportionately impact selected racial and ethnic groups. This information may have continuing individual employment rights implications once it is collected affecting current and future employment opportunities of not just the individual but offspring and other family members.

Screening applicants or employees for genetic traits that may make them more vulnerable than the average person to workplace toxins is still in its infancy. Two types of genetic tests may be used in the workplace. These are: 1) genetic monitoring or cytogenetic testing; and 2) genetic screening.

Genetic monitoring or cytogenetic testing checks the number of broken or damaged chromosomes in the employee's somatic cells. Cytogenetic testing can show when employees have been exposed to a higher than normal dose of radiation or chemicals that can cause chromosome breakage. Some researchers believe that high chromosome breakage levels indicates a greater cancer probability. However, those with chromosome breakage are not necessarily the ones who will get cancer.

Genetic screening collects information regarding specific genetic traits that indicate the applicant or employee has a risk of occupational disease from workplace exposure that is significantly greater than those without the genetic trait. These genetic traits may include:

1. Glucose 6 phosphate dehydrogenase deficiency, an inherited trait leading to hypersusceptibility to hemolytic agents;
2. Debris oquine-sparteine oxidation which enhances the danger from liver activated carcinogens;
3. Wilson's disease, a genetic disorder that markedly increases the toxicity of copper; and
4. Serum alphal antitrypsin production which can lead to significantly greater damage from exposure to respiratory irritants. [See McConnell, *Genetic Testing's Conflict with Discrimination Laws,* 9 Nat'l L. J. 14 (No. 22, February 9, 1987).]

The Occupational Safety and Health Act (OSHA) of 1970s regulations on at least fourteen workplace toxins requires the employer to provide each employee with a medical examination, including genetic tests, before putting the employee in a work situation where there may be exposure to a hazardous substance. While the fourteen substances currently covered by genetic screening regulations all present a cancer or sterility risk, it is possible of genetic screening requirements being extended to other risks as scientific knowledge develops.

OSHA regulations require that medical examination of genetic factor results be provided to the employee. Some state "right to know" statutes and OSHA right to know regulations require the chemical supplier to give each employee information about hazards encountered in handling toxic substances.

Because the OSHA regulations for genetic factors do not specify which genetic factors are to be examined, it is generally up to the employer and the examining physician to determine which genetic traits to test. The medical and scientific judgment of whether a particular genetic test has sufficient validity, specificity, and predictive value to be of use in the workplace is complicated.

Genetic testing may disqualify otherwise medically fit applicants. The more tests performed on a healthy subject, the more likely is the discovery of an abnormal result. Handicapped employees may have even less chance of being hired, regardless of their ability to perform.

Currently, little statutory protection exists for employees subject to genetic testing. OSHA permits the Secretary of Labor to require the use of measures to protect employee health, including genetic screening and monitoring. Unions could also include employee genetic screening restrictions in collective bargaining agreements.

This could constitute discrimination under federal and state fair employment practice (FEP) statutes. A screening program for the sickle-cell trait, even if it included all employees, could have a disparate impact on blacks. This would be "fair in form but discriminatory in operation" because blacks are more likely to have this trait. The employer would have to prove that:

1. The test predicts the likelihood of future illness;
2. The lower risk of future illness is a legitimate job qualification; or
3. Excluding susceptible employees is a legitimate business necessity.

Federal and state FEP statutes prohibiting handicapped discrimination might prevent employees from being excluded from employment. Employees would have to establish that "handicap" covers a genetic trait and that future illnesses are not a legitimate inquiry for employers.

There is no clear scientific evidence that genetic screening programs benefit employers. Using genetic screening for arbitrary employment exclusion is not legitimate. This testing may violate FEP laws because certain genetic characteristics occur disproportionately among certain racial or ethnic groups. Labor, privacy, health and safety, and age discrimination statutes may pose genetic screening problems. Should genetic screening information not be properly collected, maintained, used, or disclosed, claims may result out of invasion of privacy, defamation, intentional infliction of emotional distress, negligent maintenance or disclosure of employment records, public policy violations, etc.

The response that an employer can make to limit liability is to reduce exposure levels at the workplace. This would obviate the need for genetic screening and the individual employment rights concerns associated with it.

Blood Testing

Blood testing has generally been considered a valid collection device. When used to extract incriminating facts without the employee's consent, individual employment rights problems could arise, especially in certain drug-related or human immunodeficiency virus (HIV) areas. Considerable medical information regarding an applicant's or employee's health can be obtained from these tests. Outside of drug or coronary problems, the employer can identify other maladies, ailments, or diseases for which exposure is not desired. This raises the same concerns over individual employment rights presented by medical and genetic screening. These are applicable to blood testing depending upon the circumstances in which this information is collected, maintained, used, or disclosed.

Skill Testing

Recent years have brought increasing concern to individual employment rights over the confusion surrounding skill testing. For employers, a desire exists to fill available positions with employees qualified for the tasks assumed. This, combined with only a vague knowledge of what the law exacts as prerequisites for skill testing presents important employment considerations. Tests may deny employment to minorities without evidence that they were related to success on the job. Yet, employers desire to continue using tests in selecting employees. This belief in skill testing as a method of employee selection and evaluation has provoked inquiry by the courts. Basic to this inquiry is the inequitable treatment accorded blacks, other ethnic minorities, women, etc. by this testing. Inadequate educational preparation to perform satisfactorily on these tests has meant for minority employees:

1. Failure to attain employment;
2. Lower pay;
3. Lower priority for promotion; and
4. Stagnation in dull positions.

Efforts to select employees by tests began early in the twentieth century. During World War II the defense industry and the military utilized tests for measuring abilities and intelligence. This was considered essential for screening vast numbers of people for assimilation into the wartime economy. Results of these attempts to place individuals into appropriately skilled positions aided psychologists. This afforded psychologists the opportunity to ascertain the validity of standardized tests and their ability to predict performance. However, not until after World War II did psychological tests receive widespread acceptance by private and public employers.

It has generally been believed that skill testing offers an objective standard to achieving a systematic degree of success in predicting performance. It has been brought to the attention of employers and others that some tests have eliminated ethnic minorities from certain positions. This awareness has focused upon the realization that some tests were developed in favoring levels of education typical of white, middle class backgrounds. Performance on these tests has been poor by the economically disadvantaged. Steps within the total employment process may each produce unfair discrimination that affects individual employment rights.

Educational and industrial psychologists have played a major role in developing tests that attempt to predict job performance. These tests remove some of the subjectivity used in employee selection. Employment testing has developed into a highly sophisticated and technical field with its own language, its own standards, and its own complex methodology.

Testing can have a significant impact on information collection, maintenance, use, and disclosure. Depending upon the test, it may reveal interests present in employee speech, beliefs, information, association, and lifestyle. These concerns are essentially protected by federal and state fair employment practice (FEP) statutes.

FEP statutes generally require that a protected classification not be a factor in employment selection. If a selection procedure has a disproportionate impact that excludes protected persons, its use is unlawful unless the procedure is demonstrably a reasonable measure of job performance; i.e., unless it is job-related or justified by business necessity.

Under the Civil Rights Act of 1964 (Title VII), the Uniform Guidelines on Employee Selection Procedures have been developed. The Guidelines define a selection procedure broadly as any measure, combination of measures, or procedure used as a basis for an employment decision.

Employment decisions include hiring, promotion, membership, referral, retention, and selection for training or transfer. Selection procedures include traditional paper and pencil tests, performance tests, training programs, probationary periods, informal or casual interviews, unscored application forms, and physical, educational, and work experience requirements.

Title VII does not prohibit employers from giving or acting on the results of a professionally developed ability test where the test, its administration, or action on its results is not designed, intended, or used to discriminate. State FEP laws also provide exceptions from their discriminatory prohibitions for employment decisions based on professionally developed ability tests.

A professionally developed test must be job-related. [*Griggs v. Duke Power Co.*, 401 U.S. 424 (1971).] The Guidelines permit selection procedures to be supported by validity studies conducted by test publishers or distributors and described in test manuals. FEP enforcement agencies consider evidence that a professional job analysis was conducted.

General reputation of a test or other selection procedure, its author or its publisher, or casual reports of its validity are not accepted absent validity evidence. Validity assumptions based on a procedure's name or descriptive labels, all forms of promotional literature, data bearing on the frequency of a procedure's usage, testimonial statements and credentials of sellers, users, or consultants, and other nonempirical or anecdotal accounts of selection outcomes are not dispositive. Testimony by an expert witness that a test is widely used by similar employers, together with conclusive opinions, is insufficient to establish a test's validity.

"Validity" involves formulating tests to actually measure what they purport to measure. A valid test would rate prospective employees in exactly the same relationship to one another as they would stand after performance on the job. Selection upon the basis of tests that have no known validity may be little different from a random selection.

Three validation methods are generally recognized. These are:

1. Criterion-related validation;
2. Construct violation; and
3. Content validation.

Criterion-related or empirical validation is preferable to other validation methods. Under *criterion-related* validation, two methods are considered: 1) predictive validation; and 2) concurrent validation. *Predictive* validation consists of a comparison between the test scores and the subsequent job performance of those applicants who are hired. *Concurrent* validation requires the administration of the test to a group of current employees and a comparison between their scores and performance on the job. The methodology uniting these two types of criterion-related validities requires two steps. First, criteria must be identified that indicate successful job performance. Secondly, test scores are matched with job performance ratings for the selected criteria.

The second recognized validation method is *construct* validation. This requires identifying general mental and psychological traits considered necessary to successful job performance. The qualifying test must then be fashioned to measure the presence of these general traits.

The third method is *content* validation. Content validity matches the job's content with the test's content. For a test to be content valid, the aptitudes and skills required for successful test performance must be aptitudes and skills required for successful job performance. It is essential that the test measures these attributes in proportion to their importance on the job and at the level of difficulty demanded by the job.

Reliability of the test concerns its consistency as a measuring instrument. If a test is reliable, a person taking it at two different times should score substantially the same. No test is of value in employee selection unless it has a high degree of reliability. This is usually determined by either giving:

1. The test to the same group at two separate times and correlating the resultant series of test scores;
2. Two or more different (but equivalent) forms of the same test and correlating the resultant test scores; or
3. The test only once by dividing the items and correlating scores on one-half of the items with scores on the other half.

Objects of measurement concerns classifying tests regarding their purpose; i.e., what is to be measured. Generally, tests seek to measure either capacity or achievement, but this is an oversimplification.

General Abilities are commonly measured by the general intelligence test. There is still some disagreement among psychologists regarding what exactly the various standardized tests of abstract intelligence measure. Experts may disagree on whether general intelligence is a combination of just a few special capacities or aptitudes or of a great range of specific abilities. However, a combination it is.

General abilities or intelligence tests are the most common instrument used in employment testing. Usually the capacities of verbal ability, abstract reasoning, quantitative reasoning, and spatial visualization are measured. Significant research and standardization have gone into intelligence test development that a number of widely known general instruments are available.

Special Abilities or Aptitudes measure other than the basic elements found within so-called general abilities tests. Some of the particular areas of capacity for which specialized intelligence tests have been developed are mechanical, number facility, memory, word fluency, and finger dexterity. These have been identified through validity studies that help determine their varying degrees of importance in a variety of occupations and activities.

Achievement measures particular skills. They are used in selecting employees already possessed of particular job skills. They are indicative of the possibilities of future development. Tests of this type are: 1) education; 2) trade; and 3) demonstration or performance.

Health and Physical determinations by a medical staff are not confined to situations requiring special strength or agility. To ensure reasonable continuity and avoid unnecessary retirement system costs, it is not uncommon to require basic health tests of individuals applying for employment. These tests customarily are given only to those selected for actual employment. Some positions require special physical attainment, strength, endurance, agility, coordination, or other qualities. Possible examples are police officers, firemen, sanitation workers, laborers, etc. In these instances, the physical test may include special features and be part of the test process on which all individuals are rated.

That *Personality and Emotional* traits are closely related to vocational success has long been recognized; however, their identification and measurement have proved difficult. Emotional stability may be particularly critical for success in certain positions. There has been widespread interest in efforts to gauge personal and emotional adaptability to the stresses of the position.

Depending upon these tests' use, individual employment right intrusions may result that are related to this information's collection, maintenance, use, or disclosure. Where a wide public disclosure of private facts occurs regarding a test's use that injures an employee, an invasion of privacy may exist. This could occur through broad disclosure of a poor test score to those not entitled to this information for the purpose of ridiculing or humiliating someone. Defamatory use of test results through a false disclosure may likewise impose employer responsibility. Where outrageous employer conduct is associated with these tests, intentional infliction of emotional distress of test results may involve negligent maintenance or disclosure of employment records.

Polygraph Examinations

Polygraph examinations and other truth eliciting devices present serious individual employment right questions. The potential for improper information collection, maintenance, use, and disclosure are always present. Lifestyle regulation is also affected in that employment opportunities and community perception can be injured.

Requiring employees to undergo an examination that will determine truthfulness and reliability initially appears harmless and even job-related. However, often it probes areas where the employee prefers privacy by eliciting statements that are offensive, insulting, or non-job related. These tests may probe employment privacy interests present in beliefs, speech, associations, and lifestyles.

In 1895, Italian psychologist Cesare Lumbroso claimed he could detect a lie by measuring changes in blood pressure. William Moulton Marston, a Harvard educated psychologist, later popularized the polygraph's use in the United States during the 1920s when he suggested using it in the Lindbergh kidnapping investigation.

The polygraph examination is intended to be a truth-verification collection device. It consists of: 1) a corrugated rubber tube that is attached to the subject's chest to measure the respiratory rate; 2) an inflated rubber cuff attached to the arm that measures blood pressure and pulse rate; and 3) two electrodes attached to the hand that measure the flow of electric current (galvanic skin response) as the rate of perspiration increases. Its intrusive nature and accuracy have been consistently disputed.

Many states regulate or prohibit its use. Similar legislation exists at the federal level. Today, the Federal Employee Polygraph Protection Act of 1988 has severely limited this examination's use throughout the United States. Courts generally consider its results inadmissible as evidence. Under collective bargaining agreements, many arbitrators also refuse to consider this evidence.

Employer security programs may involve not only polygraph examinations for those suspected of rule violations, but may also include applicants and current employees. This is done even though restricted or prohibited by statutes, courts, and arbitrators.

Under the National Labor Relations Act (NLRA), an employer's use of a polygraph examination to discover union sympathies or protected activities of employees constitutes an unfair labor practice. All polygraph examinations in the employment setting, however, are not precluded. Where statutorily permitted, an employer may promulgate rules requiring employees to submit to polygraph examinations regarding serious or theft related employment misconduct. A known union adherent can be required to submit to a polygraph examination when the request's motivation is wholly unrelated to matters protected by the NLRA. If the employee refuses, the NLRA does not prevent the employer from terminating the employee because of a refusal to cooperate. Where an employee agrees to a polygraph examination concerning unprotected activities, however, the employee may be terminated for failing the test where the failure was not a pretense for anti-union sentiment.

Although an employer can use a polygraph examination to investigate employee misconduct without violating the NLRA, it is obligated to negotiate with the union before implementing it. This is sufficiently related to "terms and conditions of employment" to constitute a mandatory collective bargaining subject. Employer unilateral implementation without any prior negotiations is an NLRA violation unless there is a management rights clause in the collective bargaining agreement that could reasonably be construed to give the employer the authority to act unilaterally with respect to this. Where the union has a chance to negotiate and fails to indicate a desire to discuss the suggested plan or reaches a *bona fide* impasse during good faith bargaining, the employer may implement its proposed policy.

Where permitted by statute and under collective bargaining agreements, an arbitrator should not indiscriminately admit polygraph examination results into evidence. To be admitted, it should have been knowingly taken by the employee under circumstances warranting compulsory examination or the employee should have voluntarily agreed to undergo the particular examination.

A general pre-employment consent form authorizing the employer to conduct polygraph examinations whenever it deems necessary should not be accepted. This is not voluntary because a prospective employee is too likely to view it as an employment prerequisite. Documents granting relatively unlimited consent should also be rejected. A polygraph examination is potentially so intrusive and damaging that one would not ordinarily grant blanket consent unless employment status was in immediate jeopardy.

The arbitrator should consider the employee's alleged involvement. Where the test was administered to an impartial witness not implicated in the alleged misconduct, there is less reason to question consent. Polygraph evidence obtained from the grievant or another employee under suspicion should be treated cautiously. This may have been consented to out of fear for employment or may have been under extreme peer pressure from other employees. The fundamental right to be free from nonconsensual intrusions should take precedence over any evidentiary benefits in these situations that might be derived. Refusal to submit to a polygraph examination should be considered evidence of employee misconduct.

The arbitrator must consider the qualifications of the expert administering the examination. Polygraph examiners range from professionally competent individuals to amateurs. The results of only an expertly administered test should be admissible. Most arbitrators have taken the view that an employee's refusal to submit to these examinations does not provide a reasonable basis for the imposition of discipline.

Before using any polygraph examination, federal and state statutes should be carefully reviewed to determine its permissibility under the particular circumstances. Where statutorily permitted, polygraph examinations should be used only when all of the following exist:

1. Serious employee misconduct is suspected involving a substantial threat to production, discipline, or safety;
2. Less drastic investigative techniques have been unsuccessfully attempted or rejected as unworkable under the particular circumstances;
3. The employer has accumulated sufficient independent evidence to create a reasonable suspicion that the employee possesses relevant information that he/she has refused to disclose voluntarily; and
4. Legal counsel has been consulted.

Even where appropriate, the inquiry should be as narrow as possible. Although the polygraph operator may have to ask personal questions not directly related to present employment for the purpose of calibrating the machine, none of the responses to these questions should be disclosed to the employer or other parties. Only answers directly related to the specific misconduct necessitating the examination should be divulged and only to appropriate persons.

Employee waivers consenting to polygraph examinations under statutes restricting their use have generally been considered invalid. [*Polsky v. Radio Shack*, 666 F.2d 824 (3d Cir. 1981).] Where polygraph examinations are statutorily permitted for certain employees, they may be prohibited until the employer provides a valid rule notifying employees of their use. [*Marion v. Green,* 95 Pa. Commw. 210, 505 A.2d 360 (1986).] Even though polygraph examinations may be statutorily permitted for certain employees, their results may not always be admissible in subsequent hearings. [*Township of Silver Spring v. Thompson,* 90 Pa. Commw. 456, 496 A.2d 72 (1985).]

Where not statutorily restricted or prohibited, polygraph examinations may be considered constitutional privacy invasions. This may also constitute an invasion of privacy. Defamation may also arise where the results are disclosed putting the employee in disrepute. Intentional infliction of emotional distress may occur where the employer's conduct is sufficiently outrageous in administering these tests. Public policy violations have been found where these were administered contrary to a statutory prohibition. The same rationale that has been used in scrutinizing polygraph examinations should be applicable to similar tests that allegedly elicit truth.

Honesty Testing

Employee dishonesty has been a continuing problem for employers. To monitor this, employers have used a variety of polygraph examinations and truth eliciting devices. Organized labor has consistently opposed the use of these devices in the employment relationship by seeking restrictions in collective bargaining agreements and statutory prohibitions. Many states have enacted legislation either prohibiting or substantially limiting the use of truth eliciting devices in the employment environment.

Employer security programs may involve the examination of those suspected of particular *honesty* infractions through the testing of applicants or current employees. Among newer truth eliciting methods are paper-and-pencil *honesty* tests.

Employers are increasingly being solicited by developers and marketers of these paper-and-pencil honesty tests. These tests are represented as being potential substitutes for the more traditional polygraph. Employers have been assured by the marketers of these tests that they do not infringe upon any federal or state fair employment practice (FEP) statutes. However, no representation is made by these marketers regarding their legality under state anti-polygraph statutes or whether privacy interests involving information collection, maintenance, use, and disclosure are impacted.

Truth-eliciting devices are subject to various federal and state FEP statutes when used in conjunction with employment decisions. The federal Civil Rights Act of 1964 (Title VII) forbids the use of an employment test that has a disproportionate impact on racial minorities, unless the employer meets the burden of proving that the test is job-related.

Paper-and-pencil honesty testing has become a multimillion dollar industry. Test marketer statements suggest that at least 5,000 employers are using honesty tests. Honesty tests are commonly used where employees have access to cash or merchandise, for example, retail stores, financial institutions, and warehouse operations. They are used for clerks, tellers, cashiers, security guards, supervisory personnel, and police officers.

Honesty tests are represented as being psychologically validated, professionally accepted paper-and-pencil test batteries that are designed to establish a profile on the behavioral and attitude tendencies of employees. They examine: 1) employer honesty; 2) violent tendencies; and 3) drug abuse. The developers claim that honesty test scores have no adverse impact on any of the protected racial/ethnic groups (Hispanic, black, American Indian, Asian), i.e., these minority groups allegedly have not scored significantly lower than whites.

These tests have been developed by psychologists, criminologists, polygraphists, legal experts, and law enforcement specialists. No representation is made regarding whether they violate any anti-polygraph statute or any individual state confidentiality or privacy laws. The marketer does not state that it will defend any employer in a suit that is brought for the alleged use of this test or for an employment decision that is made as a consequence of it. Research studies have been conducted that apparently demonstrate that honesty tests can be used to predict employee dishonesty, drug abuse, and violence.

Honesty tests purport to evaluate a prospective employee's honesty and/or veracity by asking a series of questions. The answers to these questions are evaluated in varying degrees. It is from these representative questions that an employee's honesty is to be evaluated. Standing alone, many of these questions would pose problems in any prospective job interview as unrelated to the job. They probe individual employment rights present in speech, beliefs, associations, and lifestyles.

Honesty tests have been questioned on ethical grounds. Extensive questioning about theft attitudes and previous theft behavior is seen as offensive and as a privacy invasion. Depending on which test cutoff an employer chooses, anywhere from 25 to 75 percent of applicants may fail an honesty test.

Of particular concern, is the use of honesty tests with current employees rather than applicants. A formerly trusted employee may unjustly lose a job or a promotion, or be constantly viewed with suspicion as a result of this test. Being rejected for a job is an unpleasant experience; however, losing one's job, status or reputation because of a test classification error has greater impact. Extreme care should be taken to ensure that access to test scores unsubstantiated by theft admissions are not disclosed. Revealing results could lead to reasoning like "I always thought highly of Joe, but the test says he's dishonest." This may provide the employee with a claim for employer defamation or invasion of privacy.

Another claim may be provided under a state's anti-polygraph statute. Pennsylvania prohibits the use of a polygraph examination or any form of a mechanical or electrical lie detector test as an employment condition or for employment continuation. Violation of this statute is punishable as a misdemeanor of the second degree. This statute does not apply to employees or other individuals in the field of public law enforcement or who dispense or have access to narcotics or dangerous drugs.

The objective of an *honesty test* is to accomplish much of what a polygraph examination would undertake. This is verified by their comparison to polygraph examinations and their validation against polygraphs. Honesty tests could be interpreted as a substitute polygraph examination.

Pennsylvania's statute may be broad enough to apply to and prohibit the use of honesty tests. *Mechanical polygraph tests* are covered by this statute. Paper-and-pencil tests are mechanical tests. These tests are normally mechanically scored through the use of a computer or a microcomputer that is brought to the testing site. Consequently, a paper-and-pencil honesty test could be viewed as a mechanical lie detector test under Pennsylvania's anti-polygraph statute.

Honesty tests are at least within the *spirit* and *intent* of this statute. They purport to evaluate the same subjects as a polygraph examination. This alone should be sufficient to prohibit their use. Criminal as well as civil liability could arise from this.

If a Pennsylvania employer suspected a theft, he would be prohibited from administering a polygraph examination under Pennsylvania's statute. Honesty tests should be accorded the same prohibition in this type of situation. It would be used for the same purpose as the polygraph; i.e., to determine the theft suspect. If the objective of an honesty test is similar to a polygraph, then it should be subject to similar statutory restrictions in its use.

How other states with anti-polygraph statutes will view honesty tests is not clear. Paper-and-pencil honesty tests were found not to be prohibited under Minnesota's anti-polygraph statute. [*State of Minnesota v. Century Camera, Inc.*, 309 N.W.2d 735 (Minn. 1981).] What is certain is that this question can be expected to be litigated because of its important individual employment right connotations. If polygraph examinations have been considered unreliable to cause their regulation, then honesty tests are likewise unreliable because no more definite proof exists over their use. The standard that should be used is the test's objective and its result. These should be the determinative considerations in evaluating whether these are substitute polygraph examinations.

Meanwhile, any employer who uses honesty tests should not use them on a blanket basis. A strong job-relatedness should be available for any position for which they are used. This should be conclusively demonstrated. The employer should obtain a representation from the marketer prior to their use. This representation should state that the testing service will defend the employer in any and all actions brought against the employer that may violate federal and state FEP, confidentiality and privacy, or polygraph statutes. The testing service should make available its personnel to assist in any employer defense of these tests along with any expert witnesses. Otherwise, the employer bears a considerable risk denoted by a feeling of "buyer beware."

Handwriting Analysis

Within the hiring process, employers are increasingly using handwriting analysis to evaluate applicants. Often this is done without the individual's knowledge. These tests attempt to ascertain honesty, truthfulness, violent tendencies, and drug dependency. The information obtained from these presents collection, maintenance, use, and disclosure problems similar to those present in polygraph and honesty testing. Because of this, similar individual employment rights considerations should be given to their use and limitation. These tests are not more accurate than polygraphs or honesty tests, but through false evaluations they may impact an employee's speech, beliefs, associations, or lifestyle prejudicing employment opportunities.

NEGLIGENT HIRING

Impacting individual employment rights is the employer's responsibility for negligent hiring. Recently, employers have incurred liability for negligent hiring and/or retention of employees who engage in criminal or other illegal acts at and outside the workplace. Liability for a negligent hiring may depend upon the:

1. Background investigation conducted by the employer;
2. The position for which the employee is hired; and
3. Risk of harm or injury to third parties, including clients, customers, and other employees.

Because the thoroughness of a background investigation is necessary to minimize employer liability, competing interests between the employee and employer must be balanced. Overzealous information collection or use of information that is not job-related should not be permitted to disqualify an applicant or terminate employment. To protect individual employment rights, a specific job-relatedness should be shown by the employer. This should safeguard the employer's concern of avoiding negligent hiring claims by preserving individual employment rights.

To establish a negligent hiring, the following must be proven:

1. The existence of an employment relationship;
2. The employee's incompetence;
3. The employer's actual or constructive; knowledge of this incompetence;
4. The employee's act or omission causing the injuries; and
5. The employer's negligence in hiring or retaining the employee as the proximate cause of the injuries.

These criteria are important because they show that the employer was put on notice of the responsibility to evaluate the employee's qualifications.

Negligent hiring claims have arisen against employers where a:

1. Young boy was sexually assaulted and murdered. [*Henley v. Prince George's County*, 305 Md. 320, 503 A.2d 1333 (1986)];
2. Tenant was raped. [*Cramer v. Housing Opportunities Comm'n.*, 304 Md. 705, 501 A.2d 35 (1985)];
3. Customer was fatally shot. [*Giles v. Shell Oil Corp.*, 487 A.2d 610 (D.C. App. 1985)];

4. Customer was assaulted. [*Abbot v. Paxne,* 457 So.2d 1156 (Fla. Dist. Ct. App. 1984)]; and
5. A known forger was employed who engaged in illegal business activity. [*Pruitt v. Pavelin,* 141 Ariz. 195, 685 P.2d 1347 (1984).]

The employer's duty to insulate itself from negligent hiring liability does not end once an applicant is selected. A continuing employer responsibility exists to retain only competent employees imposing ongoing individual employment rights considerations.

3

Employment Records

Employers collect, maintain, use, and disclose considerable employment information. This information is used to hire, discipline, terminate, place, transfer, promote, demote, train, compensate, provide full or partial fringe benefits, etc. It may be collected or disclosed without employee notice, knowledge, or consent.

Employment record privacy and integrity is important for individual employment rights. These records generally contain the employee's personal, employment, and medical history. Personal history concerns prior background and work history. Employment history details current work history regarding wages, promotions, disciplinary actions, commendations, sick days, vacation days, positions held, and performance evaluations. Medical history reviews the employee's past and current health status. Collectively, these records are usually referred to as personnel files.

EMPLOYMENT RECORDS

Federal and state statutes regulate certain employment record aspects. They generally provide the employee access along with right to review and copy the employment record's contents. Some statutes permit the employee to place a counterstatement in the record where information is incorrect, disputed, or challenged.

The methods used for collecting, maintaining, and using employment information differs among employers based upon custom, business needs, and applicable statutory requirements. Various statutes mandate that certain employment information be maintained by employers. Individual employment rights are affected in the collection, maintenance, use, and disclosure of these records. Speech, beliefs, associational, and lifestyle interests are impacted. Individual employment rights are more seriously affected as employers, despite legal restrictions, use polygraph examinations, detailed application blanks, counseling interviews, and similar questionable information collection devices.

Employers frequently receive requests for employment information. Inquiries may come from other employers, social workers, insurance companies, credit bureaus, government officials, union business agents, etc. This information was initially revealed to obtain employment or collected during the employment relationship to maintain it. Disclosure may occur for a purpose unrelated to employment that is against the employee's best interest.

Through these disclosures the employee loses control of sensitive personal information along with the ability to verify this information's accuracy. The possibility of disclosing inaccurate employment information is great because each employer has its own record keeping system. Employee dependency upon the employer's good will or personal values creates problems over what confidentiality means for employment records. Overall considerations for preparing employment record privacy procedures and policies should include:

1. A uniform system of collecting, maintaining, accessing, using, and disclosing employment information;
2. Preserving and protecting confidentiality;
3. Collecting employment information by reviewing—
   - the number and types of records maintained,
   - information items,
   - information uses made within the employer's decision-making and nondecision-making structure,
   - information disclosure made to those other than the employer, and
   - the extent to which employees are aware and regularly informed of the uses and disclosures that are made of this information;
4. Fair information collection procedures and policies concerning applicants, employees, and former employees that—
   - limit information collection to that which is job-related,
   - inform what records will be maintained,

- inform of the uses to be made of this information,
- adopt procedures to assure information accuracy, timeliness, and completeness,
- permit review, copying, correction, or information amendment,
- limit internal use,
- limit external disclosures, including disclosures made without authorization, to specific inquiries or requests to verify information,
- provide for a regular policy compliance review,
- contain an employment application with a waiver authorizing the employer to disclose employee file contents to those to whom the employee grants access; that is, reference checks by subsequent employers, and to make a credit check where applicable,
- indicate on the file when and where these employee reviews took place,
- restrict information access to those with a need to know and those who are authorized outside of the employer; that is law enforcement officials, government agencies, etc.,
- ensure that information retention conforms to applicable law, and
- contain a privacy clause [See Privacy Protection Study Commission, *Personal Privacy in an Information Society* 235, 237-38 (1977).]

An employee's right to inspect his/her personnel file, however, is not absolute. Statutes may not grant an employee a right to inspect any records relating to an investigation of a possible criminal offense or to reference letters maintained by the employer. The employer is entitled to impose reasonable restrictions upon an employee's access to his/her personnel file. These may take various forms, including:

1. Requiring the employee to submit a written request to inspect his/her personnel file;
2. Allowing inspection only by appointment;
3. Allowing inspection only during regular business hours;
4. Allowing inspection only on the employee's own time;
5. Allowing inspection only in the presence of an employer representative;
6. Limiting inspection frequency;
7. Allowing employees to copy or obtain copies of their own personnel files;

8. Permitting employee amendment of this information; and
9. Documenting inspection dates by the employee. [*Id.* App. 3 at 35-43.]

Government agencies may statutorily access employment information for various reasons. The Occupational Safety and Health Act of 1970 (OSHA) permits its inspectors during a safety inspection or investigation to access and obtain all evidence that may aid them. The Civil Rights Act of 1964 (Title VII) provides that the Equal Employment Opportunities Commission (EEOC) may access all information related to alleged discrimination investigations. Sometimes statutory provisions permit government officials to obtain information from the employer's personnel files. Despite these statutory requirements, the amount and type of information to be disclosed can be somewhat controlled. The employer can challenge the information's relevancy and curtail or restrict automatic government agency access.

Union employment information requests create unique confidentiality problems. Employers must generally furnish to a union information that is relevant for collective bargaining, processing of grievances, or contract administration. This may include sensitive information found in medical records, wage histories, test results, investigation reports, etc. Supervisory personal diaries where secret notes on employee performance are maintained may also be accessed.

The employer's claim that this is personal, private, or confidential information is generally irrelevant. Good faith bargaining duties under the National Labor Relations Act (NLRA) includes supplying information by the employer that is relevant and necessary for bargaining in allowing the employees' representative, the union, to perform its functions adequately. Refusal constitutes an unfair labor practice. Confidential information may only be withheld by an employer where the private and sensitive nature of the information outweighs the union's need for the information.

Employee consent is not required to review this information. If it is relevant to union functions, the employer must release it. This relevancy concept has been broadly interpreted. Where a union requested information about employees excluded from the bargaining unit, the "... requested information had a 'probable' or 'potential' relevance to that issue, and therefore met the union's burden of relevancy." [*General Electric Co.*, 199 N.L.R.B. 286 (1972).] This sacrifices individual employment rights for the union's obligation to act on behalf of all employees.

However, where an employer bargained with the union for a privacy protection policy that employment records could not be released absent employee authorization, union access could be denied. When the employer refused to release attendance records to the union for a grievance hearing the union filed a refusal to bargain charge. The employer's conduct was not illegal. It did not have to release these records because the employer's policy was instituted to protect employee privacy and not hinder the union. Employee consent was a minimal burden on the union. [*New Jersey Bell Telephone Co. v. NLRB*, 720 F.2d 789 (3d Cir. 1983).]

Employer confidentiality policies will not necessarily protect employment information from a union whose interest in disclosure outweighs an employee's legitimate privacy expectation. Where an employer has not guaranteed absolute confidentiality of specific employment information, it will normally be released when needed to evaluate a grievance. If the employer has used this information, the union's access claim is considerably enhanced.

Insurance companies, credit bureaus, private investigators, mailing firms, debt collectors, etc. may receive access to this information. No statute requires employer disclosure to these groups and nothing prevents disclosure. The employer has complete discretion. However, the employer should assure that only accurate information is disclosed.

To enforce individual employment rights, the employee must have a reasonable privacy expectation in the information collected, maintained, used, or disclosed. This expectation may arise from the information's type or the employer's confidentiality representations. Various litigation theories may protect these rights. Among these are constitutional, tort, and contract theories.

Employment records contain data collected directly from the employee and others that the employee knew or did know were providing information at the time of hiring involving past employment, medical, educational, and family. After hiring, they include information collected about the employee at the workplace regarding payroll data, job performance reports, medical problem documentation, and disciplinary actions. References, recommendations, psychological information, and general comments may also be found in these files. It is this information's variety and quantity that attracts those who seek access to these records.

Individual employment rights in these records should be assessed regarding their *confidentiality* and *disclosure*. Regarding confidentiality, it should initially be ascertained whether the employee has a reasonable privacy expectation in the employment information. Where this reasonable privacy expectation exists, information should not be released absent employee consent or authorization. In evaluating disclosure interests, it should be determined:

1. Who is making the request?;
2. What is the request's purpose?;
3. What is the relationship between the employee and employer regarding any third party requesting this information?;
4. How can disclosure be restricted to only necessary information?;
5. Is this employment information accurate?;
6. Does the employee have a privacy interest in not releasing this information?; and
7. Is the employer under a statutory or other duty to disclose this information?

Answers to these inquiries will assist in evaluating whether individual employment rights have been breached.

A state constitutional privacy right may protect personnel files from disclosure to third parties. Employee requests to review personnel files of co-employees may violate the co-employee's privacy right guaranteed by a state constitution. The employer, as the custodian of private information, cannot waive employee rights that are constitutionally guaranteed this protection.

Invasion of privacy, defamation, intentional infliction of emotional distress, negligent maintenance or disclosure of employment records, fraudulent misrepresentation, and public policy violations are applicable to individual employment right challenges arising out of the collection, maintenance, use, and disclosure of these records.

Invasion of privacy may result through placing an employee in a false light or publicly disclosing personal private facts contained in employment records. This may affect individual employment rights present in speech, association, beliefs, and lifestyles.

Defamation can be readily applied to privacy problems arising out of employment records. Even though an employer possesses certain conditional privileges to protect legitimate interests, these are often not followed or waived.

Internal documents concerning employee performance are subject to a conditional employer privilege. Secretaries who type or receive mail as part of their duties are entitled to this privilege. Employees performing human resource functions are likewise protected. Similarly, a conditional privilege applies to performance evaluations sent by an employee's supervisor to the supervisor's superior. In these instances where the conditional privilege applies, the employee receiving the information about another employee has an interest in or a duty relating to this information that correlates with job functions.

Where employment record disclosure is not necessary to the employer's functioning, the conditional privilege may not be available. Employers may not reveal to other employees the reason for an employee's discipline or termination to improve employee morale or to eliminate rumors. Information disclosure in these circumstances does not serve a legitimate employer duty corresponding with any legal, moral, or social interest.

A conditional privilege may apply to information disclosure to third parties. It may protect communications between an employee's former employer and a prospective employer. This privilege may not be exceeded. Where the former employer's disclosures are false, liability will result. Disclosures should not embellish the seriousness of employee misconduct or add unnecessary derogatory information.

Statutes or collective bargaining agreements may insulate employers against defamation claims. Some state statutes provide that disclosures about an employee to a state's unemployment compensation department are privileged. A termination notice required by a collective bargaining agreement and released only to those directly involved with the grievance arbitration process is privileged. The employee's union membership constitutes consent to release this.

MEDICAL RECORDS

Medical records often contain sensitive and confidential employee information. Should this be disclosed, this information could cause embarrassment, humiliation, damage family relationships, or lead to employment termination while infringing individual employment rights.

Medical record technology changes through third-party payment, government medical care participation, and record-keeping system computerization have expanded this information's amount, type, and accessibility. These records may be sought for various reasons. They may be important to legal actions, public health evaluation and occupational health research, third-party payment, employment, credit rating, and for use by other health care providers.

Need for a medical record may not always outweigh individual employment rights. It may require employee notification that their records will be examined unless they raise objections. Occupational health studies often require employee health record disclosure. Subpoenas of these records are usually upheld against employer assertions of employee privacy interests.

Access to medical information may also be required for nonresearch public health purposes. State health departments may require medical information reporting about venereal disease, child abuse, injuries caused by deadly weapons, fetal deaths, abortions, and prescriptions given for dangerous drugs. Private parties may also seek medical records for public health purposes. Consumer health organizations under federal and state freedom of information acts may gain access.

Medical records may be useful in litigation. They are often subpoenaed for administrative and grand jury investigations. Where disclosure is necessary for important public purposes, including investigations of possible medical misconduct, non-payment of taxes, employee health and safety, or Medicaid fraud, the request is usually granted. This information generally remains unavailable to the public minimizing its impact on individual employment rights.

These records may also be sought through discovery procedures in civil actions. They are often necessary in litigation involving personal injury, insurance policy disputes, malpractice, divorce, and contested wills to determine damage showing pain and suffering, negotiating settlements, or proving causation, negligence and competency. These requests may be opposed by asserting statutes making this information privileged under the physician-patient privilege or state statutes protecting state-conducted health emergency study confidentiality. Concerns over individual employment rights are valid where entire medical files are disclosed, rather than just the minimum information necessary.

Medical record requests that do not require identifiable details or that use codes instead of names are the least intrusive. Other parties, including the National Institute for Occupational Safety and Health (NIOSH), public health researchers, and grand juries, often need these identifiers. These requests are granted where important public interests exist and safeguards are provided against sensitive public information disclosure. Where little or no confidentiality would remain, requests are not likely to be granted because medical confidentiality remains significant.

In developing medical record procedures, the employer should consider the following:

1. Medical information disclosure;
2. The relationship between the employee and employer regarding any third party requesting the information;
3. The employee's privacy interest in not releasing the information;
4. The employer's statutory or other duty to disclose the information;
5. Identity of the person making the request;
6. The request's purpose;
7. Restricting disclosure to only necessary information; and
8. When an employee who is the subject of medical information maintained by an employer requests correction or amendment, the employer should—
   - Disclose to the employee, or to a person designated by him/her, the identity of the medical information's source,
   - Make the correction or amendment within a reasonable time period of the person who was the information's source concurs that the information is inaccurate or incomplete, and
   - Establish a procedure for an employee who is the subject of employer medical information to present supplemental information for inclusion in the employer's medical information, provided that the supplemental information's source is also included. [Privacy Protection Study Commission, *Personal Privacy in an Information Society* 263 (1977).]

Employer authorization for disclosure of medical records should:

1. Be handwritten by the employee;
2. Be separate from any other language present on the same page;
3. Be signed and dated by the employee;
4. State the names, employer functions, or persons authorized to disclose the information;
5. State the names, employer functions, persons, or entities authorized to receive the information;
6. State the limitations on the medical information's use by those authorized to receive it;
7. Provide a date after which the employer is no longer authorized to disclose the information; and
8. Provide the employee with a copy of the authorization.

In maintaining medical record confidentiality, the employer must consider:

1. Record types involved;

2. The information;
3. The potential for harm should disclosure occur;
4. The disclosure's effect on the physician-patient relationship;
5. Safeguards against inadvertent or accidental disclosure; and
6. Statutory or public interest reasons requiring disclosure.

Different results have been accorded to individual employment rights in medical records. Violations may occur where employer representatives obtain medical information from the employee's physician absent employee authorization and convey it to supervisors.

Employees may have recourses for medical record breaches similar to those applicable for employment records. This may depend upon who is seeking or who obtained access to these records, the purposes for which the records are sought, and whether there are common law, statutory, or constitutional protections available. In *Bratt v. International Business Machines Corp.*, 785 F.2d 352 (1st Cir. 1986), a supervisor suggested that Bratt consult with a physician under contract with IBM. Following a medical visit, the physician called Bratt's supervisor telling her that Bratt was paranoid and recommending that he see a psychiatrist. The supervisor relayed this information to her supervisor, who informed an IBM Manager assigned to handle internal grievances previously filed by Bratt. Several internal memoranda and telephone calls were initiated among IBM supervisory and medical personnel regarding Bratt's psychiatric and medical status' effect on Bratt's work performance.

Bratt filed suit in federal district court charging IBM, the physician, and an IBM supervisor with a privacy breach. The district court granted summary judgment for IBM. On appeal, the First Circuit Court of Appeals certified questions regarding Massachusetts law's interpretation of a privacy right to the Massachusetts Supreme Judicial Court. The Massachusetts state court found that there was no employer communication privilege for employment medical information and that intracorporate communication could constitute publicity sufficient to breach an employee's privacy. The determine this, a court must balance the employer's legitimate business interest in disseminating the information against the nature and substantiality of the intrusion.

Applying the Massachusetts court's balancing test, the First Circuit sustained the lower court's dismissal of Bratt's claims that his privacy right had been violated when the supervisor informed other managers of Bratt's internal grievance procedure use and when internal memoranda were sent to other supervisors stating that a physician considered Bratt paranoid. This information was not so personal that the disclosure could invade Bratt's privacy. Likewise, internal disclosure of Bratt's alleged paranoia to four supervisors who had a legitimate business interest in receiving information regarding Bratt's ability to do his job was not unreasonable and did not violate Bratt's privacy.

However, IBM breached Bratt's privacy by allowing the physician to discuss the medical condition with IBM management without authorization. The physician violated this privacy right by discussing her examination of Bratt with IBM staff without his permission. IBM's internal regulations protecting the medical information confidentiality and requiring employee authorization prior to disclosure heightened Bratt's legitimate privacy expectation regarding this information. This along with this information's highly personal nature outweighed IBM's legitimate business interest in discussing the information with the physician.

Bratt's legitimate privacy expectation included establishing a confidential physician/patient relationship. This coupled with IBM's internal regulations regarding this information's disclosure heightened Bratt's privacy interest in the medical examination's results. A reasonable fact finder could conclude that the state's privacy statute was violated.

By contrast, in *Eddy v. Brown,* 715 P.2d 74 (Okla. Sup. Ct. 1986), summary judgment for the employer was affirmed where the employee claimed that a supervisor had disclosed to a group of co-workers that the employee had been undergoing psychiatric treatment. The supervisor's review of Eddy's employment medical records did not constitute "unreasonable intrusion" into his personal life because the employment medical records were "of legitimate concern" to his supervisor. Discussion between supervisory personnel of medical information affecting job performance is protected. Information disclosure to Eddy's nonsupervisory co-workers, who presumably lacked a legitimate interest in the information, was not the type of publicity that would establish a claim for public disclosure of private facts.

Employers should take precautions to protect employment medical information confidentiality by restricting access only to managerial employees who have a legitimate business interest in obtaining the information. Except in emergency situations, employers should avoid seeking medical information directly from an employee's physician without prior written employee consent. Employee hospital records should be accorded similar deference.

Information about an employee's medical condition and diagnosis should be kept confidential and never revealed to those, like co-employees, who have no need to possess the data. Revealing this information could also expose the unionized employer to costly invasion of privacy, defamation, or intentional infliction of emotional distress litigation outside of the collective bargaining agreement's grievance arbitration procedure.

4
Medical Concerns

Increasingly, individual employment rights that are present in workplace medical concerns are gaining importance. With the growing awareness of alcohol and drug abuse along with the uncertainty over the human immunodeficiency virus (HIV), employees and employers are confronted with serious questions regarding how their respective rights should be balanced. These medical concerns arise out of issues relating to physical examinations, health and safety, smoking, employee assistance programs, alcohol and drug abuse, the human immunodeficiency virus (HIV), and sterilization.

PHYSICAL EXAMINATIONS

The employer's right to require applicants to undergo a physical examination is considered basic to the hiring process. Due to their cost, physical examinations are usually administered at the final hiring process step after the offer has been made. Situations also arise that necessitate requiring physical examinations during the employment relationship.

Employers may, unless restricted by a collective bargaining agreement require employees to have physical examinations under legitimate job-related circumstances. This need may arise where an employee desires to return to work following an accident, sick leave, or extended layoff, has exercised a bid on a job requiring greater physical effort, etc. This right is not absolute exercisable at the whim of the employer. It cannot be arbitrarily insisted upon without reasonable grounds. Unreasonable requests for physical examinations could expose employers to liability under federal and state FEP statutes.

To ensure that proper medical information is obtained, employers should consider the following concerning physical examinations:

1. Establishing relationships with one or more physicians because the physician—
   - Understands the job's physical requirements,
   - Is able to provide a faster conclusion regarding employment eligibility,
   - Is familiar with the employer's required paperwork, and
   - Provides a more convenient means for dialogue with the human resources staff; and
2. Employing a full or part-time physician on a retainer and/or one of a group of physicians.

HEALTH AND SAFETY COMPLAINTS

The Occupational Safety and Health Act of 1970 (OSHA) was enacted to assure every employee safe and healthful working conditions. Rights afforded by OSHA to employees include:

1. Informing OSHA of unsafe conditions and to request a federal inspection;
2. Assisting on a limited basis in OSHA inspections;
3. Aiding a court in determining whether certain imminently dangerous conditions exist; and
4. Bringing an action to compel the Secretary of Labor to seek injunctive relief.

It is the only comprehensive statute addressed to workplace hazards and is the primary vehicle for hazard elimination.

An individual employment right arises in an employee's reasonable belief that a real danger of death or injury exists in work that may be performed. Under a regulation promulgated by the Secretary of Labor, employees have the right to refuse hazardous job activity performance in certain circumstances.

Employees who reasonably believe there is a real danger of death or injury and there is no time to resort to administrative action to remedy the danger are protected. However, employees risk termination should it subsequently be determined that the employee acted unreasonably or in bad faith.

Concerns may also arise over what employer medical job requirements may constitute hazards. OSHA requires employers to provide workplaces free of serious recognized hazards. A hazard is considered recognized if it is known to be a hazard by the employer or generally is so recognized by the employer's industry.

Concerns may also arise regarding records that are required to be maintained under OSHA. The Secretary of Labor is directed to issue regulations requiring employers to maintain accurate records of employee exposures to potentially toxic materials or harmful physical agents which are required to be monitored or measured. Employees are permitted access to their exposure and medical records to enable them to play a meaningful role in their own health management. Any current or former employee or an employee being assigned or transferred to work where there will be exposure to toxic substances or harmful physical agents has a right of access to four kinds of exposure records:

1. Environmental monitoring records;
2. Biological monitoring results;
3. Material safety data sheets; and
4. Any other record disclosing the identity of a toxic substance or harmful physical agent.

The employee may designate a representative to exercise access rights. Labor unions that are recognized or certified collective bargaining representatives are automatically considered designated representatives and have access rights to employee exposure records without individual employee consent. OSHA also has an access right to exposure records.

Employees can access their entire medical files regardless of how the information was generated or is maintained. Excluded from an employee medical record are certain physical specimens, records concerning health insurance claims, and records concerning voluntary employee medical assistance programs. Limited discretion is given physicians to deny access where a diagnosis of a terminal illness or psychiatric condition exists. Collective bargaining representatives must obtain written consent before gaining access to employee medical records.

Corrections or removal of inaccuracies must be made under a state employment record statute. OSHA's access procedures do not provide for this. This access rule does not violate an individual employment right because there is security for dealing with personally identifiable information and the rule carefully limits information use.

SMOKING

Smoking in the workplace no longer is viewed as a non-issue, a situation accepted by nonsmokers as an inevitable part of employment or by smokers as a right. What was once an individual decision is today becoming increasingly regulated by private and public sector employers through work rules or statutory requirements. As an individual employment right this requires balancing the affected employee's interests with employer responsibilities toward other employees.

Tolerance of smoking in the workplace is changing rapidly. Employers of virtually every size and description are taking steps to curtail workplace smoking. While the majority of employers have not yet restricted workplace smoking, the growth of nonsmoking policies is unmistakable.

Awards for unemployment, disability, and medical treatment have been made to nonsmokers while union grievances under collective bargaining agreements are increasingly dealing with this issue. Employers permitting or not regulating workplace smoking are highly vulnerable to challenges by nonsmoking employees. Mounting concern over smoking's effects on the health, productivity, and morale of smokers and nonsmokers has combined with changing social attitudes about smoking reversing the notion that smoking is an acceptable public practice.

Smoking is becoming an activity that an employee does within the confines of his/her home, but not at the workplace or in public. This is similar to the taboo associated with sexual activities.

In evaluating workplace smoking, the following should be considered:

1. Establish a smoking policy, which may be either voluntary or a total prohibition;
2. For unionized employers, meet with the union to discuss the smoking policy;
3. Consult employees for their input;
4. Communicate the policy;
5. Require all employees to follow the policy;
6. Establish smoking and nonsmoking areas;
7. Make smoke cessation classes available for persons who want to stop smoking;
8. Improve ventilation to minimize smoking's health hazard;

9. Where employees have a medically proven reaction to smoke, separate those persons from smokers, but do not terminate them;
10. Where smoking presents a work safety hazard, due to paints, chemicals, or explosives, adopt and implement a smoking ban that is reasonable; and
11. Investigate smoking complaints.

While discrimination against smokers does not rise to that prohibited by federal and state fair employment practice (FEP) statutes, it certainly affects individual employment rights. It may be a non-job-related criteria that controls employment distribution, especially where employers do not hire smokers or restrict smoking outside the workplace. By not confining job-relatedness to the workplace, employers could deny opportunities for what occurs outside it. When using the powerful employment incentive to control how employees act at home they decide or circumscribe what is done in private. This could be a guise to discriminate where statistics establish that certain minority, national origin, or age groups smoke more than others. Before banning workplace smoking, it may be wise for employers to consult their employees or the union where a collective bargaining agreement exists.

Connecticut's smoking statute is typical of those that have been enacted. This statute requires restaurants seating seventy-five or more to provide a nonsmoking area and prohibits smoking in government buildings. Employers of fifty or more must establish written rules regulating smoking. It does not require separate areas but permits employers to establish separate areas. Rules must be posted where employees can see them and a copy must be made available to those who request them.

Besides posing a health risk, smoking can also affect sensitive technical equipment and can be safety hazard. The rights of smoker and nonsmoker must be balanced with the nonsmoker's rights prevailing when reasonable accommodation is not possible. Courts are strongly suggesting this.

Individual employment rights in obtaining a smoke-free workplace environment may be enforced through statutory, constitutional, tort, and contractual litigation theories. Statutory remedies may exist under federal and state (FEP) statutes where handicap is covered. Under the federal Vocational Rehabilitation Act of 1973, handicap includes those who are usually sensitive to tobacco smoke. Hypersensitivity to smoke limits a major life activity by being unable to work in a smoke-free environment. The employer is not required to provide a completely smoke-free environment. A reasonable accommodation in separating smokers from nonsmokers or offering an alternative job is sufficient.

State unemployment compensation statutes can be used to recover benefits where workplace smoking is a compelling and necessitous reason for terminating employment. Likewise, state workers compensation statutes may be used to assert employer liability.

As yet, constitutional protections have been found inapplicable. Injunctive relief, however, has been successful. Nonsmokers have been granted injunctions where it was the employer's duty to provide a workplace environment reasonably free of recognized hazards and smoking was classified as a recognized hazard. [See *Smith v. Western Elec.*, 643 S.W.2d 10 (Mo. Ct. App. 1982).]

Defamation may arise where a smoker or nonsmoker is held in disrepute among fellow employees. It may also arise where a smoker or nonsmoker who asserts his/her rights is terminated for a false reason. A false imprisonment could possibly occur where a nonsmoker is required to work in a smoke filled environment. The false imprisonment exists because the employee cannot remove himself/herself from the environment without risking employment loss. This is the confinement that is necessary; however, the employer must be aware of the employee's condition and should have refused a reasonable accommodation. Public policy violations may arise where a nonsmoker asserts rights under a state smoking statute and suffers disciplinary action. However, an employee with a written employment contract was not promised a smoke-free environment merely because her employer was aware at the time it signed her contract that she preferred this. The contract did not mention the subject. The employee was provided with a smoke-free environment for a time and the employer knew of her preference for a smoke-free environment. Nothing showed that the employer entered into a contractual obligation to supply a smoke-free environment either temporarily or permanently. "Mere knowledge of her preference is not tantamount to . . . assent," the court concluded. [*Bernard v. Cameron and Colby Co., Inc.*, 397 Mass. 320, 491 N.E.2d 604 (1986).]

Where employers implement smoking policies they may be under a duty to enforce these. This may even extend to preventing employees from entering a smoking designated area because they could be injured.

EMPLOYEE ASSISTANCE PROGRAMS

Employee assistance programs (EAP) aid employees and their families to recognize and overcome personal problems that interfere with employee work performance. They are an extension of the performance evaluation process.

Initially, EAPs dealt with alcoholic employees. Today, they have been broadened to include career and personal problem counseling components. Problem areas covered may involve job dissatisfaction, supervisor or co-worker conflicts, job performance anxiety, alcohol and drug abuse, emotional problems, marital problems, gambling problems, financial problems, etc.

EAPs can be developed by the employer or contracted through agencies that provide these programs. Privacy and confidentiality are essential elements of any EAP. Unless this can be guaranteed, the EAP will not be utilized. A supervisor should not be privy to the details of the employee's EAP participation. EAP record keeping should assure personal privacy. Records of participation should be coded to prevent inadvertent identification of those who are enrolled. All EAP records should be kept separate from employee personnel or medical records. It is through this that individual employment rights are affected by the collection, maintenance, use, or disclosure of EAP information.

Because employer *confidentiality* is required to make EAPs function properly, breaches of this may result in individual employment rights litigation. [See *Brotherhood of Maintenance v. Burlington Northern*, 802 F.2d 1016 (8th Cir. 1986).] Due process constitutional arguments arise where an employee is disciplined without making the EAP available. [*Leininger v. City of Bloomington, et al.*, 299 N.W.2d 723 (Sup. Ct. Minn. 1980).] A similar claim exists under employment handbooks and policies where these are considered to be binding commitments and the employee has not been permitted to enter the EAP or EAP procedures were not followed. Employees may base unemployment compensation claims on EAPs where they were terminated for reasons unrelated to the EAP.

Confidentiality breaches expose employers to defamation claims. [See *Doe v. U.S. Dep't of Justice*, 602 F. Supp. 871 (D.D.C. 1983).] Negligent infliction of emotional distress has been alleged against an EAP treatment provider for which the employer may subsequently be liable. [*Crivellaro v. Pa. Power and Light Co.*, 341 Pa. Super. 173, 491 A.2d 207 (1985).]

EAPs can be developed by the employer or contracted through agencies providing these programs. Privacy and confidentiality are essential EAP elements. Regarding the EAP, the following should be considered:

1. Confidentiality and privacy in—
   - Record keeping,
   - Coding records to prevent inadvertent identification of those who are enrolled,
   - Limiting supervisor access, and
   - Keeping EAP records separate from employee personnel or medical records;
2. Communicating EAP services to employees and their families by—
   - Employee education, and
   - Orientating managers, supervisors, and union representatives;
3. Procedures for individuals referred by managers, supervisors, and/or union representatives;
4. Procedures for use by employees and their families;
5. The EAP's location;
6. The EAP's coordination with medical and disability benefit plans; and
7. Outside agency versus Company provision of the EAP regarding—
   - The EAP provider's malpractice liability insurance, and
   - The EAP staff's qualifications.

ALCOHOL AND DRUG ABUSE

Employees with an alcohol or drug problem may have an absentee rate sixteen times greater than the average employee and an accident rate four times greater. The United States Public Health Service has estimated that between three and seven percent of American employees use some form of illegal drug on a regular basis. Surveys indicate that much of this use occurs at the workplace where it adversely affects performance.

A growing number of employers are developing alcohol and drug abuse programs to increase workplace productivity and safety. Testing procedures are a significant part of these programs. It has been estimated that 25 percent of Fortune 500 companies, as well as many other private and public sector employers, have implemented a testing program.

Regardless of the benefits that testing may provide concerning workplace productivity and safety, it presents important individual employment rights considerations. By its very nature, testing intrudes upon the employee's solitude and physical integrity. When administered to detect employee alcohol or drug use, intrusiveness increases in complexity and degree. Like all other individual employment rights, however, this right is not absolute. It must be balanced against competing interests and objectives.

Even though workplace drug usage is costly, attempts to control it are also expensive. Unions and civil rights groups have questioned testing's usefulness amid medical controversy over what certain drug detection tests actually establish. False results indicating drug use can occur through human error, chain of custody problems, or test manipulation.

Three basic methods are generally used in conducting alcohol and drug screenings. *Pre-employment screening* subjects all or selected applicants to testing, usually as part of a physical examination given prior to a final employment offer. Applicants should be informed of the screening test and should be questioned regarding prescribed medication use during the examination, including the dosage, the expiration date, and the reason for having the prescription. Prescribed medications can be abused as easily as illegal substances. The prescription should be verified to ensure that it is for the person taking the medication.

For cause testing is conducted when a supervisor has a reasonable suspicion that an employee is under the controlled substance's influence. While the supervisor's suspicion may arise through an employee's erratic behavior, lethargy, mood swings, etc., for cause testing usually occurs after a workplace accident.

Random testing involves selecting an appropriate, scientifically determined, random sampling of the employer's work force to undergo testing. Screenings are conducted on different employee samplings at various times during the year. Random screening is intended to serve as a drug use deterrent. Employees usually have no advance notice of the testing. It is the most controversial testing method and is susceptible to legal challenges.

The enzyme multiplied immunoassay technique (EMIT) urinalysis test is the most popular screening device. This test measures the presence of delta-a-tetra hyrocannibinal (THC), the primary active cannabinoid metabolite. Because the EMIT test is relatively inexpensive, quick, and easy to use, it has become popular. However, the EMIT test, like other urinalysis tests, has two potential defects; i.e., inaccuracy and imprecision.

Although studies by the EMIT test's developers have shown fewer than 5 percent positives other studies have shown lower accuracy. The test's predictive value depends on marijuana usage's prevalence in those screened.

What is disturbing about marijuana screening is that the tests are highly sensitive. A subject may have a positive EMIT test with as little as 75 nanograms (billionths of a gram) of THC per milliliter of urine. The tests can detect a casual usage within the last fourteen days and chronic usage for longer periods following usage discontinuance. In one study, six chronic marijuana users had THC in their urine fourteen to thirty-six days following usage discontinuance. There is still disagreement that passive inhalation would have a positive test. Because intoxication lasts only one to four hours, even the test's developers caution that the test is useful only as an indicator of the marijuana use, not as an intoxication measure.

Urinalysis tests cannot be used to: 1) determine the degree of the drug's effect; or 2) distinguish between recent drug use outside the workplace and current workplace impairment. The Center for Disease Control reached the conclusion that: "If an effect on performance is the main reason for screening [for marijuana], the [EMIT] test result alone cannot indicate performance impairment or assess the degree of risk associated with the person's continuing to perform tasks." [32 *Morbidity and Mortality Weekly Rep.* 469 (1983).]

Urinalysis testing procedures are prone to certain abuses that impact individual employment rights, especially those involving association or lifestyles. Through unregulated access of an employee's urine specimen, the employer can learn physiological secrets from the specimen outside of drug use. Urine specimens can be analyzed to reveal employee pregnancies, illicit medication usage, treatment for a heart condition, manic-depression, epilepsy, diabetes, or schizophrenia.

Employers may rely on urinalysis tests to administer disciplinary action up to and including termination. This is particularly unfair when urinalysis testing may create false positive readings for amphetamine use of therapeutic cold medicines such as Contac or Sudafed. Over-the-counter cough medicines such as dextromethorpan can show a false positive for morphine use while amoxicillin, a prescription antibiotic, has been reported to cause a false positive for cocaine. Based solely on urinalysis testing, employers should not be permitted to take adverse employee actions. A follow-up confirmation test should be required to protect individual employment rights.

This follow-up test may either be a gas chromatography/mass spectrometry (GCMS) test or a blood test taken along with the initial urine specimen. The GCMS reduces the constituent chemicals to their molecular level and identifies the *fingerprint* of a specific drug. They are 99.9 percent accurate in confirming amphetamines, barbiturates, benzo-diazephines (librium and valium), cocaine, marijuana, opiates, PCP, methaqualone, and methadone. Another follow-up test is the radioimmunoassay (RIA) with a high but not perfect reliability. Because an initial or follow-up GCMS costs between $100 to $200 per specimen, some employers have not used it before adversely affecting employees. However, like urinalysis testing, the GMCS test indicates only that a drug has been used. It does not establish or verify workplace drug usage.

Only a blood test can detect workplace drug use. It can yield information specific to current use and exposure degree. Complementary blood tests can be used to eliminate the problems associated with other testing. Even though it is more intrusive regarding individual employment rights, a complementary blood test to a urine or other test has been endorsed. Like urine and other testing, a blood test's use should be limited to the specific purpose for which it is collected; i.e., drug use determination. Unless consent is explicitly granted, a blood or other tests should not be used to determine employee physiological information. To ensure that individual employment rights are balanced against the employer's desire to provide a productive and safe workplace absent alcohol or drug abuse, the employer should use or make available to applicants and employees a complementary blood test to verify or disprove urinalysis test results. All testing should be administered by an independent, unaffiliated, certified laboratory.

Controlling workplace alcohol and drug abuse generates similar concerns over individual employment rights as those that arise when an employer searches an employee's person or possessions. Chemically testing an employee's urine, blood, or breath provides the employer with knowledge about employee associations and lifestyles outside the workplace.

Concerns consistently arise in any private or public sector employer's involvement with alcohol and drug programs. Private and public sector employers implementing these programs are subject to privacy limitations under the United States Constitution and certain state constitutions. The United States Constitution's fourth amendment proscription against unreasonable searches and seizures requires proof of a "reasonable suspicion" to validate the taking of blood, urine, or breath sample from a public employee. Despite this high standard, several public employers have successfully enforced screening programs over employee challenges. Probable cause has been required. At times, testing has even been permitted without a reasonable suspicion or probable cause. [See *Skinner v. Railway Labor Executives Ass'n*, 489 U.S. 602 (1989) (body fluid testing of railroad employees was a reasonable search).]

Proponents of drug testing maintain that they are constitutional because they do not involve an "unreasonable search or seizure." Requiring someone to provide a urine sample, particularly in the presence of another, presents a major intrusion upon privacy and dignity.

State action outwardly operates to deny private sector employees constitutional protection. Private sector employers have successfully raised the state action requirement to defend against constitutional claims by employees disciplined for drug use. Where a private sector employer's conduct created clear and outrageous constitutional violations, state action may not be required. These constitutional issues could also be asserted as *public policy* tort violations.

State constitutions may protect these employment privacy interests. In California, private sector employers are limited by a constitutional employment privacy right's protection. To overcome California's Constitution, information obtained and collected about employees must be: 1) necessary and cannot be overboard; 2) properly used for a legitimate purpose; and 3) subject to a reasonable check to establish its accuracy.

Random, unannounced *spot-check* urine or blood testing is the most risky employer program. Adoption of a November 1985 ordinance by the San Francisco Board of Supervisors expressly prohibits random or employer-wide testing in the City and County of San Francisco. This ordinance represents the legislative trend toward individual employment rights protection. Within San Francisco, an employer must prove reasonable grounds for believing that an employee's faculties are impaired at the workplace and prove that this impairment presents a clear and present danger to the employee's physical safety, another employee, or the public before an employer-provided test can be required.

Random screening precludes meaningful notice that affects the employee's constitutional and common law privacy rights. A written copy of the employer's policy to implement random testing should be provided. The policy should be based on employee and workplace safety concerns. It should expressly state that refusal to provide samples or cooperate with the testing program could be grounds for discipline up to and including termination.

Pending litigation concerning drug testing involves claims disputing the accuracy of results obtained from the employee's sample. Care should be taken to select a reputable testing laboratory or clinic. Test results showing low alcohol or drug levels in the employee's system are suspect. The employee may maintain that these results occurred from use outside the workplace. Because an employer's right to regulate alcohol and drug use relies on the employee's potential impairment at the workplace, low levels of alcohol or drugs may not impair the employee's workplace abilities.

Prior to hiring, employers may inquire regarding whether an employee uses or distributes drugs. The constitutional protection against self-incrimination only applies to situations where the state is involved. Absent test results, observations of lay witnesses may be sufficient to establish that an employee is under alcohol or drug influence. Symptoms of intoxication include:

1. *Speech* — thick, slurred, loud;
2. *General appearance* — dishevelment, flushed face, poor grooming;
3. *Appearance of eyes* — red, watery, heavy lids, fixed pupils;
4. *Breath* — foul, distinctive odor of various intoxicants;
5. *Gait* — walking unsteadily, deliberately and over-carefully, swaying, weaving, stooped; and
6. *Behavior* — excessive silliness or boisterousness.

Testimony of a supervisor that an employee was intoxicated because his breath smelled of alcohol, his clothes seemed disheveled, and he staggered a little when he walked has been found in some arbitration awards to warrant termination without any medical tests. [*Kaiser Steel Corp.*, 31 Lab. Arb. (BNA) 832, 833, 835-36 (1958) (Grant, Arb.).]

While alcohol usage is usually identifiable and its effects generally recognized, drug presence may not be. When there is no sample to be tested, eyewitness testimony may provide some drug usage evidence. This may include the observance of rituals where employees pass cigarettes around after each puff, the detection of marijuana odor, and finding cigarettes or butts. Other symptoms of drug abuse and overdose can include watery or red rimmed eyes, dizziness, runny nose, and slurred speech. These effects are often similar to the symptoms of illness, however, and may not be easily distinguishable. Depending upon the facts, circumstantial evidence or constructive possession may be sufficient to sustain discipline. Some employers have utilized private and undercover investigators to detect alcohol and drug use in the workplace. Because hired investigators are employer agents, improper conduct by the investigator will expose the employer to liability, including those involving infringement of constitutional rights. Former employee testimony may also be suspect. Written tests that inventory an examinee's drug attitudes and behavior are also available.

Statutory obligations may exist regarding an employer's requirement to rehabilitate employees who are under alcohol or drug abuse. Treatment providers are not permitted to disclose information about employees in substance abuse programs absent employee consent. The Comprehensive Alcohol Abuse and Alcoholism Prevention, Treatment and Rehabilitation Act of 1970, the Drug Abuse Office and Treatment Act of 1972, and the Public Health Service's Confidentiality of Alcohol and Drug Abuse Patient Records regulations require this. The employee must sign a release authorizing the treatment center to disclose any information, including the employee's admittance. This release must specify what information can be released, to whom, the disclosure's purpose, and the consent's duration. The consent is revocable at any time. However, the treatment program's director may release information with or without consent where reason to believe exists that the employer will use the information for assisting in rehabilitation and not for denying employment or advancement. Employee Assistance Programs (EAPs) must abide by these confidentiality requirements.

Arbitrators have sustained employee grievances who were not given the opportunity to seek rehabilitation before being terminated. [*Veterans Administration Medical Center*, 83 Lab Arb. (BNA) 51 (1984) (Denson, Arb.).] The federal Vocational Rehabilitation Act of 1973 and the Comprehensive Alcohol Abuse and Alcoholism Prevention, Treatment and Rehabilitation Act of 1970 were violated when an employee was terminated for alcohol-induced absences that occurred before and after entering an alcohol counseling and hospitalization program. [*Walker v. Weinberger*, 600 F. Supp. 757 (D.D.C. 1985).] Reasonable accommodation of an alcoholic employee requires forgiveness of past alcohol-induced misconduct in proportion to his/her willingness and favorable response to treatment.

Once an employer has given an employee the choice of rehabilitation or termination and the employee refuses to undergo rehabilitation, most arbitrators uphold the termination. [*Pacific Telephone and Telegraph Company,* 80 Lab. Arb. (BNA) 419 (1983) (Killion, Arb.).] Employees may be given a second chance to enter a rehabilitation program. Arbitrators generally uphold terminations when an employee has a post-rehabilitation reoccurrence of alcohol or drug abuse. [*Tecumseh Products Co.,* 82 Lab. Arb. (BNA) 420 (1984) (Murphy, Arb.).]

Due to the lack of clear statutory or judicial authority regarding an employer's right to require an employee to take urinalysis or blood tests when suspected of alcohol or drug usage, an employee's refusal to submit to these tests may not warrant discipline or termination. State Constitution privacy provisions and other state statutes may protect employees. Employee refusal to take a blood test may not by itself justify discipline even where the collective bargaining agreement or employer policy specifically require the test. Arbitrators have been willing, however, to draw an adverse inference from an employee's failure to take the opportunity to disprove the allegation of being under the influence by taking a test. [See *Stokely-Van Camp,* 64 Lab. Arb. (BNA) 859, 860-61 (1975) (Foster, Arb.).]

There are not statutory directives regarding the appropriate discipline of an employee who is found to be under the influence. Statutes only address an employer's obligations to accommodate rehabilitation.

Adopting alcohol and drug screening programs does not affect the employer's right to prohibit workplace possession or consumption of intoxicants. Discipline resulting from provable alcohol or drug use at the workplace should be explained in employer policies.

Three main approaches have developed among employers and arbitrators regarding alcoholism. The traditional model wherein employees are judged solely on the basis of their job performance without regard to clinical explanations of their shortcomings. The therapeutic model where the alcoholic employee is deemed to be the victim of a disorder and offered opportunities to recover, including leaves of absence and appropriate treatment. A modified corrective discipline approach where the employee is viewed as suffering from an illness but ultimately may be subject to termination, perhaps after being given one second chance.

Employers can generally require employees to submit to a urine test while being observed by clinic personnel. In the absence of a showing that this observation intrudes unnecessarily upon privacy interests, this monitoring serves a permissible purpose in assuring the integrity of the sampling process. Ordinarily, where the collective bargaining agreement prescribes immediate termination for refusal to take an alcohol or drug test, the employee's refusal would constitute just cause for termination.

After exhibiting some bizarre behavior during her early morning shift, a woman who worked as a waiter's helper at a restaurant was ordered by her supervisor to undergo a drug test at an independent medical clinic. [*Union Plaza Hotel,* 88 Lab. Arb. (BNA) 528 (1986) (McKay, Arb.).] Initially, the employee signed consent forms agreeing to take urine and blood tests. She became reluctant to take the urine test after learning that she would be required to urinate in the presence of a female nurse. The employee, who planned to attend a dance rehearsal immediately following her shift at the restaurant that day, was wearing leotards and would have been required to undress completely to provide a urine sample. Declining to urinate in the nurse's presence, the employee said she "would rather be fired" than do so. She asked to be permitted to take the test in a room without a water source, where there was no possibility that she could contaminate the sample. This was denied. She then asked the nurse for a robe. This was also denied. Ultimately, the employee refused to submit to the test as required and was terminated.

Just cause was lacking in this case. The nurse's refusal to provide the grievant with a robe made the conditions of the test unreasonably onerous. The employer exceeded its rights by requiring the employee to take the test in an unusually embarrassing manner.

Discipline for drug abuse is also the result of several different views. Whereas alcoholism as a treatable disorder is gaining ground, there is more resistance to rehabilitating drug dependent employees. One reason for the different views on alcohol versus drug abuse is that the drug involvement carries a criminality taint. This may influence the discipline imposed. A *hard* drug such as heroin and other opium derivatives might warrant greater discipline than a *soft* drug such as marijuana. Other factors considered by arbitrators are whether there is a clearly promulgated contract provision or employer rule against drug possession or use and whether the employer is attempting to deal with acknowledged drug use.

Discipline for drug use or possession outside the workplace has involved arbitrator consideration of whether this adversely affected the employer's business or reputation, threatened the welfare or morale of other employees, or rendered the employee unfit to perform his/her duties. A person who uses or sells drugs may be considered an accident and health risk to himself/herself and others in the workplace, as well as a potential crime source. Possession of drugs does not necessarily demonstrate use and may be considered a lesser offense. Arbitration awards generally have no precedential value, however, they provide some insight into what other decision-makers consider appropriate discipline where alcohol and drug abuse are involved.

Various federal and state statutes may affect drug testing. Fair employment practice (FEP) statutes may apply where drug testing has a disproportionate adverse effect. Under the federal Civil Rights Act of 1964 (Title VII), a claim may be viable where an alcohol or drug policy disproportionately affects a minority group and the employer cannot establish job relatedness. Employers should have a valid nondiscriminatory reason for selecting employees for testing. Similarly, employers who are inconsistent in their disciplinary enforcement are vulnerable to a disparate treatment claim.

The Vocational Rehabilitation Act of 1973 is another federal restriction on employer decisions concerning workplace drug use. Discrimination against a former alcoholic or drug user is prohibited. This may, likewise, be prohibited under state FEP laws as handicap discrimination.

Under worker's compensation statutes, a potentially more threatening expense may arise. Where an employee claims that his/her alcohol or drug addiction is due to an industrial injury, an employer may be held liable for causing the employee's problem. [*California Microwave, Inc. and Pacific Indemnity Co. v. Worker's Compensation Appeals Board*, 45 Cal. Comp. Cas. 125 (1980)], exemplifies this problem.

In *Microwave*, an employee claimed he was disabled as a result of a drinking problem which was created and aggravated by workplace pressures was awarded benefits by the California Worker's Appeals Compensation board (WCAB). When the employee began his job as a mailroom clerk, he was a nondrinking alcoholic. The employer grew in size over the next several years and as a result, the employee's workload increased.

After requesting help from his employer, and being refused, the employee began to drink again. The employee's drinking problem became so problematic that on one occasion he attempted suicide while intoxicated. The employee was hospitalized for a short time period and then returned to work. However, soon after his return, the employee began to drink again and was rehospitalized.

The diagnosis showed that the employee was suffering from depression and organic brain damage causing a total disability. Benefits were awarded by the California WCAB because an industrial injury had occurred, through the nervous tension that caused his drinking problem, ultimately totally disabling him.

Searching or testing employees may subject employers to liability under various litigation theories. The invasion of privacy tort may provide protection. It safeguards an employee's solitude, seclusion, and private affairs. Invasion of an employee's privacy right potentially subjects an employer to actual, compensatory, and punitive damages. Voluntary employee consent, however, waives any employment privacy right.

Before conducting a drug search, an employer should limit the employee's privacy expectation by giving prior notice that searches can occur. Where the employer creates a privacy expectation through a handbook or employment policy it may be required to follow it. The search's scope may impose employer liability. Publicly disclosing private facts about a drug test's results may impose liability.

Defamation litigation may be based on an inaccurate drug test interpretation. To minimize defamation exposure, employers should be careful of all comments made to or about any employee tested. Employer information use or misuse can result in defamation.

Other tort litigation theories that may give rise to employer liability include:

1. False imprisonment where the employer restrains the employee during a search or seeks to extract urine or blood absent employee consent;
2. Intentional infliction of emotional distress where the employer's conduct is outrageous during a search or seeks to extract urine or blood absent employee consent;
3. Negligent maintenance or disclosure of employment records where erroneous information exists;
4. Fraudulent misrepresentation where the reason for testing is not correctly disclosed; and
5. Intentional interference with contractual relations where a former employer releases erroneous alcohol or drug use information to a prospective employer.

Where employees are under alcohol or drug influence outside the workplace employer liability may arise. This could occur where an employer knowingly sends an employee under alcohol or drug influence home and an accident results. It may also be alleged where the employee commits criminal acts during employment while under the influence. Likewise, the employer can be held liable for its agent's acts committed during a search or testing.

Implementation of alcohol and drug testing policies are subject to negotiation as a "working condition" under the National Labor Relations Act (NLRA). [See *Johnson-Bateman Co.*, 295 N.L.R.B. No. 26 (1989).] Discipline or termination resulting from these policies will generally be subject to grievance arbitration.

Nobody questions an employer's right and duty to ensure that employees are not working while impaired by any substance. Alcohol and drug tests do more than that. They may become unwarranted intrusions when they detect matters unrelated to safe and efficient job performance. Legal challenges to the use of these tests continue to pend. Out of this, the following has emerged regarding balancing individual employment rights with the employer's needs for a productive and safe workplace:

1. *Private or public employer.* Public employers face greater restrictions when implementing alcohol and drug screening programs because of constitutional requirements involving due process and standards for reasonable search and seizure.
2. *Job applicant or present employee.* Employers have greater latitude with job applicants than with current employees.
3. *Union or nonunion.* Employers have greater latitude with non-union employees than union employees because of statutory collective bargaining obligations.
4. *Type of position.* Employers have greater latitude with job positions that pose an injury risk to the public or to employees, such as pilot, driver, security guard, police officer, etc.
5. *Written policy and notice.* Employers who provide precisely written policies and proper notice to employees and applicants will have greater latitude than those with unwritten policies.
6. *Standard by which test or search is triggered.* Employers who limit testing and searches to defined situations involving a reasonable suspicion of job impairment have a better chance of sustaining their action than those with random testing or searches.
7. *Type of test or search.* Less intrusive testing and searching methods involving breathalizers, searches of items on a desk

top, etc. are more likely to be approved than intrusive methods like blood tests and body searches.
8. *Confirmation of test.* Employers have greater latitude in acting on test results where they have been confirmed by a second test.
9. *Standard by which adverse action is triggered.* Employers can more easily justify adverse action for workplace possession of large amounts of an illegal drug than for small amounts of alcohol or marijuana in a urine sample.
10. *Type of adverse action.* Employers with rehabilitation programs can more easily defend their policies than those who terminate employees after a first offense. [24 Gov't. Employee Rel. Rptr. (BNA) 1549 (Nov. 17, 1986).]

Employers contemplating the adoption of alcohol and drug testing programs should seriously consider the program's scope, purpose, and effect regarding:

1. Drug testing necessity;
2. Employee group or category to be tested;
3. Giving notice to all affected employees;
4. Receiving employee consent to test and to disclose test results;
5. Selecting a reputable laboratory to analyze employee samples;
6. The employer's response to employees who have a positive test result or who refuse to take a test;
7. Arranging for a confirming test on positive samples;
8. Guarding against information disclosure about employees obtained through the tests;
9. Limiting alcohol or drug testing to situations where on-the-job impairment is evident;
10. Having supervisors document behavior that suggest alcohol or drug impairment;
11. Interviewing employees about illnesses or prescription drugs that may adversely affect their job performance;
12. Implementing or strengthening restriction on the use or possession of alcohol or drugs on employer property during work hours;
13. Ensuring that the facts and circumstances that created the reasonable suspicion are documented where testing is performed based on a reasonable suspicion;
14. Providing an opportunity for the union to participate in establishing an alcohol and drug testing program, by bargaining with the union over the changes in work rule or practices resulting

from adopting a testing program under a collective bargaining agreement. [See Littler, Mendelson, Fastiff and Tichy, *Responding to Drug and Alcohol Abuse in the Workplace,* in The 1987 Employer B, B-31 (1987).]

To minimize employer liability for employee claims arising out of alcohol and drug testing, the following should be considered:

1. *Obtain a release/authorization.* Before an applicant/employee is tested for alcohol or drugs, the employer should obtain test consent. The consent form should solicit information regarding prescription drug use or nonprescription medication to eliminate false positives. For example, therapeutic cold medicines such as Contac and Sudafed, can create a false positive for amphetamine use. The consent form may help protect the employer against claims for invasion of privacy, defamation, false imprisonment, assault and battery, etc.
2. *Do a follow-up test.* An initial screening test indicating positive result should be verified by a confirmation test for all employees. Employers may wish to perform confirmation tests for applicants where:
    - There are few applicants, to minimize an additional test's costs;
    - The initial test is positive regarding an otherwise highly qualified applicant; and
    - The applicant desires confirmation in contesting an adverse employment decision.
3. *Safeguard the specimen.* The specimen should be marked in the applicant's/employee's presence and a documented chain of custody maintained to ensure that the specimen is correct. Selecting a reliable laboratory is essential.
4. *Restrict test disclosures.* Test results should not be publicized. Even when the drug tests are considered accurate and there is no risk of publication of a false fact, they should not be disclosed.
5. *Use split samples.* The specimen should initially be split into two samples. Every sample should be preserved for a reasonable time period; such as sixty to ninety days. During this period, the employee who provided the sample should be permitted to have the sample evaluated independently by a confirmation test at his/her own expense. An employee who has the opportunity to confirm the test results independently may be less likely to challenge those results. Where applicants are not permitted independently to confirm their test results because they may not be

informed of the test's results, a separate sample should be retained in case the applicant challenges an adverse employment decision. [See Redeker and Segal, *Drug and Alcohol Testing: Legal and Practical Considerations,* 7 Bureau of Nat'l Affairs Communicator 2, 20 (Fall 1987).]

HUMAN IMMUNODEFICIENCY VIRUS (HIV)

Over the past several years the rapid global spread of the human immunodeficiency virus (HIV) has quickly become a significant employment issue. It is raising concerns that may not be resolved until after many of its victims' deaths. This will require employers to balance the needs of those afflicted with a fatal disease against concerns of other employees, clients, or consumers.

HIV's uncertainty, its tragic consequences, and the public fear that it engenders prevents it from being solely a health issue. It has become a major employment issue regarding the HIV afflicted employee's entitlement to a workplace free from discrimination involving physical disability or handicap. Recent reports are that deaths from this disease will be 54,000 in 1991 alone against 9,000 in 1986. No HIV patient has lived more than three years.

HIV is a disease that affects the body's immune system rendering it vulnerable to infections and viruses. It is caused by a virus that has been given a number of names, including Human T-Lymphotrophic Virus, Type III (HTLV-III), Lymphadenopathy-Associated Virus (LAV), and AIDS-Related Virus (ARV). HIV attacks the body's immune system, leaving it incapable of defending against certain unusual fatal illnesses. These diseases are termed *opportunistic* infections. They include Kaposi's sarcoma (KS) (a rare skin cancer) and pneumocytis carnii pneumonia (PCP) (an uncommon lung ailment). The HIV's viral agent is transmitted through blood or semen during sexual intercourse, blood transfusions, or shared needles used by drug users. It is allegedly not spread by casual contact of the type that occurs at the workplace. These infections generally result in death.

Individuals infected with HTLV-III/LAV differ significantly in symptoms and physical conditions. These differences present employment problems because HIV afflicted employees cannot be treated uniformly. There are those:

1. Who have been exposed to the virus but exhibit no symptoms;

2. Who develop an HIV-related complex and exhibit HIV symptoms but have not yet developed the full syndrome; and
3. Who have an impaired immune system and have contracted an opportunistic infection, such as KS or PCP.

HIV cannot be diagnosed from symptoms alone. There are several symptoms that in combination for an extended time period may suggest the possibility of HIV, and are cause for checking with a physician. These symptoms are:

1. Unexplained, persistent fatigue;
2. Unexplained fever, shaking chills, or drenching night sweats lasting longer than several weeks;
3. Unexplained weight loss greater than ten pounds;
4. Swollen gland (enlarged lymph nodes usually in the neck, armpits, or groin) which are otherwise unexplained and last more than two months;
5. Pink or purple flat or raised blotches or bumps occurring on or under the skin, inside the mouth, nose, eyelids, or rectum that may resemble bruises but do not disappear and are usually harder than the skin around them;
6. Persistent white spots or unusual blemishes in the mouth;
7. Persistent diarrhea; and
8. Persistent dry cough which has lasted too long to be caused by a common respiratory infection, especially if accompanied by shortness of breath. [Allstate Forum on Public Issues, *AIDS: Corporate American Responds* 20 (1988).]

It is important to note that this list includes many items that are very similar to the symptoms of other diseases; some, for example, may be symptoms of stress. Only a doctor is capable of making an HIV diagnosis, and he/she will need supporting laboratory tests.

Employees who exhibit no symptoms will be in good health and physically capable of job performance. These employees are not threatened by common workplace illnesses. However, these employees can transmit it to others, regardless of whether the symptoms are exhibited. Because HIV is allegedly not transmitted through casual contact, these employees should pose no employer problem.

Other HIV afflicted employees provoke greater employer concern. These individuals will be especially susceptible to infection by common workplace viruses raising a health concern. They may eventually develop multiple infections that make them incapable of job performance. Many will require prolonged hospitalization, making regular employment difficult.

Tests have been developed to determine whether an employee has been exposed to HIV. These tests detect HIV antibodies. The most widely used test is the Enzyme-Linked Immunosorbent Assay (ELISA). The other test which is more accurate and expensive, is the Western blot test. These tests raise similar employment privacy concerns as those that exist regarding drug testing.

The methods by which HIV can be spread from person to person are:

1. Sexual intercourse with a person who is infected with HIV. HIV is essentially a sexually transmitted (venereal) disease. Semen can transmit the virus. Vaginal fluids can also transmit the virus. Although sexual transmission of HIV has been more common among homosexual men than among heterosexuals, cases of HIV transmission between heterosexuals during sexual intercourse are gradually increasing. Men can transmit the virus to women during sex, and women are able to transmit the virus to their male sex partners. As in the case of other sexually transmitted diseases, the proper use of condoms may reduce the risk of transmission, but are not 100 percent effective.
2. Sharing drug needles with an infected person. Sharing an intravenous (IV) drug needle with someone can inject the virus directly into the user's bloodstream. Needle use transmission is not limited to drug addicts. Occasional or recreational use of intravenous drugs is more common than is generally supposed, and can be the basis for HIV needle transmission.
3. Injection of contaminated blood products, such as in blood transfusions. This transmission method should be extremely rare now because of blood-screening programs. It also applied in the past to hemophiliacs, who are medically required to inject themselves with a blood-clotting medication called Factor 8, which was made from the blood of other people.
4. A woman infected with HIV who becomes pregnant or breast feeds can pass the virus to the baby. A woman may have none of the HIV symptoms and may only become aware of her infection because of her baby's condition. [Allstate Forum on Public Issues, *AIDS: Corporate America Responds* 20 (1988).]

What these transmission methods have in common are that they all involve the most intimate human contacts; i.e., all require some type of deliberate interaction.

The Center for Disease Control has issued HIV guidelines for the workplace (CDC Guidelines). The guidelines are directed to:

1. Health care employees;
2. Personal service employees having close personal client contact;
3. Food service employees, such as cooks, and food handlers; and
4. "Other workers" including persons in offices, schools, factories, and construction sites. [Center for Disease Control, *Recommendations for Preventing Transmission of Infection with HTLV-III/LAV in the Workplace,* 34 Morbidity and Mortality Weekly Report No. 45, at 682-94 (1985).]

They are based on the assumption that HIV is a blood borne, sexually transmitted disease that is not spread by casual contact, except for rare cases by blood transfusion, by an infected mother to her infant, or by accidental needle stick injury. The guidelines state that HIV is transmitted only by sexual acts or by sharing drug abuse equipment.

Regarding health care employees, the CDC Guidelines include certain recommendations. They concern managing exposure to blood or other body fluids, precautions to be taken with needles and sharp instruments, appropriate use of gloves and other protective garments, use of equipment to minimize the need for mouth-to-mouth resuscitation, sterilization and disinfection procedures, and disposal of infected body wastes.

Personal service employees include those having client body contact; i.e., barbers, hairdressers, cosmetologist, manicurists, massage therapists, and acupuncturists. The CDC Guidelines recommend that employees be aware of infection possibility through an open or oozing lesion that may come in contact with an infected person's blood or body fluid. There could also be a transmission risk when instruments contaminated with blood are not sterilized or disinfected. Personal service or health care employees who have open or oozing lesions should refrain from direct contact with individuals or others until the condition clears. The CDC Guidelines point out that transmission has not been documented in personal-service settings, indicating that the risk of transmission may be minimal or nonexistent.

The CDC Guidelines indicate that HIV is not transmitted through food preparation or service and that there have been no documented cases of Hepatitis-B or HIV transmission in this manner. Food service employees should follow established standards and practices of good personal hygiene and sanitation. They should not prepare or serve foods when they have open or oozing lesions and they should take care to avoid injury to their hands when preparing food. Food service employees known to be HIV infected need not be restricted from work, according to the guidelines, unless they have another infection, condition, or illness for which there should be a restriction.

The CDC Guidelines for other employees emphasize that HIV is not spread by the nonsexual, contact that occurs among employees, clients, and consumers in offices, schools, factories, construction sites, etc. Employees known to be HIV infected should not be restricted from work based on this, nor should they be restricted from using telephones, office equipment, toilets, showers, eating facilities, and water fountains.

Although employers are currently considering HIV testing policies for applicants or employees, states are enacting statutes restricting this. California prohibits persons, except as specified, from testing a person's blood for HIV without written consent. Because employers are not excluded, this is most likely prohibited in the employment setting.

Florida protects a person who submits to a serologic test for infectious disease from unauthorized test result disclosure. These test results may not be used to determine if a person may be insured for disability, health or life insurance, or to screen, determine suitability for or terminate employment.

Wisconsin prohibits an employer or an employer's agent from directly or indirectly soliciting or requiring as an employment condition for an applicant or employee an HIV blood test. Insurers may not condition coverage on whether or not an individual has obtained an HIV blood test or what the test revealed. Test result confidentiality is also protected.

Constitutional privacy considerations that arise out of drug testing are applicable to HIV testing. Mandatory HIV blood testing infringes the employee's protected privacy "interest in avoid disclosure of personal matters." Blood testing's physical intrusion is similar to compulsory immunizations. Unlike a vaccination, a positive HIV blood test could have a devastating impact on an employee's life and associations. Significant psychological trauma might accompany an erroneous diagnosis. The employee's most intimate personal relationships could be affected by a positive test. Disclosure to others could have serious results. A positive reading might be construed falsely to perceive an employee as a "gay" or a drug user. Through this, federal constitutional protections arising out of the first amendment's associational rights, the fourth amendment's guarantee against unreasonable searches, and the fifth amendment's protection against self-incrimination are impacted. State constitutional relief may also exist. [See *Glover v. Eastern Neb. Community Office of Retardation,* 686 F. Supp. 243 (D. Neb. 1988), *aff'd,* 867 F.2d 461 (8th Cir.), *cert. denied,* ____ U.S. ____, 110 S.Ct. 321 (1989) (mandatory HIV testing at a facility for the mentally retarded is a constitutionally impermissible search and seizure).]

Federal and state fair employment practice (FEP) statutes may recognize HIV as a protected handicap. While these statutes contain differences, their underlying intent is similar; i.e., employees who are capable of performing, without endangering themselves or others, should be allowed to do so regardless of physical or medical condition which is, or is perceived to be, disabling. FEP statutes generally consider someone physically handicapped where there is a physical condition substantially limiting one or more major life activities, a record of this impairment, or they are regarded as having this handicap. *Physical handicap* is considered as an impairment of sight, hearing, or speech; or the impairment of physical ability because of either a function loss; coordination loss; or an amputation. It also includes any other health impairment requiring special education or related services. Conditions that have been found to be handicaps include: 1) hypersensitivity to tobacco smoke; 2) high blood pressure; 3) high blood sugar levels; and 4) a missing kidney.

Current thoughts indicate that HIV is a protected handicap. [See *Shuttleworth v. Broward County,* 639 F. Supp. 654 (S.D. Fla. 1986).] This is especially so where a physical handicap includes any bodily condition that has a disabling effect or that may handicap in the future. There can be no doubt that HIV constitutes a physical handicap because HIV will at some point impair physical ability.

HIV is similar to handicap discrimination against individuals with contagious diseases. Recurrent tuberculosis has been considered a protected handicap. [*School Board of Nassau County, Fla. v. Arline,* 772 F.2d 759 (11th Cir. 1985), aff'd, 480 U.S. 273 (1987).] It limits one or more major life activities.

States with broadly defined physical handicap FEP statutes will probably conclude that HIV is a protected handicap. Coverage under FEP statutes should not be presumed. Several states do not prohibit handicap discrimination and other states have handicap discrimination statutes that may not cover HIV. Georgia and Kentucky expressly exclude persons suffering from communicable diseases, which HIV is considered to be.

Where HIV is considered a protected handicap, employers will have to make reasonable accommodations when HIV affects the employee based upon the particular situation. It may involve granting the employee time off for doctors' appointments, reducing work hours, restructuring job duties, or placing the employee on medical leave. As the HIV infected employee becomes more susceptible to diseases, the employer may have to accommodate the HIV infected employee by isolation from other employees when the HIV infected employee's health or safety is endangered by working near others.

Most state handicap FEP statutes provide an employer defense for *bona fide* occupational qualification ("BFOQ"). Where an employer can demonstrate that after reasonable accommodation the employee cannot perform essential job functions by not endangering health or safety, or the health or safety of others, the employer may have a permissible defense. The job and handicap together may create an *imminent and substantial risk* to health or safety.

Should HIV be considered a physical handicap, an HIV infected employee's protection from discrimination would apply at all levels of the employment relationship. Applicants could not be asked whether they have HIV or have been exposed to HIV unless this was job-related. Current employees should not be required to take an HIV test or to provide proof that they do not have HIV unless job-relatedness can be directly established. Some states already prohibit testing for HIV.

State statutes restricting employee medical information use and disclosure may impose liability. Additionally, the right of privacy guaranteed by some state constitutions has been interpreted to protect employee personnel files. The employer, as the custodian of private information, cannot waive constitutionally guaranteed employment privacy rights.

HIV infected employees may argue that any termination based on their physical handicap violates the implied covenant of good faith and fair dealing. In some states, this may not be available because claims based on physical handicap discrimination must be processed through to the state's FEP statute and not by a separate wrongful termination lawsuit.

Fear of HIV may also create employer problems. Employees who voluntarily leave work due to a reasonable, good faith, and honest fear of harm to health from the work environment may assert this in claiming unemployment compensation benefits. These employees have certain rights under federal and state statutes concerning the protected status of certain activity regarding health and safety matters should they assert this. Termination or discrimination because of this activity is protected. [See *Stepp v. Indiana Employment Sec. Div.*, 521 N.E.2d 350 (Ind. 1988) (laboratory technician's refusal to perform chemical examinations on body fluids from HIV patients was just cause for termination and proper denial of unemployment compensation benefits).]

Employers with unionized work forces face additional problems. Refusal to work with a fellow employee afflicted with HIV may be considered engaging in protected activity. This would depend on the reasonableness of the employee's protests and whether HIV creates an abnormally dangerous working environment.

Employers may be concerned about consumer reaction that it employs persons with HIV. Generally, however, customer preference is no defense to employment discrimination.

Litigation theories may safeguard individual employment rights relating to HIV. Where an employer alleges or discloses that an employee has HIV, liability can be premised upon:

1. Invasion of privacy where a sufficient public disclosure of an employee's HIV condition occurs;
2. Defamation;
3. Intentional infliction of emotional distress where the conduct is outrageous;
4. Negligent maintenance or disclosure of employment records;
5. False imprisonment could occur where the employee is unwillingly detained to obtain a blood sample for an HIV test;
6. A false reason for obtaining or using a blood test may establish a fraudulent misrepresentation; and
7. Intentional interference with contractual relations results where an employer alleges or discloses that an employee has HIV to a prospective employer and this information is erroneous, not job-related, or maliciously disclosed.

In a case illustrating the HIV defamation problem and employer liability for information disclosure, an employer improperly terminated an employee for allegedly having been exposed to HIV. [*Little v. Bryce*, 733 S.W.2d 937 (Tex. Ct. App. 1987).] The employee told another employee that his roommate was being treated for HIV. The co-employee subsequently informed supervisors that the employee had been exposed to HIV virus and that he might have HIV. Without verifying the accusation's truth, one of the supervisors confronted the employee and immediately terminated him. It was subsequently learned that neither the employee nor his roommate had HIV.

In addition to the potential liability for handicap discrimination and violation of the employee's rights by terminating him without any substantiation that he had HIV, the employer could also be held liable for defamation, even if the employer had raised the qualified privilege defense. Being mistakenly accused of having a contagious and loathsome disease creates a claim for defamation because of the inherent damage to reputation that results. Even if an employer establishes that a communication is made under a qualified privilege, the privilege is lost if the communication is made with "malice or want of good faith." Malice is defined not only as "ill will," but also a "reckless disregard for the truth or falsity of a statement. If someone is so motivated by fear or prejudice against a person that he/she become reckless about the truth or falsity of defamatory information about the person, then the defamatory remarks are made with malice.

The following procedures should be considered in avoiding workplace HIV conflicts:

1. Consider initial planning for dealing with HIV;
2. Do not feel compelled to announce an HIV policy, absent genuine workplace concerns, because—
   - Prematurely adopting an HIV policy may lead employees to believe that the employer knows something that may create undue concern about an HIV workplace risk,
   - Not knowing the circumstances of how the HIV issue will arise, it is difficult to make a premature commitment to any particular course of action, and
   - Unless some special risk of transmission exists; i.e., needle stick injuries, the best policy is a case-by-case approach;
3. Designate a small group of senior managers to deal with the HIV issue, which should include people knowledgeable about the medical, human resource, and legal issues;
4. Should the HIV issue require action, institute employee HIV education as the first step;
5. Institute a reasonable HIV policy that treats HIV victims like those with any other degenerative, noninfectious disease, to minimize legal liability;

MEDICAL CONCERNS / 115

6. Recognize that, given current technology, screening applicants or employees for HIV may not be effective, because the most common blood serum HIV antibody tests provide almost no useful information. In some states this testing is unlawful;
7. Determine whether any federal, state, or local regulation would prohibit certain employee classes with infectious diseases from working in or near certain areas;
8. Require an employee who is diagnosed with HIV, or any other infectious or communicable disease—
   - To provide a physician's certificate outlining whether the employee should work under any particular restrictions, and
   - To provide a statement regarding whether the employee's being subject to exposure to common viruses carried by other employees might pose an imminent and substantial risk to his/her health;
9. If the physician requires that work or exposure to others be restricted, make efforts to reasonably accommodate the HIV-afflicted employee by—
   - A job redefinition,
   - Transfer, and
   - Consultation with the physician attending a pregnant employee might also be indicated;
10. If the physician imposes no restriction, and assuming that there are no other health or safety restrictions imposed by law with respect to the employee, permit the employee with HIV to continue working;
11. Advise employees, based on the consensus of medical opinion, that there is no risk of contracting HIV in a normal workplace environment;
12. If an employee refuses to work with an HIV victim, follow alternative courses, such as—
    - The employee may be treated in accordance with counseling or progressive discipline procedures,
    - Reference may be made to employer policies regarding insubordination or harassment of employees who are members of a protected class,
    - The employer may wish to avail itself of the conciliation and remedial powers of a FEP Agency to resolve the situation,
13. Treat HIV victims who, by virtue of their illness, no longer are able to work, the same as any employee who has a long-term, debilitating disease;

14. Respect privacy rights and statutory rights to medical information confidentiality of HIV-afflicted employees, in that disclosing that an employee has HIV beyond those individuals with a need to know, can lead to—
    - Costly litigation, and
    - Increased anxiety among co-employees. [See Littler, Mendelson, Fastiff and Tichy, *Acquired Immune Deficiency Syndrome: The Problem of Accommodating Individual Rights with the Concerns of the Workplace,* in The 1987 Employer O, O-23 to O-24 (1987).]

Out of this the following has emerged regarding HIV:

1. HIV is a new disease requiring behavioral changes and extensive educational efforts;
2. HIV is a worldwide epidemic;
3. HIV results from the human immunodeficiency virus (HIV);
4. HIV transmission occurs through sexual contact, exchange of infected blood or blood products, or from mother-to-child in utero or at birth, but not through the air or by social or casual contact, saliva, tears, insects, or by eating food prepared by an HIV-infected person;
5. No vaccine or drug has proven effective in preventing or curing HIV;
6. HIV has been concentrated among homosexual/bisexual males and intravenous drug users;
7. HIV has severe psychological, social, and economic consequences;
8. The ELISA or initial blood test for HIV antibodies can produce false positive results, requiring confirmation by a more specific test known as the Western Blot; in some instances, an HIV- infected person may have a negative test result;
9. Mandatory testing should be for blood, tissue, organ, and semen donors only and all other testing should be voluntary;
10. Public disclosure of HIV-related information constitutes a most serious personal privacy invasion;
11. Discrimination should not be permitted; and
12. Except for the area of confidentiality, protective measures should be taken through regulations promulgated by the

appropriate governmental agencies, rather than through statutory enactments. [See Pennsylvania Bar Association Task Force on Acquired Immune Deficiency Syndrome, *AIDS: Law and Society* 2-4 (May 11, 1988).]

Regarding HIV and its workplace impact, the following can be indicated:

1. People with HIV infection are entitled to the same rights and opportunities as people with other serious or life-threatening illnesses;
2. Employment policies must, at a minimum, comply with federal, state, and local laws and regulations;
3. Employment policies should be based on the scientific and epidemiological evidence that people with HIV infection do not pose a transmission risk of the virus to employees through ordinary workplace contact;
4. The highest levels of employer and union leadership should unequivocally endorse nondiscriminatory HIV employment policies and educational programs;
5. Employers and unions should communicate support of these policies in simple, clear, and unambiguous terms;
6. Employers should provide employees with sensitive, accurate, and up-to-date education about risk reduction in their personal lives;
7. Employers have a duty to protect the confidentiality of employees' medical information;
8. To prevent work disruption and rejection by co-employees of an employee with HIV infection, employers and unions should undertake education for all employees before any incident occurs and as needed thereafter;
9. Employers should not require HIV screening as part of general preemployment or workplace physical examination; and
10. In those special occupational settings where there may be a potential risk of exposure to HIV (for example, in health care, where workers may be exposed to blood or blood products), employers should provide specific, ongoing education and training, as well as the necessary equipment, to reinforce appropriate infection control procedures and ensure that they are implemented. [See *Workplace Bill of Rights,* 1 Personnel Directors' Legal Alert 8 (May, 1988).]

STERILIZATION

Employers generally may prescribe the medical criteria for a particular job. However, these criteria must be job-related. Sometimes, these criteria are quite controversial by affecting individual employment rights. Sterilization is one of these. It affects one's most personal interest procreation.

Until recently, disagreement existed regarding whether fetal protection policies were lawful, and if so, under what conditions. [See e.g., *Wright v. Olin Corp.*, 697 F.2d 1172 (4th Cir. 1982) (upholding fetal protection plan); but see *Zuniga v. Kleberg County Hospital*, 692 F.2d 976 (5th Cir. 1982) (rejecting employer's fetal protection plan).] Those accepting the business necessity defense for these policies placed considerable emphasis on whether the employer, in implementing a fetal protection policy, failed to use an available, less discriminatory alternative of achieving its business purpose. A policy in which employees are transferred and made financially whole for their losses meets the less discriminatory alternative test. However, a more onerous policy that automatically terminates fertile females or prohibits their hiring would violate Title VII.

A fetal protection policy that barred women who were capable of bearing children from working in jobs where there is a high level of lead exposure violated Title VII. [*United Auto Workers v. Johnson Controls, Inc.*, ___ U.S. ___, 111 S.Ct. 1196 (1991).] Even though exposure to lead may pose a substantial risk of harm to the fetus, the policy was found to be illegal by the United States Supreme Court [*Id.*].

The employer, a battery manufacturer, implemented a policy that barred childbearing women from production and maintenance jobs where their blood level could rise above 30 micrograms. Women were presumed capable of bearing children until they medically proved otherwise. Under the policy, women who were required to transfer out of jobs were paid medical removal protection benefits to compensate for lost earnings.

Citing medical evidence that fetuses are particularly vulnerable to lead exposure—more so than grown men or women—and that fetal exposure could occur before a mother was aware of her pregnancy, the policy was still found to be facially discriminatory. Acceptable alternatives existed that would protect fetuses from lead exposure.

Some states prohibit an employer from requiring an employee to be sterilized as an employment condition. Sterilization problems normally arise where hazardous working conditions exist. In making metal products, including lead shot and bullets, an employer adopted a rule prohibiting fertile female employees aged eighteen to fifty from working in the exposed area because of possible reproductive hazards. One female transferred to another job while another had a tubal ligation and returned to work. The union filed a grievance but the arbitrator upheld the employer's action. [*Olin Corp.*, 73 Lab. Arb. (BNA) 291 (1979) (Knudson, Arb.).]

Despite this, workplace sterilization policies as employment conditions should be closely scrutinized. They should not be permitted to abridge constitutional rights or those that exist under fair employment practice (FEP) statutes or health and safety statutes.

5

Information Collection Procedures

After hiring, information collection continues at the workplace. Much of this employer information collection involves updating and maintaining information that has already been obtained. However, in other instances individual employment rights are affected through searches, monitoring, surveillance, and literature solicitation and distribution.

SEARCHES

Employer security problems have broadened from concerns over property and information theft to safeguarding the workplace from alcohol and drug abuse. This raises questions over:

1. Screening potential employees;
2. Investigating and handling workplace theft, dishonesty, and substance abuse problems; and
3. Protecting employer confidential information from disclosure.

Searches or the potential for searches can create individual employment rights problems. Employees who are stopped and searched may assert several claims against employers. Among these are:

1. Invasion of privacy;
2. Defamation;
3. False imprisonment;
4. False arrest;
5. Malicious prosecution;

6. Intentional infliction of emotional distress; and
7. Constitutional right infringement.

False imprisonment poses a significant individual employment rights intrusion when detaining employees to search their bags, cases, purses, or person. This generally requires a total employer restraint on freedom to move that is against the employee's will. Merely stopping an employee is not a total restraint. Keeping the employee in an office or on the employer's premises is a total restriction. The restraint need not be lengthy or physically confining; i.e., the employee need not be locked in a room. Generally, the employee must be aware of the restraint, but awareness may not be necessary where substantial damages result from confinement. The employee can satisfy this by showing that he/she was ordered not to leave.

Confinement is determined by finding whether a reasonable person placed in these circumstances by an employer believed that they were being restrained? This could occur by:

1. Placing physical barriers;
2. Using force or the threat of force to restrain the employee; or
3. The appearance of force or other intimidation means to restrain the employee.

Where an employee remains free to leave, despite being asked questions or being accompanied to or from work during an investigation, no false imprisonment occurs.

Generally, not until the employer causes an arrest, does it incur false arrest liability potential. False arrest does not occur where the employer gives truthful information to law enforcement authorities and allows them to determine the ultimate course. Where the information disclosed to the police is known to be false and the employer insists on arrest, liability may result. Probable cause for an arrest is a valid defense to a false arrest claim. "Probable cause" concerns a good faith, reasonable belief in the arrest's validity. A signed uncoerced statement admitting employee responsibility protects the employer from liability. [See *Jacques v. Firestone Tire and Rubber Co.*, 6 Cal Rptr. 878, 183 Cal. App.2d 632 (1960).]

Malicious prosecution arises where the employer:

1. Makes a false accusation;
2. Knows the statement's falsity or a reckless disregard for its truth; and
3. Causes arrest, confinement, or other damages.

This may arise in search situations where theft is alleged.

Defamation arises during a search where accusation of a crime or some other adverse act is:

1. Made that would bring disrepute to the employee;
2. Made falsely or with reckless disregard for its truth; and
3. Communicated to others orally or in writing.

Where the search leads to conduct or to an accusation causing emotional upset with outrageous manifestations, a claim for intentional infliction of emotional distress may be made.

Searching employee property that is brought onto the employer's premises may affect constitutionally protected privacy interests. Here the employee's privacy interest must be balanced against the employer's interest in productivity, the well-being of its workforce, and the security of its premises. This individual employment right depends upon the employee's privacy expectation in the particular workplace setting and circumstances, including whether the employee's right to privacy will adversely impact legitimate employer interests in a healthy and productive workforce or the integrity of its premises.

Searches at the police's request may deem the employer the police's agent where constitutional protections would apply. The United States Constitution's fourth amendment protects against unreasonable searches and seizures by government agents where the individual maintains a reasonable privacy expectation from governmental intrusion. Police must have a valid search warrant to search an employee's locker. However, an employer must have a valid search warrant where it is acting as the police's agent. A warrantless search at the police's request would violate the employee's fourth amendment rights. Evidence obtained through an improper search could be excluded from a criminal proceeding. The employee could also bring an action for damages against the employer for a constitutional violation. Waiver of fourth amendment rights could, however, occur by the employee consenting, without coercion, to the search.

Formal notice should be provided to employees that lockers, desks, and vehicles may be searched without their consent or awareness. Unwritten but established employer practice of searching lockers and trucks may not be sufficient. A twelve-year record of inspecting lockers that included three or four actual inspections for cleanliness and at least one inspection for the purpose of finding an illegal weapon, was not sufficient to counter an employee's reasonable privacy expectation in a locker. [*United States v. Speights,* 557 F.2d 362 (3d Cir. 1977).]

Search of employee purses, lunchboxes, and pockets should only be undertaken after clear notice of intention to do so has been provided. The employer should obtain employee consent prior to conducting these searches. Privacy expectations in these items are a substantial intrusion into the employee's affairs. It is important that an employee's knowledge of a rule and assent to a search be established prior to any disciplinary action to counter claims that consent was coerced and not valid.

Because of the search criteria developed by arbitrators under collective bargaining agreements, they may offer additional guidance in evaluating these individual employment rights. Evidence obtained in violation of the unreasonable search-and-seizure provisions of the federal Constitution's fourth amendment is inadmissible in federal and state criminal proceedings. It is not uncommon for employers to present at arbitration proceedings evidence that has been obtained through a search of an employee's person or effects. Sometimes employers receive this evidence from police officers who have uncovered it during a search pursuant to a criminal investigation. In others, employers obtain evidence through their own searches.

Employers may impose reasonable rules regarding searches where they are made an employment condition. Some arbitrators permit employers to use evidence obtained without the employee's knowledge or consent if it is obtained from employer property, even if the property is momentarily under the employee's control. Although exclusionary rules are not automatically applicable in the arbitral proceeding, few arbitrators permit the employer to use evidence obtained by breaking and entering an employee's personal property, even though the property is located on the employer's premises.

Arbitrators confronted with evidence that was obtained from a police search must determine whether the evidence's admissibility should be reviewed under the fourth amendment. Some arbitrators have concluded that the exclusionary rule, which precludes using impermissibly seized evidence in a criminal proceeding against the search's victim, should be applied. Where an employee is aggrieved by police misconduct, evidence should be excluded from any criminal prosecution and liability imposed against those responsible for the illegal search.

Although many searches are intended to discover evidence pertaining to specific employee misconduct, some inspections are preventive rather than accusatory. Often employers conduct regular examinations of employees as they enter and leave to prevent the introduction of contraband onto their premises or the theft of property. These inspections are similar to international border searches. The inherent authority of a sovereign nation to conduct these border inspections without complying with the fourth amendment's probable cause requirement has been recognized. Arbitrators have also acknowledged the employer's right to conduct reasonable employee searches of their person and belongings as they enter or leave the workplace, particularly where there are *bona fide* reasons involving theft or workplace drinking. [See *Dow Chem. Co.,* 65 Lab. Arb. (BNA) 1295 (1976) (Lipson, Arb.).]

Generally, the security procedure must be clearly established, fairly administered, and understood by all employees. Where an arbitrator determines that an inspection rule has not been consistently applied or has been promulgated without sufficient notice to employees regarding their obligations, the disciplinary action may be modified.

Where an employer's search policy is not used to obtain information about statutorily protected employee rights and is not applied discriminatingly to inhibit the exercise of these rights, it should be permissible under the National Labor Relations Act (NLRA). Search policies usually significantly impact employment conditions that may constitute mandatory collective bargaining subjects. The employer may be obligated to afford the union an opportunity to negotiate over the proposed policy's implementation and its limitations.

As long as employees are informed of their obligations under search policies, an employer may prescribe compliance with them as an employment condition. Where a carefully defined policy required employees to permit large purse inspections brought onto the employer's premises, the arbitrator sustained the employee's termination for refusing a pocketbook search. [*Aldens Inc.,* 51 Lab. Arb. (BNA) 469 (1968) (Kelliher, Arb.).]

Certain employee privileges may be made contingent upon the employer's right to conduct searches. Providing locker space to employees can be conditioned on the employer's right to inspect locker contents at any time.

Policies requiring employees to submit themselves and their personal property to security examinations as an employment condition should be unambiguous and should be narrowly construed to avoid unnecessary and unanticipated privacy intrusions. Before conducting a search of an employee or his/her personal effects, an employer should always try to obtain permission. Employers should exercise caution in examining an employee's belongings that are not situated in an employer container. The employer should have probable cause to believe that relevant evidence will be uncovered.

Arbitrators generally support discipline where the employer has a well established and clear work rule prohibiting drug use or possession, especially at the workplace. The employer has the right to implement strict enforcement of its theft prevention procedures through inspections.

Two civilian government employees who parked on the military reservation where they worked were disciplined for marijuana possession and drug related paraphernalia seized from their cars. These searches were conducted either with employee consent or under a search warrant. They were deemed necessary when security dogs trained to detect the presence of drugs alerted an accompanying security officer. Both employees received written reprimands. [*U.S. Air Force Logistics Command*, 78 Lab. Arb. (BNA) 1092 (1982) (Feldman, Arb.).]

A locker search used by guards stationed at a nuclear power plant to discover marijuana was proper. Though the guards were not, as a group, notified of the search, the union acknowledged the employer's right to search guards' lockers as part of the employer's efforts to maintain discipline and safety. The arbitrator emphasized that the grievant was charged with a violation of plant rules and regulations and not the criminal offense of marijuana possession. [*Burns Int'l Security Service*, 78 Lab. Arb. (BNA) 1104 (1982) (Traynor, Arb.).]

Employers may conduct business-related searches within the plant, even though intrusive, as long as clearly defined rules govern these procedures, and the investigative activity does not violate the collective bargaining agreement or worker rights protected under the NLRA. Arbitrators will accord probative value to most evidence relevant to a grievance, provided that it was obtained pursuant to lawful, good faith security techniques undertaken by an employer.

Where the circumstances surrounding a search suggest duress or deception, however, arbitrators will give the evidence little weight. Evidence obtained through acts of coercion or deception, or pursuant to an improper employer search, will be excluded. To avoid problems with individual employment rights problems that are present in searches, the following principles emerge:

1. Employment applications should clearly provide that employees agree to subject themselves to employer searches;
2. The search policy should be given wide dissemination and be fully explained to all employees;
3. Employees should be informed that the purpose of searches is to serve as a deterrent and that the employee being searched is not under suspicion; and
4. Employees should not be selected for searches in a random, arbitrary, capricious, or discriminatory manner.

In investigating alleged workplace thefts, the human resource staff should consider the following:

1. Upon learning of theft allegations—
   - Notify and consult with legal counsel,
   - Structure the theft investigation to maximize the likelihood that the attorney-client and the attorney work product privileges apply, and
   - Consider whether legal counsel should participate in the investigation,
2. Evaluate the need for special expertise in theft situations involving—
   - Time mischarging, purchasing fraud, travel pay fraud, and so forth, where an accountant may need to be involved, and
   - Theft of computer services, where a computer expert may be necessary,
3. Establish the alleged theft's essentials regarding—
   - By whom,
   - Against whom,
   - Persons involved,
   - Nature of the improper act, and
   - When it occurred;
4. Determine whether to inform the suspected employee of the investigation and suspend him/her pending the outcome, or leave the employee at the workplace to obtain additional evidence of any wrongdoing;
5. Investigation procedures—
   - Interview all potential witnesses, including employees and outside third parties,
   - Consider obtaining signed statements from persons who may later take a position adverse to the employer,
   - Examine all pertinent records and documents,

- Avoid group interviews,
- Be impartial and take care not to convey a prosecutorial image, and
- Take thorough, detailed, and exact notes by—
  —Using the witness's language,
  —Including proper names, job titles, salary grades, and reporting relationships for persons interviewed and mentioned, and
  —Reviewing notes with the person interviewed to fill gaps or make necessary corrections.

MONITORING

Monitoring involves the use of mechanical devices to obtain employment information. Computer, telephone, and video technology are the most common types of workplace monitoring; however, they are not the only types. Biometric identification involving hand geometry and retinal patterns are being used to limit access to secure rooms and sensitive equipment or information. Hand geometry is the bond structure and webbing between the fingers that is thought to be unique in each individual. Retinal patterns are the configuration of blood vessels in the retina.

The extent of workplace monitoring is unknown because it is done without employees realizing it. Anytime computers or telephones are used in the workplace there is monitoring potential.

Title III of the federal Omnibus Control and Safe Streets Act of 1968 (Title III) prohibits all private individuals and organizations, including employers, from intercepting wire or oral communications of others. Similar prohibitions exist under state intercept statutes. These prohibitions have been narrowed in the employment context by the statute's "extension phone exemption." This permits employers to intercept certain employee workplace conversations and impact individual employment rights.

Employers may monitor employee conversations by listening on an extension to the employer's telephone system where this is done in the ordinary course of the employer's business. Monitoring of an employee based on the suspicion that business matters with a competitor might be discussed has been permitted. [See *Briggs v. American Air Filter Co., Inc.*, 630 F.2d 414 (5th Cir. 1980).] Employees handling telephone transactions with the public may be monitored. Personal calls may also be intercepted.

Where the employer violates Title III, the employee has a private right of action for actual and punitive damages, plus costs of attorneys' fees. Title III does not prohibit photographic surveillance of employee performance or honesty.

State statutes contain eavesdropping provisions similar to Title III. However, Title III's "extension phone" exemption does not apply under some state statutes.

Employers affect individual employment rights, at the workplace through various monitoring devices. These monitoring devices may include:

1. Wiretaps;
2. Transponders and beepers;
3. Pen registers and touchtone decoders;
4. Diodes;
5. Voiceprint identification;
6. Cordless telephones; and
7. Spotters.

Wiretaps are governed by Title III. They must be based on probable cause. This includes establishing that normal investigatory techniques have or will not be successful. Court authorization and approval by the Attorney General or Assistant Attorney General is required. They can be authorized for limited time periods not to exceed thirty days and are restricted to certain crimes; i.e., drug trafficking, currency reporting, bribery, etc. States have similar prohibitions on wiretapping.

Should wiretaps be used on an employer's premises, they probably would arise through a law enforcement agency's request. When this occurs, "state action" requirements would be present and certain constitutional protections would apply to safeguard individual employment rights.

Transponders and beepers transmit a traceable signal. They are generally used to locate a vehicle's or airplane's presence. Law enforcement agencies sometimes use transponders as a surveillance aid. Transponders are not regulated by Title III because they cannot transmit speech and do not intercept oral communications. However, use of a beeper has been held to constitute a search under the fourth amendment requiring a prior court order for law enforcement authorities.

These devices could be used by employers to locate employees and their vehicles who are suspected of deviating from scheduled delivery routes, spending time at home and not on the employer's business, etc. Depending how they are used by an employer, they offer the potential for a constitutional violations as an illegal search.

Pen registers and touch tone decoders record outgoing telephone calls disclosing the date, time, and number dialed. They may be used to trace non-toll employee calls. Title III generally does not prevent use of these devices. No oral communication interception is involved. The Federal Communications Commission (FCC) Act and Title III do not regulate pen registers, but fourth amendment considerations require a prior court order by law enforcement authorities. States may also regulate their use. Texas amended its wiretap statute to require prior court approval of pen registers.

Because employers may be concerned about employee personal telephone calls, these devices may be used as a verification. Employers using these devices should be careful. They could be exposed to a fourth amendment challenge as a public policy violation.

Diodes permit a telephone call to be traced. They prevent a disconnection and are useful in tracing local telephone calls. They are not prohibited by Title III because they do not record. They merely locate the call's source. For individual employment rights similar constitutional considerations apply regarding search and seizure.

Voiceprint identification involves analysis of recorded speech through a graphic representation to assist in identifying the speaker. It is not prohibited by Title III when not obtained by improper means; i.e., a wiretap. Voice spectrogram analysis has reached the standard of scientific acceptance and reliability necessary for evidence admissibility.

Cordless telephones operate similar to a radio. Conversations over cordless telephones can frequently be overheard by others over their telephones or AM and FM radio receivers. Whether these unintended interceptions violate FCC regulations, Title III, or state statutes has not been determined. However, the eavesdropping prohibition contained in FCC regulations provides that no person, directly or indirectly, may use a radio frequency device for the purpose of overhearing or recording private conversations of others unless all parties of conversation consent. Employers could be subject to an individual employment right intrusion where these are knowingly used to obtain information for employee disciplinary purposes. Defamation, invasion of privacy, or public policy violations could be alleged.

Employers are also subject to state statutes that regulate the use of human agents; i.e., *spotters* posing as customers to monitor employees. These statutes generally prohibit employee discipline or termination based on a spotter's report, unless the report is provided to the employee, or the spotter is employed exclusively by that employer to conduct the entire investigation.

Through these and other methods an employer may monitor employee job performance or other activities. This could occur at the workplace or outside of it. Use of any of these methods raises significant concerns over individual employment rights. These concerns are similar to those that these methods engender when used for law enforcement activities. Because of this, the same standards and protections for their use should apply for employment as for law enforcement use. This would prevent their arbitrary or discriminatory use. For their use, the employer should show a legitimate business necessity based directly on a workplace health, safety, or preservation of production need. Otherwise, the use of these methods should be carefully scrutinized as affecting individual employment rights endangering employee speech, beliefs, information, associations, and lifestyles.

Workplace monitoring may be used to measure and document employee transactions involving:

1. Planning and scheduling personnel and equipment;
2. Evaluating employee performance and personnel decisions concerning promotion, retraining, termination, etc.;
3. Increasing productivity by providing feedback on speed, work pacing, etc.;
4. Providing security for employer property, including intellectual property and personnel records;
5. Investigating incidents of misconduct, crime, or human error; and
6. Increasing employer control, discouraging union organization activities, identifying dissidents, etc.

Before undertaking monitoring, the employer should:

1. Review the applicability of any federal or state statutes regulating the proposed monitoring;
2. Ensure that the monitoring is job-related;
3. Clearly notify employees that job performance may be subject to monitoring;
4. As a condition of employment, obtain the employee's written consent to monitoring job performance;
5. Disclose to employees what mechanical or electronic devices may be used for monitoring job performance;
6. Disclose to employees when, where, and how these mechanical or electronic devices may be used for monitoring job performance;
7. Consider the fairness of work performance standards—
   - Do they fairly reflect the particular work force's abilities?,

- Will they create stress for many employees?,
- Do they account for recurring system difficulties and other workplace problems?,
- Do they include quality as well as quantity goals?,
- Do they represent a fair day's pay for a fair day's work?, and
- Do employees share in productivity gains achieved through new technology?;

8. Consider the fairness of the measurement process—
   - Do employees know and understand how the measurements are being done?,
   - Can the measurement system be defeated, impairing morale of those willing to follow the rules?,
   - Do employees receive statistics on performance directly and in time to affect their work rate?,
   - Is the relationship between quality and quantity communicated by supervisors when discussing problems with performance?,
   - Do supervisors communicate clearly that they are taking system/workplace problems into account?,
   - Are group rather than individual rates used when this approach is more equitable?, and
   - Is there a formal complaint process for contesting how work data is used?

9. Consider the fairness in applying the measurements to performance evaluations—
   - Are there meaningful recognition programs for superior performance?,
   - Is work quantity only one of a well-rounded and objective set of evaluation criteria?,
   - Does the employee see and participate in the performance evaluation?,
   - Is there an appeal process from the supervisor's performance evaluation?, and
   - Is there a performance-planning system to identify and help performance problems? [Office of Technology Assessment, *The Electronic Supervisor: New Technology, New Tensions* 29, 38 (1987).]

SURVEILLANCE

Unlike monitoring, surveillance generally involves physical observation of employees without their knowledge. This may arise by observation, extraction, or reproduction. Observational surveillance involves viewing the employee at the workplace, although the employee may not be aware of this. Surveillance by extraction generally involves employee information collection through questionable testing; i.e., by a polygraph examination, honesty testing, etc. Reproduction surveillance generally involves employee information collection through photographic, recording, or other similar devices.

Employers use surveillance for various purposes. These may include:

1. Determining the extent of union organizational activity;
2. General workplace surveillance for job performance purposes;
3. Manipulating employees;
4. Photographing employees; and
5. Electronic surveillance.

Before undertaking surveillance, the employer should:

1. Review the applicability of any federal or state statutes regulating the proposed surveillance;
2. Ensure that the surveillance is job-related;
3. Clearly notify employees that job performance may be subject to surveillance;
4. As a condition of employment, obtain the employee's written consent to job performance surveillance;
5. Disclose to employees what mechanical or electronic devices may be used for job performance surveillance; and
6. Disclose to employees when, where, and how these mechanical or electronic devices may be used for job performance surveillance.

Union Meeting Surveillance

The right to engage in union activity is an individual employment right that arises out of associational protections. Employers may affect individual employment rights by attending or observing union meetings through their presence or a representative's. Refusal to engage in unlawful surveillance is also protected. Generally, this illegal employer surveillance is remedied by resorting to federal or state labor relations statutes.

The uninvited attendance of an employer's representative at a union meeting is generally unlawful because it interferes with employee rights under federal and state labor relations statutes. Under the National Labor Relations Act (NLRA), an employer did not engage in unlawful surveillance when its supervisor openly attended a union meeting and left when asked. [*Litton Educational Pub., Inc.,* Am. Book Div., 214 N.L.R.B. 413 (1974).] However, where a school board member insisted, without union permission, upon being present at union membership meetings in the school's auditorium this was unlawful despite a public meeting law. [*Whiteboro Central School Dist.,* Pub. Bargaining Cas. (CCH) ¶41,642 (N.Y.L.R.B. 1980).]

When a supervisor arrived at a union meeting, a union official told the membership that he could be asked to leave. The membership said nothing. The union official then invited the supervisor to stay because the meeting was not secret and he knew a *stooge* would carry any desired information to the employer. Through this invitation, the surveillance was lawful. [*NLRB v. Computed Time Corp.,* 587 F.2d 790 (5th Cir. 1979).]

Illegal surveillance may occur where the employer's representative is near or in close proximity to a union's meeting place. A sheriff and a county correctional officer did not attend a union meeting, however, they unlawfully surveilled union activities by remaining in a parked car outside a union meeting. Driving a car slowly near a union's meeting to observe employees entering and leaving by a supervisor was unlawful. [*Filler Products, Inc., v. N.L.R.B.,* 376 F.2d 369 (4th Cir. 1967).] Sitting in a parked car near a union hall's entrance, without a legitimate purpose by an employer was improper. [*Custom Coating and Laminating Corp.,* 249 N.L.R.B. 765 (1980).]

A public university's representative did not unlawfully observe a union meeting by walking past the meeting room's open door because a legitimate reason existed for passing by the room. He was on his way to prepare another room for inspection by a university benefactor. [*Univ. of Maine,* Pub. Bargaining Cas. (CCH) ¶41,346 (Me. L.R.B. 1979).] Likewise, a private sector supervisor's chance presence at a restaurant during a union meeting to pick up food was lawful. [*C and M Sportswear Mfg. Corp.,* 183 N.L.R.B. 230 (1970).] A company president did not unlawfully view a union meeting by arriving at a parking lot meeting while delivering rent for the parking lot to its owner. [*Aircraft Plating, Inc.,* 213 N.L.R.B. 664 (1974).]

Workplace Surveillance

Mere employee observation by an employer does not in itself cause an individual employment right violation. Where employer surveillance becomes overzealous it may become actionable. Employers sometimes avoid the National Labor Relations Act (NLRA) proscription against surveilling union activities by observing employees at the workplace. One employer observed through a one-way mirror a union card solicitor during working hours and followed the card solicitor without committing a violation. [*J.C. Penney Co., Inc.*, 209 N.L.R.B. 313 (1974).]

A supervisor's desk location may be a legitimate method to ensure that employees are working. Moving a desk next to two known union adherents to ensure the employees were working and not spending work time on union or other outside activities was permitted. [*East Side Shopper, Inc.*, 204 N.L.R.B. 841 (1973). Even though a known union activist had been watched, a supervisor's elevated office was also lawful. From the elevated office, supervisors could observe all employees during working hours. [*Tartan Marine Co.*, 247 N.L.R.B. 646 (1980).] Using a desk in an employee work area while a plant superintendent was on crutches was lawful. This was not in response to union organizational activity, but resulted from the supervisor's physical infirmity. [*U.S. Industries, Inc., Durango Boot Div.*, 247 N.L.R.B. 361 (1980).]

Instructing a supervisor to remain at the workplace near union meetings may be lawful. This may be permissible because of past theft, fire, and employee disciplinary problems. [*Peerless of America, Inc.*, 198 N.L.R.B. 982 (1972).] Possible employee sabotage cannot be used as a pretext for unlawful surveillance. [*Alexander Dawson, Inc., dba Alexander's Restaurant and Lounge*, 228 N.L.R.B. 165, *enforced on other grounds*, 586 F.2d 1300 (9th Cir., 1978).]

Assigning employees to work together may be legitimate where quality control problems exist. This is appropriate where employee warnings had been issued for defective work.

Publicly observing union activities may not be unlawful. Where supervisors stood behind the employer's glass door entrances and watched the union distribute literature to employees leaving work no violation occurred. The union's literature dissemination was conducted in full public view. [*J.H. Block and Co., Inc.*, 247 N.L.R.B. 262 (1980).] Observing employees signing union authorization cards in the employer's parking lot in full public view was also lawful. [*Chemtronics, Inc.*, 236 N.L.R.B. 178 (1978).] Even where a plant superintendent observed union card solicitation occurring on a public road from the employer's parking lot, no violation occurred. The superintendent was in the parking lot for a lawful purpose and did not take notes or hide his presence. [*Phillips Industrial Components, Inc., Subsidiary of Phillips Ind., Inc.*, 216 N.L.R.B. 885 (1975).]

Workplace surveillance has been attempted by retaining certain information in employee personnel files. Retention of material in an employee's personnel file naming the employee as a union officer was unlawful. [*State of Illinois, Department of Personnel and Children and Family Service*, Pub. Bargaining Cas. (CCH) ¶40,214 (Ill. Ofc. of Collective Bargaining 1977).] Designating employees electing dues checkoff of an employee performance evaluation constituted unlawful surveillance. This served no legitimate purpose and was a violation even though the surveillance was secret and unknown to the employees. [*Illinois Bureau of Employment Security*, Pub. Bargaining Cas. (CCH) ¶41,229 (Ill. Ofc. of Collective Bargaining 1979).]

Employee Manipulation

Employee manipulation involves employer attempts to circumvent employee rights to engage in protected union activity under federal and state labor relations statutes. This affects individual employment rights present in beliefs and associations. Employer activity is evaluated by considering the:

1. Background,
2. Nature of the information sought,
3. Identity of the questioners,
4. Location, and
5. Interrogation method used.

Generally, an employer cannot ask employees to report union attempts to obtain authorization cards or to report union organizer names. A supervisor unlawfully told employees to report union harassment to sign authorization cards. [*Poloron Products of Mississippi, Inc.*, 217 N.L.R.B. 704 (1975).] However, an employer lawfully invited employees to report if they were *threatened* during a union campaign. The employer maintained the right to assure that its workforce was free from union coercion. The same employer's request to a newly hired employee to report union *harassment* was unlawful. This was so vague as to invite employees generally to inform on fellow workers who were engaged in union activity. [*Massey Stores, Inc., dba Kermit Super Value*, 245 N.L.R.B. 1077 (1979).]

A supervisor's request for an employee to report "anything going on" was not unlawful. The supervisor was referring to sabotage or wanton negligence suspected as causing defective products. No reasonable basis existed for believing that the supervisor was referring to a union organizational campaign. [*Randall's,* 157 N.L.R.B. 86 (1966).]

Camera Surveillance

The most ominous surveillance method is the camera. This may occur through film or videotape. It may affect individual employment rights present in speech, associations, beliefs, and lifestyle when done to circumvent employee rights to engage in union activity.

Camera surveillance of lawful union picketing can constitute unlawful interference even though not used to retaliate against the picketing employees. This may intimidate employees and is not justified to compile a historical record. Even though employer surveillance films are never developed, a violation can occur. [*Faulhaber, Co.,* 129 N.L.R.B. 561 (1960).]

It is not even necessary to take photographs. Illegal surveillance occurred where an employer approached pickets with a camera. Raising the camera and focusing can be sufficient to coerce and restrain the striking employees. [*Electri-Flex Co.,* 238 N.L.R.B. 713 (1979).] Displaying a camera and appearing to take pictures of union handbilling activities was unlawful. [*Fluid Chemical Co., Inc.,* 203 N.L.R.B. 244 (1973).]

Camera surveillance by a union may not be unlawful. A representation election was not set aside where a union business agent photographed employees. The union lacked the employer's power to retaliate against employees. [*AFSCME, Local 1584 v. Manatee Cty.,* Pub. Bargaining Cas. (CCH) ¶41,111 (Fla. L.R.B. 1979).]

Where litigation potential exists, an employer may take photographs for court proceedings. Photographing strikers on the picket line was lawful where these were taken to assure compliance with a consent decree. [*Pittsburgh and New England Trucking Co.,* 238 N.L.R.B. 1706 (1978).]

Photographs are proper where the employer seeks rule violation evidence. A department store lawfully photographed union organizers talking with employees during store hours. The store had the right to prevent union solicitation on the selling floor. [*Franklin Stores, Corp.,* 199 N.L.R.B. 52 (1972).]

Electronic Surveillance

Related to camera surveillance is surveillance by electronic or mechanical means. This may involve the use of tape recorders.

Employers can be liable for electronic surveillance by their middle-management executives. Employees may also be disciplined where they use a concealed tape recorder at meetings with their employer. [*Yoder v. Com., Dep't of Labor and Industry*, 92 Pa. Commw. 177, 498 A.2d 491 (1985).]

LITERATURE SOLICITATION AND DISTRIBUTION

Individual employment rights are affected through an employer's regulation of workplace literature solicitation and distribution. This curtails certain aspects of constitutional speech, association, and right to information. It may cause employees to refrain from exercising union organizational rights under federal and state labor relations statutes. Employees should be able to review and form opinions regarding literature brought into or distributed at the workplace. This should be permitted unless it interferes with the employer's legitimate ability to effectively operate its business by maintaining production levels and quality.

These individual employment rights normally arise when literature is brought into or distributed at the workplace. How far can an employer regulate this; i.e., does it extend to prohibiting the reading of *adult* literature and soliciting donations for a charitable organization during lunch periods?

Employer concerns commonly arise when a union attempts to solicit or organize employees. These actions cause employers to evaluate their literature solicitation and distribution policies because a threat exists to the employer's autonomy. The National Labor Relations Act (NLRA) regulates this at the federal level. It has been interpreted as providing the right to distribute union literature and to solicit union membership in the workplace.

The National Labor Relations Board (NLRB) has set certain presumptions regarding employer rules regulating union solicitation and distribution. These are generally applicable absent any showing of employer anti-union access or discrimination. They provide that it is presumptively valid for an employer to promulgate a rule prohibiting:

1. Union solicitation by employees in work areas during working time. [*Veeder-Root Co.*, 192 N.L.R.B. 973 (1971).]
2. Solicitation by employees during nonworking time, even if on employer property. [*Peyton Packing Co.*, 49 N.L.R.B. 828 (1943)];

3. Literature distribution by employees in work areas at any time. [*Rockingham Sleepwear, Inc.*, 188 N.L.R.B. 698 (1971)]; and
4. Literature distribution by employees in nonwork areas during nonwork time. [*Republic Aviation Corp. v. N.L.R.B.*, 324 U.S. 793 (1945).]

Solicitations should be distinguished from conversation. Discussing a subject, even if that subject is the union, may not permit an employer to apply its no-solicitation rule. Handing out union authorization cards that are to be signed and returned to a union organizer is considered solicitation. All other literature dissemination is considered distribution. Although literature distribution may be prohibited in work areas, the employer may only prohibit employee literature distribution during nonwork time in nonwork areas where a necessity to maintain discipline or production exists.

Employer rules may be found invalid where they discriminate against union organizing activities by allowing more permissive solicitation and distribution for other activities. Employer policies that attempt to control this should restrict all solicitation and distribution to nonwork areas during nonwork times equally, regardless of the material's content.

Individual employment rights may generally be enforced through recourse to the administrative procedures under federal and state labor relations statutes. Should employers retaliate against employees for engaging in literature solicitation and distribution where invalid rules or no rules exist, the discipline may be overturned. Reinstatement and back pay orders may result.

6

Employee Concerns at the Workplace

Workplace personal concerns affecting individual employment rights generally involve exercising certain duties, choices, or rights along with the employer's accommodation of these. Personal concerns may arise out of jury or witness duty, voting time, whistleblowing, dress and grooming codes, spousal policies, nepotism, third party representation, performance evaluations, name changes, identification tags, religious accommodation, privacy misconduct, and language requirements.

JURY OR WITNESS DUTY

Individual employment rights extend to general society obligations with which an employer cannot interfere. Jury or witness obligations are among these. A strong public policy implicit in federal and state constitutions, statutes, and decisional law encourages jury service. This also pertains for responding to a subpoena. Statutory protections for this interest generally entitle an employee to take time off for jury duty or for a court appearance as a witness where reasonable notice is given to the employer. The employer is prohibited from terminating or discriminating against an employee for taking time off for this purpose. This can cause employer liability even in the absence of a statute prohibiting employer interference with jury service. [See *Nees v. Hocks*, 272 Or. 210, 536 P.2d 512 (1975).]

In evaluating jury or witness duty, the following should be considered:

1. Review federal and state statutes for any requirement regarding time off, payment, etc.;
2. Proof of jury or witness duty should be presented; and
3. Requests for jury duty should be made in advance so as not to interfere unnecessarily with employer staffing requirements.

VOTING TIME

Voting is a general society obligation to which individual employment rights extend. It affects speech, beliefs, and associational interests. A strong public policy implicit in federal and state constitutions, statutes, and decisional law encourages voting. [See *Bell v. Faulkner*, 75 S.W.2d 612 (Mo. Ct. App. 1984) (refusing to vote as employer wished).] Some states require that an employee be given time off to vote.

California provides that when an employee does not have sufficient time outside work hours to vote, the employee may take work time off to vote. The employee is entitled to no more time off than is necessary to vote and the employer must pay up to two hours of any time taken off for voting. This time may be minimized through the employer's scheduling of voting time at the beginning or end of a shift. Employees can also serve as election officials without being disciplined or terminated, but are not entitled to pay for these absences.

In evaluating voting time, the following should be considered:

1. Applicable federal and state statutes should be reviewed for any requirements regarding time off, payment, etc.;
2. Requests for voting time should be made in advance of the election date so as not to interfere unnecessarily with employer requirements;
3. Proof that voting time was used by the employee; and
4. Voter registration verification, by having the employee sign an authorization-to-vote form indicating—
    - That the employee is an eligible, and registered voter for the subject election, and
    - That falsification may result in employee discipline up to and including termination.

WHISTLEBLOWING

Whistleblowing involves required participation or reporting of employer or fellow employee unlawful and/or improper conduct to the employer or to government authorities. [See *Tameny v. Atlantic Richfield Co.*, 27 Cal.3d 167, 610 P.2d 1330, 164 Cal. Rptr. 839 (1980).] Protective or active whistleblowing may be involved. Protective whistleblowing occurs when the employee is asked to commit a crime. Active whistleblowing involves the employee seizing the initiative and disclosing the employer's activities. This has been recognized for reporting to either government or employer authorities conduct that may violate the law, but for which no statute requires an employee to report.

Federal and state statutes increasingly protect whistleblowing. California's statute prohibits an employer from retaliating against an employee for disclosing information to a government or law enforcement agency where the employee has reasonable cause to believe that the information disclosed is a violation of noncompliance with a state or federal statute or regulation. Employers are prohibited from adopting policies or rules preventing employee disclosure of this information. Information that might violate the confidentiality of the lawyer-client privilege, the physician-patient privilege, or information considered a trade secret is not permitted to be disclosed. Absent a statute, whistleblowing violations may be enforced by asserting a public policy claim.

Regarding whistleblowing, the following should be considered:

1. Applicable federal and state statutes protecting whistleblowing;
2. Internal complaint procedures for resolving whistleblowing incidents;
3. Offering protection for legitimate whistleblowing complaints; and
4. Prohibiting retaliation for legitimate whistleblowing complaints.

DRESS AND GROOMING CODES

There is no rule of dress that does not in some way inhibit the employee's personal freedom. These rules may designate the type of clothing or uniform that must be worn by employees or that may not be worn at the workplace. Personal taste of style may be one of the more significant individual employment rights that an employer seeks to affect at the work place. It deals directly with speech, association, and lifestyle interests.

Dress and grooming standards may be imposed by the employer as part of health and safety requirements, customer relations, image, or business type. These may also arise informally through employee peer pressure; i.e., the work place norm among employees becomes a dress and grooming standard that they have established for themselves over a given time period with which new employees must conform or be ostracized.

Employment is not required to be continued where an employee affects some whim of style that is inappropriate to the employer's legitimate business image. In obtaining employment, one impliedly consents to abide by the employer's "reasonable" rules. However, the employer's actual business necessity may be required to be shown. This may be considered sufficient where there is an overall need for discipline, esprit de corps, and uniformity, depending upon the employer's business and the policy's relationship to the particular job duties involved.

Despite an employer's right to set these policies, certain individual employment rights may be adversely affected. These primarily involve violations of fair employment practice (FEP) statutes. The federal Civil Rights Act of 1964 (Title VII) defines religious beliefs to include observances and practices. Religious beliefs may be protected by Title VII's reasonable accommodation requirement, constitutional guarantees, or other FEP statutes.

Requiring female employees to wear sexually provocative uniforms violates Title VII. [*EEOC v. Sage Reality Corp.*, 507 F. Supp. 599 (S.D.N.Y. 1981).] However, an employer could not terminate an employee for sexually provocative attire where her dress appearance was similar to other employees. [*Atlantic Richfield Co. v. DCCHR*, 515 A.2d 1095 (D.C. App. 1986).]

Under collective bargaining agreements, arbitrators have recognized that an employer's dress code may restrict individual employment rights. For an employer's policies to be considered reasonable, they must be related to either health and safety or to a legitimate business interest or necessity of the employer. A dress or grooming code cannot be imposed that is the result of an arbitrary decision based on personal taste. Where an employer maintained the same dress code for twenty years that required female employees to wear white dresses, shoes, and stockings, it was not violated when the employees wore pants suits. [*Oxford Nursing Home*, 74 Lab. Arb. (BNA) 1300 (1980) (Wolff, Arb.).] However, where the policy has a direct effect upon production, safety, sales, or relationships with public consumers, an arbitrator will normally sustain it.

Depending upon the circumstances, other litigation theories may give rise to claims where individual employment rights are affected by dress and grooming codes. Where an employer's comments about an employee's dress are particularly derogatory, denigrating, or malicious and are communicated to others, defamation or intentional infliction of emotional distress may be asserted.

The following should be considered regarding dress and grooming codes:

1. Health and safety requirements;
2. Customer relations;
3. Employer image;
4. Business type; and
5. Job-relatedness.

SPOUSAL POLICIES

Employer spousal policies may encompass various prohibitions. They may restrict or deny employment with the same employer because one is or becomes husband and wife. This may result in a failure to hire, transfer to another department, or termination. As an individual employment right, it affects associational considerations. One is restrained or penalized for taking part in life's basic relationship of husband and wife. However, these policies have generally been permitted as a reasonable employer method of eliminating possible employee conflicts or favoritism that may grow out of the husband and wife relationship.

These policies have not escaped scrutiny. They are generally impacted by federal and state fair employment practice (FEP) statutes; however, constitutional claims may also be asserted. The federal Civil Rights Act of 1964 (Title VII) does not expressly prohibit discrimination based on marital status, however, the Equal Employment Opportunity Commission (EEOC) and the courts have recognized that sex discrimination comprehends a *sex-plus* job requirement when imposed on one sex and not the other.

Policies that are applied to employees based on their sex are discouraged. Rules that forbid or restrict a married woman's employment, but do not apply to a married man violate Title VII. The variable is sex making the discrimination invidious and unlawful.

It is an unlawful employment practice for an employer to discriminate against any individual because of sex unless sex is a *bona fide* occupational qualification reasonably necessary to the employer's business operation. Employment rules that adversely affect one sex over the other are *per se* discriminatory.

No-spouse rules that are job-related are not discriminatory where they plausibly improve the work environment. Job-relatedness may be established by showing that a no-spouse policy is necessary because:

1. The marital relationship often generates emotional outbursts that can hamper job performance;
2. Spouses working together can be expected to support each other when problems arise with the employer or fellow employees that could hinder dispute resolution;
3. Problems can arise where spouses work together and one is promoted to a supervisory position; and
4. It prevents one spouse from using his/her position to secure favoritism for the other to the detriment of the more highly qualified.

Spouse has been interpreted to include persons who are not legally married but who live together with all the attendant marriage responsibilities and commitments. Similarly, under the EEOC's Executive Order 11246's Sex Discrimination Guidelines, any distinction between married and unmarried persons of the opposite sex is considered an impermissible distinction made on the basis of sex.

Where a no-spouse policy has a neutral effect on both sexes and it can be proven, it will be upheld when a justifiable business reason existed for instituting it. No-spouse rules that do not forbid employment of or require termination when marriage occurs are likely to be approved.

It is a Title VII violation to deny employment because of marriage to someone of a particular national origin group or because a spouse's name is associated with a national origin group. Title VII sex discrimination occurred where an employer terminated a black female after discovering that her husband was white. The employer stated an assumption that a black woman who was married to a white man did not need the job. [*Vuyanich v. Republic Nat. Bank*, 409 F. Supp. 1083 (N.D. Tex. 1976).] A white person is protected by the Civil Rights Statutes's Section 1981 from discrimination motivated by marriage to a black. [*Faraca v. Clements*, 506 F.2d 856 (5th Cir. 1975), *cert. denied*, 422 U.S. 1006 (1975).]

It is legitimate business practice to protect business confidentiality and competitive position by uniformly disqualifying male and female applicants or employees who are married to a competitor's employees. Termination of an employee who was married to a competitor's employee did not violate Title VII. This policy was applied to men and women equally. The employer's business was highly competitive that gaining inside information would be destructive. [*Emory v. Georgia Hospital Service Assoc.*, 4 Fair Empl. Prac. Cas. (BNA) 891 (M.D. Ga. 1971), *aff'd*, 446 F.2d 897 (5th Cir. 1971).]

Policies against hiring or continuing spousal employment are lawful under Title VII when they are applied equally to male and female employees. Terminating the spouse with the least seniority where married workers cannot decide who should leave did not violate Title VII under either a discriminatory treatment or a disparate impact theory. [*Harper v. Trans World Airlines, Inc.*, 385 F. Supp. 1001 (E.D. Mo. 1974), *aff'd*, 525 F.2d 409 (8th Cir. 1975).] A school board's decision to transfer a male department head's wife to a new school under its policy of not employing spouses in the same school did not violate Title VII where the couple agreed to let the school board pick who would transfer and the choice was based on the best interests of the educational program. [*Meier v. Evansville-Vanderburgh School Corp.*, 416 F. Supp. 748 (S.D. Ind. 1975), *aff'd without op.*, 539 F.2d 713 (7th Cir, 1976).]

No-spouse rules cannot be used as a pretext to discriminate. Assertion that a wife, rather than her husband, was being terminated because the husband was the head of their household was rejected. [*Georgia v. Farmers Electric Cooperative, Inc.*, 715 F.2d 175 (5th Cir. 1987).] A *sensitive position*, policy where female secretaries who were married to male employees were required to transfer to prevent confidential employer information disclosure violated Title VII. The policy of protecting confidential information was not even handedly applied between men and women. Men who were employed at the same level as their spouses's supervisors were not required to transfer. [*EEOC Decision No. 79-59*, 26 Fair Empl. Prac. Cas. (BNA) 1774 (1979).]

Arbitrators have reviewed this under collective bargaining agreements. *Just cause* or like phraseology is used in many collective bargaining agreements. When not specifically contained in a collective bargaining agreement a just cause standard for disciplinary consideration is, absent a clear proviso to the contrary, implied. Two aspects of just cause are relevant for considering no spouse policies. First, there ordinarily must be some reasonable cause to justify disciplinary action or termination involving an offense against employer policies that are actually or constructively known to the employee. Offenses usually involve employee wrongdoing or culpability, either of commission or omission.

Under just cause concepts, an employee may be subjected to disciplinary action only if the offense has been committed. If an employee is not guilty, the employer has no "cause" to impose discipline. "Marriage" patently does not involve wrongdoing. It does not ordinarily come within the class of offenses that will justify disciplinary action, provided the marriage is legal. A "bigamist" or "fraudulent marriage" might be viewed differently.

The second aspect of just cause is non-disciplinary. It involves substantial impairment of the employment relationship. Here the employer cannot be reasonably expected to continue the relationship, notwithstanding that the employee is guilty of no-fault, wrongdoing, or culpability. This may arise where the employee, through no fault:

1. Is unable to perform work with reasonable efficiency;
2. Has excusable absenteeism that is so extensive that it impairs the employment relationship; or
3. Develops an irreconcilable conflict of interest with the employer, even though he/she is not guilty of wrongdoing.

The usual standards for non-disciplinary termination are that:

1. The cause or reason for the non-disciplinary termination substantially impairs the employment relationship;
2. The cause has been chronic or, by its inherent nature clearly will be so; or
3. There is no reasonable prognosis that the cause will be removed in a reasonable time period.

Marriage, close family relationships, and nepotism may, in some appropriate cases, fall within this second aspect of "cause" for non-disciplinary termination under just cause concepts.

Employer policies must be fair, reasonable, and not unduly intrude into employee personal lives beyond that reasonably required by the employment. To be fair and reasonable, the policy must be related to the employer's business needs. In applying to a no spouse policy, the inquiries must concern whether:

1. Marriage of two employees prior to hiring or after hiring substantially impairs the employment relationship;
2. The employer has a legitimate interest in its employees' marriage status to justify regulation as an intrusion into the private affairs of its employee during non-paid, off-premises hours; and

3. It violates concepts of "just cause." [See *Ritchie Industries, Inc.*, 47 Lab. Arb. (BNA) 650, 656 (1980) (Roberts, Arb.).]

Where the policy is contained in a collective bargaining agreement, an arbitrator will probably not examine the policy's reasonableness. This is because the parties have, themselves, agreed that it does not violate just cause.

This may be true also of a policy that has been acquiesced in by the union. Here its reasonableness and acceptability is established by mutually binding custom and past practice. Where there has been a long-standing policy against employee marriage and the continued employment of spouses has not been challenged by the union, then custom and past practice may support the policy. Further inquiry regarding its reasonableness is unnecessary. However, the union must be aware or be made aware of this policy.

As a hiring policy only, an arbitrator may possibly approve its reasonableness. It may not be approved where it is applied to existing employees who subsequently marry, especially where the policy by its own wording is limited to "hiring."

A policy prohibited continued employment of relatives of spouses. It required the resignation of one employee within 30 days of becoming related to another employee or termination of the employee with the least seniority should neither resign. The policy was contained in an internal employer document that was not collectively bargained, was not part of the employer's published work rules available to employees, and was not posted.

One month after two employees who had been living together for six months, and who had been employed for periods of approximately five and seven years, were married, the junior employee was terminated. During the time they lived together, neither employee presented any disciplinary problem.

Acknowledging that the policy could not be set aside because it existed separate and apart from the collective bargaining agreement, this became a question of application. The theoretical future harm that married employees might cause was not sufficient for termination considering the employees' record of service, attendance, and loyalty. [*Distribution Center of Columbus, Inc.*, 83 Lab. Arb. (BNA) 163 (1984) (Seidman, Arb.).]

Employer policies regarding no spouses will have the best chance of being sustained where they do not outright forbid employment of or force a married spouse's termination. Those that continue spousal employment, but not in the same department are preferred. Otherwise, a strong business justification for the policy must be established that it is neutral in impact on both sexes. The policy must be a fair, reasonable, and a necessary intrusion into the employee's private lives.

In evaluating spousal concerns, the following should be considered to avoid conflict:

1. Equal application to both sexes;
2. Neutral effect on both spouses;
3. Confidentiality considerations; and
4. Job-relatedness by evaluating that:
   - Spouses may support one another,
   - The marital relationship may generate emotional problems detrimental to job performance,
   - Favoritism may exist between spouses, and
   - A spouse in a supervisory position over the other spouse may be less inclined to recognize or deal with unsatisfactory job performance.

NEPOTISM

Nepotism is the practice of favoring relatives over others. As an individual employment right, it affects associational considerations prohibiting or restricting working relationships with relatives similar to spousal policies. They have generally been permitted as a reasonable employer method of minimizing employee conflict or favoritism arising out of close family relations.

They are usually challenged under federal and state fair employment practice (FEP) statutes. The federal Civil Rights Act of 1964 (Title VII) is not violated unless nepotism policies discriminate against a particular national origin or some other protected class. Granting preferences to children of deceased employees if they were the deceased's widow's sole support, were over eighteen, and applied within thirty days of the father's death or of reaching age eighteen, was neutral and not discriminatory. [*Scott v. Pacific Maritime Assoc.*, 695 F.2d 1199 (9th Cir. 1983).] Allowing friends and relatives of employees to apply for work without being referred by an employment service does not discriminate where the effect was only to afford easier access to applications. [*United States v. Hayes International Corp.*, 456 F.2d 112 (5th Cir. 1972).]

Impermissible nepotism practices were found where:

1. Preferences were granted to stockholders, all of whom were the employer's relatives or friends and members of a particular national origin group. [*Bonilla v. Oakland Scavenger Co.*, 697 F.2d 1297 (9th Cir 1982)]; and
2. Preferences were granted to friends and relatives of employees while black females were underrepresented in the employer's work force. [*Lea v. Cone Mills Corp.*, 438 F.2d 86 (4th Cir. 1971).]

To remedy a past nepotism history, an employer may be required to recruit previously excluded groups. Discrimination caused by nepotistic practices can be negated by the number of blacks entering an apprenticeship program under an affirmative action plan.

Giving preference for summer work to college students who are employee children is unlawful where most of the employer's work force is white and past discrimination in hiring has not been corrected. Summer hiring preference to employees' sons is sex discrimination.

Prohibiting relative employment does not violate Title VII unless it disproportionately affects protected groups or is used unfairly against particular individuals. This did not occur where a woman claimed she was denied a promotion that was given to the daughter of the employer's president because she failed to establish that she was qualified for the position. [*John Fabick Tractor Co.*, 532 F. Supp. 453 E.D. Mo. 1982).] However, an employer's anti-nepotism rule violated Title VII where the employer disqualified a woman after it had made exceptions for male applicants. [*Lindebaugh v. Auto Leasing Co.*, 18 Fair Empl. Prac. Cas. (BNA) 752 (W.D. Ky. 1978).]

In asserting nepotism claims, FEP statutes offer the best litigation likelihood. Outside of remote constitutional implications, nepotism claims might conceivably be asserted as a public policy violation or as intentional infliction of emotional distress where the employer's conduct was particularly malicious, willful, or outrageous.

Regarding nepotism, the following should be considered:

1. Applicable federal and state statutes;
2. Neutral effect on all national origins;
3. Job-relatedness; and
4. Confidentiality considerations.

THIRD PARTY REPRESENTATION

The right to representation at investigatory interviews for union and non-union employees is an important individual employment right. This concept allows an employee a limited opportunity to safeguard certain work place interests when discipline or termination arises.

Private sector employees have a qualified right to union representation during employer initiated investigatory interviews. [*NLRB v. J. Weingarten, Inc.*, 420 U.S. 251 (1975).] This right arises when the employee reasonably believes the investigation will result in disciplinary action, but only if the employee specifically requests union representation. When an employee demands union representation, the employer has two alternatives. First, the investigation may be pursued without an interview. Second, union representation may be allowed, but the union representative's participation may be restricted. There is no obligation to bargain with the union at the interview and the employer may insist upon hearing only the employee's version.

A qualified right to union representation during investigatory interviews can be justified by its elimination of the power imbalance that arises when employees confront employers without assistance. A union representative's presence shields an employee from any threat to employment while safeguarding the bargaining unit's interests.

This right may also include non-union employees. Non-union employees should be entitled to a co-employee's presence because the representative not only safeguards that particular employee's interests, but also the interests of other employees by guarding against unjust or arbitrary employer action; and, in addition, by providing assurance to other employees that, when and if they are subjected to a like interview, they too can obtain the assistance of a representative. The role of the co-employee is the same as the union representative. Recent federal court decisions have discussed this right's possible extension to non-union employees. [See *E. I. DuPont de Nemours & Co.*, 289 N.L.R.B. No. 81 (1988), *pet. for review denied*, 876 F.2d 11 (3d Cir. 1989) (representation right does not apply to non-union employee under NLRA; however, employee may ask for presence of a fellow employee at a disciplinary interview).]

The employee's request that a co-employee be his/her representative at an investigatory interview builds solidarity and vigilance among employees absent a union no differently than it does where a collective bargaining representative has been recognized. In the non-union context, it also serves to help eliminate the bargaining power inequality between employees and employers. The perception by employees of an imbalance of power may be heightened in the absence of a union, and the risks of improper or even unintentional employee intimidation by the employer may be accentuated. Similarly, the co-employee's presence may facilitate a more expeditious, efficient, and equitable disposition of disputes, and perhaps serve to settle them informally.

The need of non-union employees to support each other through this type of conduct may well be greater than that of union represented employees. Non-union employees normally do not have the benefit of a collective bargaining agreement that serves as a check on an employer's ability to act unjustly or arbitrarily. They also usually do not have the protection of a grievance arbitration procedure to challenge or enforce problems arising out of the employment relationship.

Correcting the imbalance between non-union employees and their employer is not achieved by forcing an employee to attend a disciplinary interview alone. To counter this, non-union employees must look after each other. When confronted with the prospect of an investigatory interview that might result in discipline, the only assistance readily available lies in co-employees. The purpose underlying the representation right is to prevent an employer from overpowering a sole employee. A co-employee's presence, even if that individual does nothing more than act as a witness, still effectuates that purpose in the same manner as the presence of an experienced union representative.

The representation right at an investigatory interview depends on a subjective rather than objective test; i.e., the employee must reasonably believe that discipline may result. It is clear that the right to representation does not arise during a routine employer/employee conversation because no reason to fear disciplinary action exists in this situation. Nevertheless, this subjective test is easily satisfied, even if the nature of the interview is nonaccusatory. The right to representation may arise during seemingly innocuous discussions concerning the employer's distribution of such benefits as overtime and holiday pay. Disciplinary actions may result from these conversations even if they cannot be characterized as terminations, suspensions, or warnings. Because of this, an employer who desires to avoid unfair labor practice charges would be wise to err on the side of representation.

Employees confronted with possible discipline must be able to present their case effectively. This may be accomplished by the presence of a representative or co-employee who is more familiar with the policy, rules, and employer customs than an employee who is intimidated by both the predicament and meeting the employer on unequal terms. Representation may deter disparate treatment of employee-offenders by insuring that equal punishment is dispensed for identical infractions. The representative or co-employee can safeguard the interests of other employees by informing them of employer decisions.

Presence of a representative or co-employee may generate a better understanding of the dispute. Early review affords an opportunity to correct errors that might produce ill feelings among employees. This is especially true today where in the non-union setting employers are increasingly susceptible to wrongful termination litigation.

This right inheres in the National Labor Relations Act (NLRA's) guarantee of employee rights to act in concert for mutual aid and protection. Denial of this right interferes with, restrains, and coerces employees and thus results in an unfair labor practice. Refusing an employee's representation request is a serious violation of this right. This compels the employee to appear unassisted at an interview possibly jeopardizing job security.

It is the employee's affirmative responsibility to request representation. No employer obligation exists to inform the employee of the representation right. The employee may voluntarily forego the right and participate in an investigatory interview unaccompanied by a representative or co-employee. However, the employee must be informed prior to the investigatory interview of the subject matter of the interview and the nature of any charge of impropriety it may encompass.

The right to representation, once asserted, includes the right to confer with a representative or co-employee before the interview. To represent effectively an employee "too fearful or inarticulate to relate accurately the incident being investigated" and to be "knowledgeable" to "assist the employee by eliciting favorable facts, and . . . getting to the bottom of the incident," the representative or co-employee must be able to consult prior to the interview. In this way, the representative or co-employee can learn the employee's version and gain familiarity with the facts. A fearful or inarticulate employee may be more likely to discuss the incident fully and accurately with a representative or co-employee. Without this information and pre-interview conference, the ability of the representative or co-employee to effectively give aid and protection would be diminished.

The employer, however, need not postpone an investigatory interview merely because the requested representative or co-employee is unavailable. The reason for the unavailability is irrelevant, especially when another representative or co-employee is available and could have been requested. There is no obligation for the employer to suggest or secure alternative representation.

Since the exercise of the right may interfere with legitimate employer prerogatives, the employer has no obligation to justify a refusal to allow representation. The employer may simply advise that the interview will not proceed unless the employee is willing to enter the interview unaccompanied. The employee may refrain from participating. This protects the employee's right, but relinquishes any benefit that could be derived from the interview. The employer is free to act on information from other sources. The employer, however, cannot threaten, coerce, or cajole the employee to remain without a representative or co-employee. It cannot be threatened that the right's exercise will lead to more severe discipline or that the employee's fate will be in more capricious and hostile hands.

A final limitation is that the employer has no duty to bargain with any representative or co-employee who might attend. Even though the representative or co-employee could attempt to clarify the facts, the employer may insist on hearing only the employee's account.

The best rationale supporting the right to representation at investigatory interviews is that it assures fairness. Fairness is not the mere resolution of factual issues, but the process used by the employer that makes a factual resolution possible. The process of representation at investigatory interviews may be less efficient than investigation without an interview or an interview without a representative's or co-employee's presence. This right is not intended to promote efficiency, but to protect the employee who reasonably believes that disciplinary action is imminent. The representation right for union and non-union employees recognizes higher values than speed, convenience, and efficiency. It safeguards these employees from unresponsive employers by protecting their fairness and due process interests. Through this individual employment rights are furthered.

The impact of existing decisional law in the public sector is limited by individual state or local statutes, court decisions, executive orders, and attorney general opinions that vary from one state to another. In the private sector, however, precedent is virtually unlimited because the NLRA is interpreted through a centralized agency, the National Labor Relations Board (NLRB). Private sector precedents provide reliable, if not analogous authority to public sector tribunals when the statutory language in both sectors is parallel. Blind deference, however, is unwarranted unless the legislature intended that the statute be so construed. Private sector precedent may provide some guidance, but it is also necessary to consider "the distinctions that necessarily must exist between legislation primarily directed to the private sector and that for public employees."

It would be anomalous to suggest that the rationale for representation during investigatory interviews for union and non-union employees in the private sector is inapposite to the public sector. Public sector employees, however are not governed by the provisions of the NLRA that make the right to union and co-employee representation possible. Nevertheless, many public sector labor relations statutes are sufficiently similar to the NLRA to guarantee the right to representation at investigatory interviews. The right also received support from the decisions of state labor relations boards. [See *Sch. Dist. of the City of Detroit, Bd. of Ed. v. Organization of Sch. Adm're and Supervisors, Local 28*, 106 Mich. App. 438, 308 N.W.2d 247 (1981), *lv. denied*, 413 Mich. 859 (1982).]

Regarding a correlative right of representation at investigatory interviews for public employees, it should be noted that the United States Supreme Court has recognized that the government, as an employer, can exert greater control over its employees than it could over the public. Despite this, the public employer's need for wide control over its employees must be balanced against the employee's interest of representation in personnel decisions affecting assignment, promotion, transfer, discipline, and termination.

A public employer's internal administration does not make it immune to statutory, fairness, or due process requirements. Its discretion cannot be merely subjective judgment, but must be controlled by clear rules governing its actions. For example, welfare benefits cannot be terminated, parole revoked, or wages garnished without established reasons. Extending representation rights to public employees at investigatory interviews where discipline can reasonably result, may make judgments over employee problems more objective.

A private or public sector employer's failure to accord the right when requested by a union or non-union employee may impair disciplinary action. This may occur through an unfair labor practice, a civil service proceeding, or an arbitration award. In all instances, the employer's paramount interest should be the preservation of disciplinary action from reversal. Employers may be wise to accord union or non-union employees the right to representation at investigatory interviews even if the situation only arguably warrants its application.

In dealing with third-party representation rights, the following should be considered:

1. An investigatory interview is a meeting in which the employee is asked questions about employee misconduct and the employee reasonably believes that this interview will result in his/her being disciplined;
2. The employee must affirmatively request representation to invoke the right;
3. The employee's request can be made before the interview or at any time during the interview;
4. There is no obligation that the employer advise the employee of the right to request representation;
5. Upon the employee's timely request, the employer should disclose the subject matter to the employee prior to the investigatory interview, and permit the employee to consult privately with a representative if he/she so requests;
6. The employer can insist that the representative remain silent until the employee gives an account of the incident, but the employer cannot insist that the representative be silent for the entire investigatory interview;
7. The representative can assist the employee and clarify any misconceptions that may arise, but the employer can insist on hearing only the employee's account;
8. The representative does not have to be brought in if the employee is simply disciplined without the occurrence of any interrogation or questioning, but if the employer wants to question the employee in the meeting after imposing the discipline, the employee can request the presence of the representative; and
9. If an employee requests a representative, the employer may decide not to have any interview whatsoever, and may simply proceed with the investigation through other means. [See American Hospital Association, *The Wrongful Discharge of Employees in the Health Care Industry* 102-103 (1987).]

PERFORMANCE EVALUATIONS

Individual employment rights in performance evaluations require that they be collected, used, maintained, and disclosed with the utmost care. These records influence employee advancement, compensation, assignment, etc. This sensitive information's confidentiality must be preserved by the employer. They also must be accurately completed.

Failure to undertake this, may result in considerable liability. Wrongful information disclosure or maintaining inaccurate information, may result in claims for invasion of privacy where a broad public disclosure of private facts occurs, defamation, intentional infliction of emotional distress where conduct is outrageous, negligent maintenance or disclosure of employment records, or public policy violations. Contractual breaches may also arise where employment handbooks and collective bargaining agreements exist.

At times, the employer's competing interest to maintain these performance evaluations' confidentiality may conflict with the union's information right regarding the bargaining unit it represents. As part of its grievance processing responsibilities, unions may be entitled to other employee's performance evaluations.

Accurate and regular employee job performance evaluation is important, and the following should be considered:

1. Performance evaluations should be conducted annually;
2. Performance evaluations should review—
   - Job knowledge,
   - Work quality,
   - Work quantity,
   - Initiative,
   - Adaptability,
   - Dependability,
   - Cooperation,
   - Improvement areas,
   - Punctuality, and
   - Attendance;
3. The performance evaluation should allow the employer to identify areas where the employee is performing adequately and areas where the employee needs to improve; and
4. The performance evaluation may be used to determine promotion, layoff, or termination.

A performance evaluation interview should be conducted in a comfortable setting and should place the employee at ease. It should not be confused with a disciplinary interview. Prior to the interview, the following should be undertaken.

1. Schedule the meeting sufficiently in advance to allow everyone time to prepare;
2. Arrange a location that provides privacy and freedom from interruptions;
3. Inform the employee of the meeting;
4. Compile the employee's last performance evaluation, job description, and the employer's current salary guidelines;
5. Allow sufficient time for the interview;
6. Choose an appropriate time that allows an opportunity to do further follow-up with the employee before the day is over;
7. Become familiar with the employee's personality and how he/she is likely to react to the interview;
8. During the interview—
   - Discuss the employee's typical performance and do not over-emphasize recent or isolated events,
   - Discuss all factors evaluated rather than scrutinizing one or two in particular,
   - Maintain consistency and objectivity,
   - Do not be overly swayed by previous performance evaluations, and
   - Discuss with the employee plans for future development and identify methods for improving in deficient areas and for gaining additional skills;
9. Take follow-up steps after the discussion by—
   - Having the employee acknowledge the review by signing it and providing any comments, and
   - Following up the review on a regular basis prior to the next performance evaluation. [See Dreesen, *The Increasing Importance of Effective Performance Appraisals*, 4 Special Focus 3, 4 (Oct. 1987).]

A performance evaluation is only as good as those who implement it. Without training, managers and supervisors will be unaware of the problem areas that they should avoid, such as:

1. A tendency toward leniency or harshness that does not produce an accurate measure of the employee's abilities;
2. The *halo effect,* the tendency to rate someone highly simply because that particular employee is well-liked or to rate someone poorly because the individual is disliked;
3. The *central tendency,* rating all employees as average;

4. The *similar to me effect,* evaluating those who are most like the rater highly and those who are not similar to the rater poorly;
5. The *most recent error effect,* the tendency to consider not the employee's typical and overall performance but only the employee's most recent performance; and
6. *Stereotyping,* rating an employee based upon a particular dislike for a particular characteristic of the employee such as dress style or hair length. [*Id.*]

Performance evaluations have several uses:

1. Enabling an employee to better understand his/her job and the areas of satisfactory and unsatisfactory performance;
2. Providing a supervisor with a formal mechanism by which to review each employee's performance and discuss it with the employee;
3. Permitting the supervisor to increase the employee's morale, by complementing the good aspects of performance, and to enable the employee to become more efficient, by pointing out weaknesses; and
4. Minimizing wrongful termination claims over job performance, in that—
   - A terminated employee who has been counselled and made aware of his/her problems will have a better perception of employer fairness, and
   - The employee will know that the employer's case is documented. [See American Hospital Association, *The Wrongful Discharge of Employees in the Health Care Industry* 40 (1987).]

The following should be reviewed by a supervisor before completing a performance evaluation:

1. Consider the employee's typical performance during the entire period;
2. Do not overemphasize recent happenings or isolated incidents that are not typical of the employee's normal performance;
3. Use accurate data obtained from records whenever possible, or from careful observation when this is not possible;
4. Compare the employee's performance being reviewed with other individuals who have performed the same job;
5. Do not let one performance factor influence other factors;
6. Each performance factor should be considered independently of the others;

7. Do not permit salary or length of service to affect the performance evaluation;
8. Consider only the employee's performance in relationship to the specific job requirements;
9. Do not rate an employee high because the employee has years of service, but performs at an average rate;
10. Do not let personal feelings bias the performance evaluation;
11. Do not attribute greater proficiency to personally well-liked employees, or because of sympathy for an employee; and
12. Do not be wrongly influenced by a prior performance evaluation. [See Bureau of National Affairs, Inc., *Performance Appraisal Programs, PPF Survey* No. 135 (Feb. 1983) at 36.]

NAME CHANGES

Employee surnames raise an individual employment right interest. Because of our society, females commonly adopt the male's surname upon marriage. However, for various reasons, a female may not wish to publicly use a male's surname. These reasons may include personal preference, identification with the "women's rights movement," a desire to maintain surname to continue family tradition, etc.

At the work place, this interest may come into conflict with the employer's policy to maintain standardized information. When this occurs, federal and state fair employment practice (FEP) statutes may be violated. Under the federal Civil Rights Act of 1964 (Title VII), an employer rule requiring married women, but not married men, to change their surnames to that of their spouses' on personnel forms was illegal. [*Allen v. Lovejoy*, 553 F.2d 522 (6th Cir. 1979).] Violations of public policy and claims for intentional infliction of emotional distress could be asserted where employer conduct was especially outrageous.

IDENTIFICATION TAGS

Many employers require employees to display their name at the work place. Employees have asserted a privacy interest in these policies. Where employee health or safety considerations regarding personal harm are not present, employers can generally require this identification to promote legitimate business practices.

RELIGIOUS ACCOMMODATION

Individual employment rights may arise around religious practices. These result from dress and grooming codes, hours of work requirements, sabbath celebration, union membership, etc.

Claims regarding religious accommodation generally involve federal and state fair employment practice (FEP) statutes. Under the federal Civil Rights Act of 1964 (Title VII), once an employer offers an accommodation to an employee's practices that is reasonable, it has satisfied its duty. It must do so unless it would result in undue hardship to the employer's business. [See *Ansonia Bd. of Ed. v. Philbrook*, 479 U.S. 60 (1986).]

Depending upon the circumstances, claims could be asserted for defamation where the employer discloses information placing an employee in a false light regarding religious practices, intentional infliction of emotional distress where employer conduct regarding religious practice is outrageous, or violations of public policy. Contractual liability may arise out of employment handbook and collective bargaining agreements.

The following should be considered in dealing with religious accommodation of employees at the work place:

1. Where a religious accommodation would affect a collective bargaining agreement's terms, the employer should contact the union;
2. Safety may be evaluated to determine whether the religious accommodation would impose undue employer hardship;
3. Undue hardship may exist where co-workers object to the religious accommodation;
4. Future impact of accommodating an employee's religious belief is insufficient to establish undue hardship; and
5. An employee requesting a religious accommodation—
   - Incurs no liability if he or she refuses to attempt to accommodate or to cooperate,
   - Must inform the employer that religious beliefs create a problem, and
   - Is not required to suggest possible accommodations.

PRIVACY MISCONDUCT

Individual employment rights may be affected by other employees. Other employees may abridge rights present in speech, beliefs, associations, information, and lifestyles. When this occurs, the employer may be obligated to take disciplinary action. Three male employees were properly disciplined where they opened the women's dressing room and observed what was occurring. [*Island Creek Coal Co.*, 87 Lab. Arb. (BNA) 844 (1986) (Stoltenberg, Arb.).]

A police officer's termination was sustained where he misused a computerized law-enforcement-information system to contact a woman whom he raped, and to disclose criminal justice information to a gas station owner regarding a recently hired attendant, whom the owner then terminated. [*City of Sterling Heights*, 89 Lab. Arb. (BNA) 723 (1987) (Keefe, Arb.).] Termination of a twenty-seven-year exemplary employee who admitted to ten incidents of petty theft from co-employees was not arbitrary. [*City of Palo Alto*, 90 Lab. Arb. (BNA) 361 (1988) (Koven, Arb.).] Likewise, a supervisor was found liable for intentionally interfering with the relations of a female employee where she refused his romantic advances and was verbally and physically harassed at the workplace. [*Lewis v. Oregon Beauty Supply Co.*, 302 Or. 616, 733 P.2d 430 (1987).]

Imposing discipline in a manner that unduly embarrasses or humiliates an employee affects individual employment rights in how one is perceived by others. [See *Klamath County & Operating Engineers*, 90 Lab. Arb. (BNA) 354 (1988) (Levak Arb.).] For example, announcing to the press that an employee was suspended without pay where the employee first learned of the disciplinary action from a neighbor who read about it in the newspaper would cause undue embarrassment. [*Id.*]

While at the workplace, employees can affect the privacy interests of nonemployees.

This may arise where:

1. A customs service officer drove beside a female pedestrian and masturbated in front of her. [*National Treasury Employees Union Chapter 165 and United States Customs Service*, [1988] Gov't Employee Rel. Rptr. (BNA) 803 (May 30, 1988) (Kanowitz, Arb.).], and
2. A telephone installer engaged in voyeurism or "peeping Tom" activities. [*General Telephone Co. of Indiana*, 90 Lab. Arb. (BNA) 689 (1988).]

In evaluating privacy misconduct, the following should be considered:

1. Employee physical privacy;
2. Employee information collection, maintenance, use, and disclosure privacy; and

3. Applicable federal and state statutes, where employer liability may result from sexual harassment, disclosure of employment records, and so forth.

LANGUAGE REQUIREMENTS

Language requirements affect individual employment rights mainly through speech regulation. This interest is afforded protection under federal and state fair employment practice (FEP) statues.

The Equal Employment Opportunity Commission's (EEOC's) guidelines cover employer rules requiring that employees speak English only. Requiring employees to speak only in English at all times while in the work place, including during work breaks and lunch periods, is a burdensome term and condition of employment. Often an individual's primary language is an essential national origin characteristic. This can create an atmosphere of inferiority, isolation, and intimidation leading toward a discriminatory work environment.

It is permitted, however, to establish a rule requiring that employees speak only in English at certain times if the employer can show that this is a business necessity. Safe and efficient business operations are important considerations in evaluating this. English-only requirements when performing dangerous work or work involving communication with the public might be acceptable.

Bilingual employees are treated differently than employees who are not equally comfortable with two languages. Specifically, it is not discriminatory for an employer to forbid a bilingual employee from speaking anything but English in a public area while on the job. [See *Garcia v. Gloar*, 618 F.2d 264 (5th Cir. 1980), *cert. denied*, 449 U.S. 1113 (1981).]

SEXUAL HARASSMENT

As an individual employment right, sexual harassment can constrain the employee through association opportunities and information dissemination. Sexual harassment is unlawful whether or not the employee suffers an economic or tangible loss. [*Meritor Savings Bank v. Vinson*, 477 U.S. 57 (1986).] This may include termination or denial of promotion. Employees can assert a sexual harassment claim where the harassment is severe and pervasive enough to create a "hostile environment." [See e.g., *Gilardi v. Schroeder*, 672 F. Supp. 1043 (N.D. Ill. 1986), *aff'd*, 833 F.2d 1226 (7th Cir. 1987).]

Employers are not strictly liable for harassment when this conduct is engaged in by managers or supervisors. [*Meritor Savings Bank v. Vinson*, 477 U.S. 57 (1986).] The circumstances of each case must be examined to determine employer liability. For example, evidence of the complaining employee's sexually provocative dress or speech may be relevant in determining whether the employee found the sexual advances unwelcome. [*Id.*]. Conduct that creates a "hostile working environment" may consist of:

1. Unwelcome sexual advances;
2. Requests for sexual favors;
3. Visual forms of harassment in cartoons or drawings;
4. Physical interference with normal work or movement in blocking or following an employee; and
5. Verbal harassment through jokes, slurs, and derogatory comments.

Unlawful harassment also exists if employment or receipt of employment benefits is conditioned on submission to sexual advances, or if rejection of these advances is used as the basis for employment decisions; i.e., *quid pro quo* harassment. Federal and state FEP statutes prohibit sexual harassment.

Sexual harassment applies to employees of either sex. Although discrimination on the basis of sexual preference is not unlawful under either federal or state FEP statutes, harassment of a homosexual on the basis of his/her sexual preference is unlawful sex discrimination. [See, e.g., *Wright v. Methodist Youth Services, Inc.*, 511 F. Supp. 307 (N.D. Ill. 1981).]

Employers have been found strictly liable in quid pro quo cases, regardless of whether the supervisor's conduct was known, on the theory that the supervisor was relying upon the supervisorial authority to hire, fire, promote, and so forth in attempting to control the employment's conditions. [See *Hensen v. City of Dundee*, 682 F.2d 897 (11th Cir. 1982).] In contrast, it has been found that employers should not be strictly liable for hostile environment harassment. [See *Rabidue v. Osceola Refining Co.*, 805 F.2d 611 (6th Cir. 1986).] An employer may be responsible even for the acts of nonemployees who sexually harass employees, where the employer knew or should have known of the conduct, and failed to take immediate and appropriate corrective action.

Employer liability for sexual harassment is consistent with the principle that an employer is liable for torts committed by one employee against another where the employer could have prevented the occurrence through reasonable care in hiring, supervising, or disciplining workers. [*Hall v. Gus Construction Co.*, 842 F.2d. 1010 (8th Cir. 1988).] Conduct need not be sexual in nature to be considered as evidence of harassment. Hostility toward women because of their gender can be manifested through incidents other than explicit sexual advances. [*Id.*]. However, employers can minimize sexual harassment liability by investigating promptly upon learning of the problem and taking remedial steps.

Remedial action may take the form of reiterating the employer's sexual harassment policy. However, the employer may not retaliate against an employee who has a good faith belief that sexual harassment is occurring and informs of this. [See *Jenkins v. Orkin Exterminating Co., Inc.*, 646 F. Supp. 1274 (E.D. Tex. 1986).]

To respond to and prevent work place sexual harassment, employers should:

1. Develop a policy that—
   - Defines sexual harassment,
   - Prohibits sexual harassment,
   - Contains a complaint or grievance, procedure where the employee is not required initially to raise the sexual harassment concern with the harasser, and
   - Imposes discipline up to and including termination for sexual harassment;
2. Discuss sexual harassment concerns at training and supervisor meetings; and
3. Investigate all sexual harassment complaints.

The following procedure should be considered for use in employee sexual harassment claim investigations:

1. Upon receiving a sexual harassment complaint, the human resources staff should—
   - Discuss it with the employee,
   - Advise the employee that, because of sexual harassment's sensitive nature, the complaint should not be discussed with co-workers or others,
   - Interview the alleged harasser,
   - Maintain confidentiality,

- Interview other persons with pertinent information; i.e., witnesses or persons who also have had problems with alleged harasser,
- Inform or reiterate to the alleged harasser the sexual harassment policy,
- Advise a supervisor, where he/she should be advised, that retaliation against the complaining employee is prohibited, and
- Hold a group meeting to discuss the problem, when an unknown person is causing the harassment;
2. Should it be determined that sexual harassment occurred, appropriate discipline up to and including termination should be imposed;
3. Upon concluding the human resources staff's investigation, the complainant should be contacted to—
    - Explain what action has been taken,
    - Request the complainant to report other sexual harassment occurrences,
    - Reiterate that the employer forbids sexual harassment, and
    - Reinforce the policy that employees with sexual harassment complaints are to inform management of these instances immediately. [See Bureau of National Affairs, Inc., *Sexual Harassment: Employer Policies and Problems, PPF Survey* No. 144 (June 1987).]

VIDEO DISPLAY TERMINALS

Video display terminals (VDTs) have become an indispensable part of the modern workplace. [See L. Lorber and J. Kirk, *Fear Itself: A Legal and Personnel Analysis of Drug Testing, AIDS, Secondary Smoke, VDT's* 43 (1987).] VDTs are an essential component of computer-based systems for data entry, data acquisition, interactive communication, word processing, computer programming, and computer-assisted design and manufacture. [*Id.*]

Employee concerns have been generated about potential health defects from video screens involving certain physical reactions to sitting in front of a video screen for prolonged periods, including eye strain, backache, headaches, and computer stress. Likewise, individual employment rights may be impacted by the prospect that general tension or anxiety at work might be elevated by computer systems that speed decisions demanded from employees and which may provide supervisors with data for performance appraisals.

Health risk investigations have focused on: 1) reproductive hazards to pregnant women or their fetuses, including miscarriages and birth defects; and 2) cataracts. [*Lorber and Kirk* at 43]. In 1979 and 1980, women employed in the classified ad department of the Toronto Star were taking part in a mini baby boom. During a one-year period, fourteen babies were born to women in this section. Four of the infants had birth defects. The mothers of the four defective babies each used a VDT. Although three other VDT users in the office gave birth to healthy babies that year, it was noted that video screens were a common denominator in this "cluster" of four birth defects. Suspicion arose that perhaps radiation from VDTs played a role in producing these reproductive accidents. [*Lorber and Kirk* at 44.]

Initial reports of suspicious clusters of reproductive problems among VDT operators led to the recognition and reporting of still other clusters. [*Id.*] A 1985 congressional report listed (13 so-called "clusters" of birth defects or miscarriages in the United States and Canada allegedly associated with the use of video screens. [See United States Congress, Office of Technology Assessment, *Automation of America's Offices* 145 (1985).]

A number of systematic investigations of the radiation emitted by VDTs and its potential health effects have been generated by the widespread public concern about VDTs. [*Lorber and Kirk* at 48]. Early investigations focused on specific work sites in which apparent clusters of health problems had arisen. Later studies sought to compare the health VDT operators and non-VDT operators more generally. Regardless of their origin or design, these studies have one thing in common: none has discovered a meaningful relationship between exposure to VDTs and adverse health outcomes. [*Id.*].

Regardless of scientific opinion or the conclusions of statistical risk assessments, fear about VDT radiation has persisted. The National Institute for Occupational Safety and Health made the following recommendations with respect to the factors which most affect VDT operator health:

1. *Workstation design*. Maximum flexibility should be designed into VDT units, supporting tables, and operator chairs. VDTs should have detachable keyboards and work tables. Chairs should be height adjustable and provide proper support;
2. *Illumination*. Source of glare should be controlled through VDT placement (i.e., parallel to windows as well as parallel to and between lights), proper lighting, and the use of glare control

devices on the VDT screen surface. Illumination levels should be lower for VDT tasks requiring screen-intensive work and increased as the need to use hard copy increases. Hard-copy material may require local lighting in addition to the normal office lighting;
3. *Work regiments.* Continuous work with VDTs should be interrupted periodically by rest, breaks, or other work activities that do not produce visual fatigue or muscular tension. As a minimum, breaks should be taken after two hours continuous VDT work and breaks should be more frequent as visual, mental and muscular burdens increase; and
4. *Vision testing.* VDT workers should have visual testing before beginning VDT work and periodically thereafter to ensure that they have adequately corrected vision to handle this work. [*Lorber and Kirk* at 51.]

7

Outside the Workplace

Individual employment rights are not limited to those that arise during hiring and at the workplace. After workplace commitments are completed, the employee may be subject to employer intrusions outside the workplace. Depending upon the employer's business and the employee's position, an employer may attempt to hold the employee accountable for or restrict the employee's activities outside the workplace.

Employer restrictions may affect employee associations, financial arrangements, employment opportunities, living arrangements, romantic involvements, etc. By not complying with these restrictions, the employee may be subjected to adverse employer action up to and including termination. Concerns pertaining to individual employment rights arise over whether activities outside the workplace are strictly a personal employee matter subject only to violation of a law that should be dealt with by the courts or involve legitimate employer interests.

It is not always clear when an employer may restrict or be concerned with employees outside the workplace. Employee personal lives should be free from arbitrary or capricious employer intervention. Generally, the employer can hold an employee accountable for and restrict activities that are directly employment related. Employers have no right, however, to impose restrictions for reasons unrelated to employment.

In evaluating the employer's right to curtail individual employment rights outside the workplace, employee and employer interests must be balanced. These respective rights may be balanced by considering their:

1. Effect on employee work performance;
2. Effect on other employees;
3. Effect on the employer's operational efficiency;
4. Direct employer injury; and
5. Indirect employer injury.

It is within these parameters that individual employment rights outside the workplace must be examined. These rights outside the workplace involve:

1. Personal associations;
2. Lifestyle regulation;
3. Loyalty;
4. Conflicts of interest;
5. Off-duty misconduct; and
6. Residency requirements.

PERSONAL ASSOCIATIONS

Freedom of association is generally guaranteed by the United States Constitution's first amendment. This often requires concealing one's associations from others preventing information disclosure regarding a particular association where it could be perceived as harmful to the individual's economic or social well-being. It includes the right to engage in advocacy of political, social, and governmental beliefs. Accountability for these personal associations outside the workplace often present concerns for individual employment rights.

Basic Associations

Freedom of association's constitutional connotations are not limited to advocating views that are popular or noncontroversial. It protects associations advocating unpopular, controversial, dissident, or unorthodox views. Association is not confined to political ideals, but extends to asserting mutual economic, legal, and social interests. Primarily protected are associations involving political affiliations, labor unions, minority organizations, social clubs, religious sects, and national origin groups. Associations that benefit legally and economically are included within its scope. Employment is one of these.

Individual employment rights are promoted by maintaining relationships that otherwise might be foregone because of hostility that could result from their disclosure. Unlimited non-job-related inquiry into employee associational relationships as well as their spouses and children curtails these rights.

Constitutionally protected association rights are recognized for public employees. They enjoy greater constitutional protection regarding their personal associations than other employees as illustrated by the following:

1. A pubic employee's rights were abridged when forced, through a polygraph examination, to disclose information regarding personal sexual matters. [*Thorne v. City of El Segundo*, 726 F.2d 459 (9th Cir. 1983)]; and
2. Constitutional privacy rights outweighed other interests where a married part-time policeman's termination was inappropriate because he was flirting with a married woman. [*Briggs v. North Muskegon Police Department*, 563 F. Supp. 585 (W.D. Mich. 1983).]

However, the rights of two police officers was not infringed where city regulations prohibited off-duty employees from cohabitation outside of marriage. [*Shawgo v. Spradlin*, 464 U.S. 965 (1983).]

These constitutional interests may or may not be given protection when private sector employees are involved. As fundamental interests, they may be protected within at-will employment's "public policy" exception. Through this, freedom of association interests outside the workplace may be extended to benefit private employees.

Employee personal association protection is also provided by federal and state fair employment practice (FEP) statutes. Under the federal Civil Rights Act of 1964 (Title VII), a violation occurs when an individual is denied an employment opportunity because:

1. Their name is associated with a national origin group;
2. Membership in, or association with, a national origin group;
3. Membership in, or association with, an organization identified with, or seeking to promote the interests of, national origin groups; or
4. Attendance or participation in schools, churches, temples, or mosques generally used by persons of a national origin group.

A white person's termination because of association with blacks is illegal race discrimination. This was found where an employer did not hire a white applicant because the applicant's sister associated with a black male by whom she had biracial children. [*Whitney v. Greater New York Corp. of Seventh-Day Adventists*, 401 F. Supp. 1363 (S.D.N.Y. 1975).] White persons are protected from job discrimination motivated by the sale of their homes to blacks. [*De Matteis v. Eastman Kodak Co.*, 511 F.2d 306 (2d Cir. 1975), *on reh'g*, 520 F.2d 409 (2d Cir. 1975).]

Termination for membership in the United Klans of America was not a Title VII violation or prohibited religious discrimination. [*Bellamy v. Mason's Stores, Inc.*, 368 F. Supp. 1025 (E.D. Va. 1973), *aff'd*, 508 F.2d 504 (4th Cir. 1974).] However, involvement in a church-related organization that promotes homosexual rights may be considered a religious belief or practice under Title VII. This was found where a bank required an employee to resign. [*Dorr v. First Kentucky National Corp*; 796 F.2d 179 (6th Cir. 1986), *reh. en banc granted, opinion vacated (see* 41 Fair Empl. Prac. Cas. (BNA) 421 *for original opinion*).]

State FEP statutes also protect employee personal associations outside the workplace. Some prohibit employers from intentionally engaging in any reprisal against a person for associating with a person or group of a different race, color, creed, religion, or national origin.

Associational interests may be protected under other litigation theories depending upon the circumstances in which they are questioned or denied. Defamation may be applicable where an employer places the employee in disrepute because of personal associations to fellow employees or the general public. International infliction of emotional distress may result where the employer commits outrageous conduct in dealing with employee personal associations.

Bankruptcy/Debtors

Private and public sector employers are prohibited by the federal Bankruptcy Code from discriminating in employment against individuals because they are or have been associated with a bankrupt or debtor in bankruptcy. This affects employee personal association rights outside the workplace.

A person who files a bankruptcy petition is protected from discrimination under the Code. The Code's protection is similar to that provided by the Civil Rights Act of 1964 (Title VII) prohibiting discrimination on the basis of race, color, religion, sex, or national origin. An employer may not terminate an employee *solely* because an employee files a bankruptcy petition. Employers who allow performance or conduct problems to continue uncorrected may be curtailed from taking adverse actions if the problem employee unexpectedly acquires a protected status under the Code. [See *Stockhouse v. Hines Motor Supply*, 75 Bankr. 83 (Bankr. D. Wyo. 1987).]

A police department rule terminating policeman for filing a bankruptcy petition was unconstitutional. [*Rutledge v. City of Shreveport*, 387 F. Supp. 1277 (D. La. 1975).] Likewise, terminating firemen for declaring bankruptcy hampered firemen from obtaining a new opportunity in life. The Code does not permit termination of debtors or short-term suspensions because of ordered wage deductions.

Additional protection for debtors may exist under collective bargaining agreements. For example, an employee could not be terminated because of his wife's debts. [*American Airlines, Inc.*, 59 Lab. Arb. (BNA) 947 (1972).]

Unions

Individual employment rights outside the workplace exist in union associations. Adverse actions against employees because of membership in or activities on behalf of unions violates the federal National Labor Relations Act (NLRA) and state labor relations statutes.

The employer must have knowledge of the union activity along with a discriminatory motive or unlawful employer intent must exist. Absent anti-union motivation, an employer may terminate an employee for a good reason, a bad reason, or no reason at all without violating the NLRA. The employer will prevail if the termination would have occurred even in the absence of union activities.

Refraining from union association can be protected under federal and state fair employment practice (FEP) statutes. Under the Federal Civil Rights Act of 1964's (Title VII's) religious discrimination guidelines, employers must accommodate an employee whose religious beliefs prohibit compliance with a collective bargaining agreement requiring joining the union or paying union dues. The employee must be excused from the membership requirement and be permitted to pay a sum equivalent to the dues to a charitable organization. The NLRA contains similar protections.

For other employees, the union dues requirement can be excused; however, they can be required to pay a fair share for the union's representation and collective bargaining activities. Where this exists, the non-union employees must be provided with a constitutionally adequate procedure that allows them to challenge any fair share fee before an impartial arbitrator.

For example, an employee whose religion allowed the support of unions but whose personal study of the Bible led her to oppose unions was exempt from paying the union dues required by her employer's union security agreement. [*Machinists, Lodge 751 v. Boeing Co.*, 833 F.2d (9th Cir. 1987), *cert. denied,* 485 U.S. 1014 (1988).] As a reasonable accommodation by her employer under Title VII, she was permitted to substitute a charity donation in the amount of the dues because the substitution did not cause undue hardship to the employer or union. [*id.*] The NLRA provides for the substituted donation only for members of *bona fide* religions that have "historically held conscientious objections" to unions. Title VII requires employers to make reasonable accommodations for their employees' religious beliefs. The union maintained that the more recent NLRA protections were intended to supersede and limit Title VII's broad protections. However, because the two statutes are not irreconcilable, the NLRA's specific protections do not limit Title VII's more general mandates against religious discrimination.

LIFESTYLE REGULATION

Employer lifestyle regulation outside the workplace generally involves cohabitation, romantic, and social relationships that center on morality standards. Protection from unwarranted employer lifestyle intrusions may have constitutional connotations as well as limitations under federal and state fair employment practice (FEP) statutes. They may arise prior to and after hiring.

Public employees enjoy more constitutional protection regarding their individual lifestyles than private sector employees. When a public employer regulates employee lifestyles outside the workplace, it must do so consistently with procedural and substantive due process mandates. A rational connection must exist between the employee's lifestyle and the employee's job requirements.

Sexual activities by public employees outside the workplace should not be considered by employers. They generally have little relationship to job performance. First amendment privacy and free association guarantees were abridged when an employee was forced, through a polygraph examination to disclose personal sexual matters. [*Thorne v. City of El Segundo*, 726 F.2d 459 (9th Cir. 1983), *cert. denied,* 469 U.S. 979 (1984), *later appeal aff'd in part, rev'd and remanded in part,* 802 F.2d 1131 (9th Cir. 1986).] Workplace sexual misconduct, however, may be prohibited.

Cohabitation or sexual activity outside of marriage at times may present legitimate employer concerns. This often depends upon the public employment's nature. More deference may be given to the state's interest in preserving the morale and integrity of law enforcement, fire protection, and teaching activities than might be appropriate in other public employment contexts. For example, the following employer actions have been found permissible:

1. A deputy sheriff was lawfully terminated for insubordination and disobedience when he continued to visit the wife of an organized crime leader contrary to a sheriff's order. [*Baron v. Meloni*, 556 F. Supp. 796 (W.D. N.Y. 1983).]
2. City regulations prohibiting police officers from engaging in any personal conduct that could result in unfavorable public criticism did not infringe individual employment rights when two employees were disciplined for cohabitation. A patrolwoman and a police sergeant were suspended because they dated and spent several nights together. These punishments were imposed even though the department failed to provide any notice that their conduct was prohibited. [*Shawgo v. Spradlin*, 701 F.2d 470 (5th Cir. 1983), *cert. denied*, 464 U.S. 965 (1983).]
3. Termination of an Immigration and Naturalization Service (INS) inspector was permitted who knowingly allowed an undocumented alien with whom she had a close personal relationship to regularly enter the United States. [*Immigration and Naturalization Service*, 88 Lab. Arb. (BNA) 105 (1986 (Marlatt, Arb.).]

However, the following employer actions have been found impermissible:

1. A statute that punished teachers for "public homosexual conduct was unconstitutional," which was defined as "advocating, soliciting, imposing, encouraging or promoting public or private homosexual activity in a manner that creates a substantial risk that such conduct will come to the attention of school children or school employees." Although a teacher could be terminated for public homosexual conduct, discipline for mere "advocacy" was barred. [*National Gay Task Force v. Board of Educ.*, 729 F.2d 1270 (10th Cir. 1984), *aff'd*, 470 U.S. 903 (1985).] However, a female teacher's demotion was upheld because of romantic involvement with a female student. This homosexual relationship was viewed as unprofessional and detrimental to the university's

best interests. [*Naragon v. Wharton*, 572 F. Supp. 1117 (M.D. La. 1983).]
2. A school board was not permitted to terminate a middle-aged female teacher who allowed a twenty-six-year-old male visitor to stay at her apartment overnight. [*Fisher v. Snyder*, 476 F.2d 375 (8th Cir. 1973).]
3. Refusing to renew a teaching contract because the teacher was undergoing a divorce was impermissible. [*Littlejohn v. Rose*, 768 F.2d 765 (6th Cir. 1985), *cert. denied*, 475 U.S. 1045 (1986)]; and
4. A married part-time policeman's termination was found inappropriate where he was flirting with a married woman. [*Briggs v. North Muskegon Police Department*, 563 F. Supp. 585 (W.D. Mich. 1983).]

Public employee lifestyles have been regulated by requiring disclosure of outside employment earnings. This does not concern intimate economic relationships of husband and wife to preserve individual employment rights. It involves financial affairs of persons who are paid by the public and who occupy public trust.

Private sector employees have also claimed lifestyle intrusions outside the workplace. Termination for having an affair with a married co-worker despite an explicit employer policy to the contrary did not violate a municipal equal opportunities ordinance. [*Federated Rural Electric Insurance Co. v. Kessler*, 131 Wis.2d 189, 388 N.W. 2d 553 (1986).] However, a "topless stripper" was improperly terminated for engaging in prostitution acts on her own time where her extracurricular activities had not so injured the employer's business reputation. [*Conway, Inc. v. Ross*, 627 P.2d 1029 (Alaska 1981).]

The employee spouse's reputation has also been considered. A nursing home that failed to promote a black nurse's aide to a certified medication technologist's position, validly considered her husband's reputation as a drug abuser. The husband's reputation as a drug abuser within the community was firmly established. [*Holloway v. Prof. Care Centers*, 42 Fair Empl. Prac. Cas. (BNA) 161 (E.D. Mo. 1986).]

A ban against single-parent pregnancies among a girls club's staffers did not violate the Civil Rights Act of 1964 (Title VII) despite its disproportionate impact on black women. [*Chambers v. Omaha Girls Club*, 834 F.2d 697 (8th Cir.), *reh'g denied en banc*, 840 F.2d 583 (8th Cir. 1988).] The club acted lawfully when it terminated an unmarried pregnant black employee who could no longer serve as a role model for the club's teenage members. A role-model rule was justified by business necessity and as a *bona fide* occupational qualification, because role modeling may help prevent teenage pregnancies, which was one of the club's main purposes. Validation of the club's rule by conducting an empirical study to prove that it prevented pregnancy among teenagers was not required. No workable alternative to termination existed when the employee became pregnant, because a temporary replacement would have taken too long to train and no position was available that did not involve contact with the club's members.

Employers at times may have legitimate interests in monitoring employee home activities. This has been found appropriate during medical leaves and while in an on-call status away from the employer's premises.

LOYALTY

Given loyalty's ill-defined nature, several circumstances exist under which employer relief is sometimes granted:

1. An employee forms a competing business before resigning from employment. [See *Bancroft-Whitney Co. v. Glen*, 64 Cal. 2d 327, 411 P.2d 921, 49 Cal. Rptr. 825 (1966).]
2. An employee quits and, either before or after quitting, solicits customers whom the employee services. [See *Aetna Building Maintenance Co. v. West*, 39 Cal.2d 198, 246 P.2d 11 (1952). *superseded by statute as stated in American Paper and Packaging Products, Inc. v. Kirger*, 183 Cal. App. 3d 1318, 228 Cal. Rptr. 713 (1986)]; and
3. When one employee successfully solicits employees of another to leave their present jobs and join a competing enterprise. [See *Frederick Chusid and Co. v. Marshall Leeman and Co.*, 326 F. Supp. 1043 (S.D.N.Y. 1971).]

Loyalty problems are so varied and complex that no set of guidelines can insulate the employer from them entirely. However, the following considerations may help to minimize loyalty problems by present and former employees:

1. Consider using restrictive covenants;
2. Prepare a written confidentiality policy; and
3. Protect the confidentiality of and access to critical employer information.

Just as every employee promises to perform work prudently and skillfully, they also impliedly promise to serve their employer faithfully and honestly. Loyalty is more a state of mind. It is a legally cognizable duty to act in a loyal fashion toward one's employer throughout an employment relationship. The extent of the employer's right to demand loyalty represents a significant concern outside the workplace that impacts employee furtherance of economic opportunities.

Employees owe their employer loyalty even though they may not be officers or directors. If the employee fails to serve the employer loyally, the employment relationship may be terminated. This normally arises when an employee engages in outside business activities resulting in less work for the employer or efforts to obtain the employer's business or customers. A balance is sought between the employer's loyalty interest and the employee's freedom to further economic interests. Areas affected include:

1. Embezzling employer funds;
2. Appropriating the employer's business opportunities;
3. Encouraging other employees to terminate employment;
4. Planning to begin a new enterprise while an employee; and
5. Carrying out preparations for other employment opportunities on the current employer's working time.

In determining whether an employee's activities impact loyalty to one's employer that can be restricted or prohibited, the following should be considered:

1. Depriving the employer of legitimate business opportunities;
2. Derogatory effect on the employer;
3. Inconsistency with the employer's interests; and
4. Devoting time and effort to the additional job such that performance on the primary job is adversely affected.

The loyalty interest arose where an ice cream wholesaler's employees formed a competing company. The employee's wives incorporated the new company. While still employed, the employees solicited the employer's customers, utilizing confidential customer lists. The employer obtained an injunction restraining the former employees from selling to their former employer's customers. [*Arnold's Ice Cream Co. v. Carlson*, 1330 F. Supp. 1185 (E.D. N.Y. 1971).]

Termination was appropriate where two supervisors started a shipdecking company. This company competed with their employer because they preformed work for their employer's competitor and solicited decking jobs from their employer's customers. [*Jacksonville Shipyards, Inc.*, 74 Lab. Arb. (BNA) 1066 (1980) (Taylor, Arb.).]

Liability may arise by recruiting other employees to leave an employer and to join the employee's new business. The employee may be liable for interfering with the other employees' contract with the employer.

Mere planning and preparation to start a competitive business is not necessarily disloyal where it is not done on the employer's time. Only when the employee commits disloyal acts of stealing trade secrets, customer lists, or soliciting the employer's customers or employees, does a loyalty breach occur. The employer may obtain injunctive relief to prevent a former employee from using trade secrets or customer lists. Profits made by an employee who appropriates a business opportunity that should have passed onto the employer may also be recovered.

Holding another job while working for an employer or *moonlighting* is not by itself disloyal. Many collective bargaining agreements permit employees to hold another job. When employee outside interests closely resembles the work done by the employer, loyalty can be questioned. A cigarette salesman's termination was upheld who operated his own vending machine company that supplied cigarettes. [*Phillips Brothers, Inc.*, 63 Lab. Arb. (BNA) 328 (1974) (Stern, Arb.).] However, a city plumber doing plumbing work on his own time without a required license was reinstated, despite work rules prohibiting outside work. The employee had not been warned and other employees who had violated the employer's outside employment rules were reinstated after a suspension. [*City of Rockville*, 76 Lab. Arb. (BNA) 140 (1981) (Levitan, Arb.).] Just like any other work rule, to be enforceable it must be consistently applied without discrimination.

Problems arise when part-time employment interferes with employee performance or attendance at the primary job. However, an employee was reinstated where he worked a second job during his sick leave. The employee had worked this job weekends for several years with the employer's knowledge. [*Merroid Corp.*, 63 Lab. Arb. (BNA) 941 (1974) (Kossoff, Arb.).]

Inquiring about position openings has also created problems. While making an emergency trip to pick up a part, an employee went out of his way to inquire at a competitor about employment. This was considered disloyal and the termination was sustained. [*Aluminum Foundaries, Inc.*, 82 Lab. Arb. (BNA) 1259 (1984) (Seidman, Arb).]

The loyalty duty may even extend after an employee resigns. A reporter's termination was appropriate for what was termed a breach of his duty of loyalty to his employer. The employee resigned due to an alleged unethical employer action. The newspaper had airbrushed the penis off the Infant Jesus in a reprint of a painting. His reasons for leaving were explained to a competitor who published a headline story of this disclosure. This resulted in the employee's termination before the two-week notice period ended. The employee then attempted to rescind his resignation. The original resignation was upheld because during this two-week notice period the employee was not released from his loyalty duty. [*Los Angeles Herald-Examiner*, 49 Lab. Arb. (BNA) 453 (1967) (Jones, Arb.).]

A loyalty duty to expose wrongdoing to the employer generally arises where an employee knows or has reason to believe that theft of employer property has occurred or is currently occurring, but the employee remains silent. Termination is proper where employees either have actual or implied knowledge of theft over areas where they exercise responsibility and fail to report this.

CONFLICTS OF INTEREST

This involves the employee's duty to avoid or disclose any actual or possible conflict of interest with their employer. Often it is not the conflict itself that results in problems. It is the failure to disclose it or to divest it when warned. The following should be considered regarding whether outside employment constitutes a conflict of interest:

1. Depriving the employer of legitimate business opportunities;
2. Inconsistency with the employer's interests;
3. Derogatory effect on the employer; and
4. Devoting time and effort to the additional job such that performance on the primary job is adversely affected.

Termination was reasonable where an employee failed to disclose a conflict of interest to a university. The employee contracted with a firm where her husband had a substantial financial interest and did not reveal this relationship. It was not unreasonable to conclude that the employee knew her conduct was improper. [*University of California*, 78 Lab. Arb. (BNA) 1032 (1982) (Ross, Arb.).]

Conflict of interest surfaced involving a sportswriter who picked favorites for horse races. The sportswriter became part-owner of a horse. Although the employee refrained from picking favorites when his horse was racing, a conflict of interest was present where horses of the same stable ran in other races. [*New York Post Corp.*, 62 Lab. Arb. (BNA) 225 (1973) (Friedman, Arb.).]

Negative information about employers raises conflict of interest concerns. A public utility company's written reprimand for an employee who had written a letter containing substantial falsehoods to a local newspaper opposing nuclear power was proper. [*San Diego Gas and Electric Co.*, 82 Lab. Arb. (BNA) 1039 (1983) (Johnston, Arb.).]

Conflict of interest may also involve marital and family relationships. Employee termination may occur because a spouse or close family member is also employed. Termination is based upon an inherent conflict of interest when family members work closely together. Employers argue that conflicts between family loyalty and employer obligations are increased when this occurs.

Generally, an employer may publish and institute a rule prohibiting married couple, sibling, and close family member employment. Problems arise when the employer has not published a rule and terminates a spouse or gives them the opportunity to resign.

Dating a sales representative from a competing employer was improper where an employer raised a conflict of interest. The employer expressed a policy of not interfering in employees' personal affairs unless it had a detrimental effect on the employee's work performance. This policy ensured employees a privacy right and to hold a job even though off-duty conduct might not be approved by the employer. No evidence of an actual conflict of interest was presented. The employee's job did not have access to sensitive information that could have been used by a competitor. [*Rulon Miller v. IBM*, 162 Cal. App.3d 241, 208 Cal. Rptr. 524 (1984).]

A former employee, however, could not recover where the employer allegedly terminated him because he was accompanied by a woman who was not his wife, but who was presented as his wife, to a company outing. Though freedom of association is an important social right that ordinarily should not dictate employment decisions, the right to associate with a non-spouse at an employer's outing without fear of termination was not within the public policy exception prohibiting an at-will employee's termination. [*Staats v. Ohio Nat. Life Ins. Co.*, 620 F. Supp. 118 (W.D. Pa. 1985).]

Federal and state fair employment practice (FEP) statutes have been used to raise conflict of interest concerns. A female employee's termination based on an insurance company's policy against employing any person whose spouse is employed by an insurance company in active competition did not constitute sex discrimination. The employer's policy applied to male and female employees and was made known to employees generally from time to time in employee meetings. [*Emory v. Georgia Hospital Service Assoc.*, 4 Fair Empl. Prac. Cas. (BNA) 891 (5th Cir. 1971).]

Where a female applicant's husband was a prime user of an airport, it was found that a city did not discriminate on the basis of sex by refusing to hire the female as the airport manager. As the owner of a flight training school and aircraft rental service, the female applicant's husband was both a prime user and tenant of the airport. The city charter provided that no employee of the city shall have a financial interest, direct or indirect, in any contract with the city, or be financially interested, directly or indirectly, in a sale to the city of any services except on behalf of the city as an employee. [*Satterwhite v. Greenville*, 395 F. Supp. 698 (N.D. Tex. 1979).]

OFF-DUTY MISCONDUCT

Employee termination for misconduct at the workplace will usually be upheld. When misconduct occurs outside the workplace, concerns regarding the employer's right to impose discipline arise. This may involve misconduct that is non-criminal and criminal.

Non-Criminal Misconduct

Certain instances arise where the employer may properly demonstrate concern for employee misconduct outside the workplace. Fights outside the workplace over personal matters would not normally be subject to employer regulation. Where the fight relates to the employment relationship and affects the work environment, the employer's concern may be legitimate.

The difficulty is in determining when an employee's rights must yield to the employer's legitimate business interests. Employers generally maintain that the employee's misconduct outside the workplace has caused an actual business loss or injured the employer's reputation. The following should be considered regarding noncriminal misconduct that occurs outside the workplace:

1. Injurious effect upon the employer's reputation;
2. The source and degree of adverse publicity;
3. The type of misconduct; and
4. The employee's position.

A bus operator was properly terminated who was publicly identified as the acting grand dragon of the Ku Klux Klan. Danger of physical violence existed along with a threatened wildcat strike by fellow employees and an economic boycott. The employee's activities, not beliefs, were at issue. [*Baltimore Transit Co.*, 47 Lab. Arb. (BNA) 62 (1986) (Duff, Arb.).] Where an injurious effect upon an employer's reputation is alleged, the source and degree of adverse publicity, the type of misconduct, and the employee's position become important.

Where an off-duty employee "streaked" in front of an airport terminal he was terminated for irresponsibility. Termination was improper because this misconduct was not viewed negatively by other employees, fellow employees encouraged it, and there was little reluctance to work with the employee. [*Air Cal*, 63 Lab. Arb. (BNA) 350 (1974) (Kaufman, Arb.).] "Mooning" or "baring of bottoms" while outside the workplace may be insufficient to support termination where not job-related. [*South Central Bell*, 80 Lab. Arb. (BNA) 891 (1983) (Nicholas, Jr., Arb.).] However, an employer's requirement to "moon" or "bare bottoms" as a workplace requirement at an employment outing may support a wrongful termination action. [*Wagonseller v. Scottsdale Memorial Hosp.*, 147 Ariz. 370, 710 P.2d 1025 (1985).]

In misconduct violations outside the workplace, a relationship must exist between the misconduct and the employment relationship. The termination of an employee was sustained who verbally assaulted his supervisor at a restaurant while both were off-duty. The assault was detrimental to the supervisor's ability to handle employees and the employee's bitterness and hostility toward supervision would carry over into the employment relationship. [*General Telephone Co. of Kentucky*, 69 Lab. Arb. (BNA) 351 (1979) (Bowles, Arb.).]

Misconduct at employer-sponsored athletic events outside the workplace and off the employer's premises may result in disciplinary action. [*Indianapolis Power and Light Co.*, 88 Lab. Arb. (BNA) 1109 (1987) (Volz, Arb.) (employee misconduct at employer-sponsored basketball game).] This may occur, for instance, where an employee threatens other employees at an employer-sponsored athletic event. In evaluating the discipline's severity, the following must be considered:

1. The athletic event's nature;
2. The aggressiveness of both sides in the athletic event;
3. Type of rivalry;
4. Verbal versus physical misconduct; and

5. The necessity to request police intervention to control the situation.

Even though an employer may properly terminate an employee for noncriminal misconduct arising outside the workplace, it may still find itself subject to unemployment compensation claims. For example, where unemployment compensation benefits were denied to drug rehabilitation counselors who were terminated for ingesting peyote during a Native American Church religious ceremony, their case was initially remanded to determine if the state prohibited the religious use of peyote. [*Employment Division, Department of Human Resources v. Smith,* 485 U.S. 660 (1988).] If the religious use of peyote was found permitted under state statutes, they would be entitled to unemployment compensation benefits in protection of their first amendment religious freedom guarantees. In a subsequent ruling, use of peyote was found to be not legal in Oregon and unemployment compensation benefits were denied. [*Employment Division, Department of Human Resources v. Smith,* ___ U.S. ___, 110 S.Ct. 1595 (1990).]

Criminal Misconduct

Arrest or conviction for off-duty misconduct can result in disciplinary action. Where an arrest or conviction has an adverse impact on the employer's business, disciplinary action is generally considered appropriate. The effect and likelihood of negative publicity along with the sensitive nature of certain pubic sector positions makes it likely that criminal activities outside the workplace of public employees will have an indirect but damaging impact on the employer's business.

Arrest, indictment, or conviction for employee activities outside the workplace that adversely affect their own or fellow employee's job performance or is directly or indirectly detrimental to the employer's business, may sustain disciplinary action. The following should be considered regarding criminal misconduct outside the workplace:

1. Negative oral or written publicity;
2. Nature of the employee's misconduct;
3. Nature of the criminal misconduct, such as arrest, indictment, or conviction;
4. Effect of the employee's or fellow employee's job performance;
5. Detriment to the employer's business; and
6. The employee's explanation, if any.

A dairy driver-salesman was one of ten people arrested in a raid on a night club and was charged with Sunday liquor sale, prostitution, pandering, and conducting obscene exhibitions involving men and women. The employee's suspension was sustained, pending outcome of the trial, because of possible damage to the employer's image and good will. The driver-salesman's duties necessitated a close personal relationship with customers and the charges' seriousness increased the employer's potential harm. [*Menzie Dairy Co.*, 45 Lab. Arb. (BNA) 283 (1965) (Mullin, Jr., Arb.).]

Where an employee grabbed a shotgun and went into the woods behind his home after a quarrel with his wife, a state trooper ordered the employee to come out. As the employee emerged, the gun discharged, slightly grazing the trooper and causing the employee's arrest. The employee was terminated because of the adverse publicity in two local newspapers. The employee was reinstated because the newspaper accounts of the incident did not reveal the employer's identity and his job did not require him to deal with the public. [*Valley Bell Dairy Co.*, 71 Lab. Arb. (BNA) 1004 (1978) (Hunter, Jr., Arb.).]

A driver employed be a county road commission for ten years was terminated after pleading no contest to a third degree criminal sexual offense. Although the one-year jail sentence had a work release provision to enable employment continuation, the driver was terminated for violating the commission's rule against conviction for penal offense and for indecent or immoral conduct. No direct relationship between the illegal conduct and the driver's job was found. Absent a job relationship, discipline was inappropriate. The employee's good work record and the imposition of a relatively light sentence with work release privileges outweighed possible problems with fellow employees and the public. [*Gratiot County Road Commission*, Pub. Bargaining Cas. (CCH) ¶49,048 (1986) (Roumell, Jr., Arb.).]

A city corrections officer was interviewed as part of a police investigation into a burglary. The corrections officer signed a statement admitting that on the night of the burglary he had been smoking marijuana with four teenage boys and that he had driven one of the boys to the home of the boy's mother where the burglary occurred. The Corrections Department terminated the officer for misconduct stemming from his purchase and smoking of marijuana in the company of teenagers and due to his role in the burglary. This behavior of smoking marijuana was sufficient to bring considerable discredit to the employer and warrant termination. Public officers relinquish some of their privacy rights when they accept their positions. Because the employee was an off-duty peace officer, his violation had a greater impact than would the same action by an average citizen. [*New York State Dept. of Corrections*, 86 Lab. Arb. (BNA) 793 (1986) (La Manna, Arb.).]

A city could not base discipline on its belief that a police officer had committed a jealousy-induced assault where a jury acquitted him of assault and battery charges. [*City of Mason*, 73 Lab. Arb. (BNA) 464 (1979) (Ellman, Arb.).] Likewise, a federal agency failed to show that termination for engaging in illegal sexual activity with a minor child promoted the efficiency of the agency. [*Social Security Administration*, 80 Lab. Arb. (BNA) 725 (1983) (Lubic, Arb.).] But an employee whose job was to administer breathalyzer tests was properly suspended for off-duty driving under the influence of alcohol. [*Polk County, Iowa*, 80 Lab. Arb. (BNA) 639 (1983) (Madden, Arb.).]

RESIDENCY REQUIREMENTS

Residency or distance requirement are frequently imposed by public employers and occasionally by private employers. Generally, a person's residence is where they reside and where they intend to stay; i.e., the domicile or abode. Physical presence for a long time period is not dispositive of "residence." Other factors include:

1. Voting place;
2. Mailing address;
3. Driver's license address;
4. Where one keeps clothes;
5. Location of property owned; and
6. Rental payment.

At issue in residency requirements are individual employment rights in choosing where one lives, a right to travel, and geographical limits curtailing access to employment opportunities. Residency requirements may result in the employer compromising applicant quality because of a constricted recruitment base. Constitutional challenges to residency requirements have focused on interference with a fundamental right to travel.

Residency requirements necessary to serve legitimate employer interests are valid. Teachers, police, and fire fighters are frequently subject to these. However, where a collective bargaining agreement recognized the employer's right to establish reasonable rules and regulations for the safe and efficient conduct of the city's business, the rule was unreasonable because the city did not specifically justify a three-mile range. [*City of Monmouth,* 79 Lab. Arb. (BNA) 345 (1982) (Harter, Arb.).]

Just cause provisions in collective bargaining agreements and statutory residency requirements may sometimes conflict. Where a city had a statutory residency requirement that provided for employee termination there was no indication in the collective bargaining agreement regarding how the just cause provision would relate to the pre-existing residency ordinance. When a street and sanitation employee moved out of the city, his employment was terminated. The arbitrator found that the residency ordinance was not contained in the contract, but was a work rule that was not reasonably related to job performance. The arbitrator ordered the employee reinstated. The city ignored the award and the union appealed. The court ruled that the arbitrator exceeded his powers in determining that the termination was not for just cause. In arbitrating whether the termination pursuant to the ordinance was for just cause, the parties used a contractual provision as a means for violating the law, and a contract provision that violates the law is void. [*WERC v. Teamsters Local No. 563,* 75 Wis.2d 602, 250 N.W.2d 696 (1977).]

Fair employment practice statutes may be used to challenge residency requirements. The Civil Rights Act of 1964 (Title VII) was violated where a municipal residency rule denied employment to blacks. [*United States v. Village of Elmwood Park,* _____ F. Supp. _____, 43 Fair Empl. Prac. Cas. (BNA) 995 (N.D. Ill. 1987).] This occurred where Elmwood Park's and Melrose Park's police and fire department residency requirements preferred residents over nonresidents for municipal positions and *word of mouth* recruitment excluded blacks from consideration.

According to the 1980 census, blacks accounted for more than 20 percent of the labor force in Cook County and about 16 percent of the labor force in the Chicago metropolitan area. Elmwood Park is in a township where blacks comprised about 13 percent of the private industry's work force. However, no blacks worked for Elmwood Park, which had about 100 employees, and the municipal manager testified that the town had never employed a black person.

In August 1985, the Elmwood Park Board of Trustees passed an ordinance requiring fire and police applicants to live in the town at least three years prior to employment. Previous to this ordinance, the Elmwood Park board of police and fire commissioners had imposed an identical three-year residency requirements on applicants. The town also followed a philosophy of preferring town residents for municipal positions outside the fire and police departments. Since 1975, it had hired only two nonresidents for city jobs, both of whom were white.

Elmwood Park maintained that its residency requirements for employment were necessary for it to hold its own, maintain a healthy community, and employ individuals who had more pride in the community because they lived there. [*Id.*] It did not normally post notices of vacancies and it relied on word of mouth as its primary recruitment source. Residency requirements along with hiring practices and philosophies were similar in the Melrose Park companion case.

These duration requirements and preference for residents in municipal employment had an overwhelming biased and disparate adverse impact on blacks that was not justified by any job-related necessity. The practices were precisely the artificial, arbitrary, and unnecessary barriers prohibited by Title VII. Moreover, the philosophy of favoring residents over nonresidents reduced the proportion of blacks in the relevant labor force from 13 or 18 percent to zero.

The word-of-mouth recruitment system posed an additional barrier to prospective black applicants. A word-of-mouth recruitment system limits information about job openings to the friends and relatives of incumbent employees. Given the all-white nature of the municipal workforces, this disproportionately deprived qualified black applicants of the information they needed to apply for positions. [*Id.*]

Residency requirements for applicants may be found suspect under FEP statutes when they have a disparate impact on minorities, unless the employer can show that there is substantial justification for the practices. [*Id.*] Although employment practices may appear fair and neutral on their face, if they are found to have a disparate impact on a protected group, they will be invalidated unless they are shown to have a "manifest relationship to the employment in question." [*Griggs v. Duke Power Co.*, 401 U.S. 424, 432 (1971).] Policies designed to "help our own" and to foster pride in the community by themselves will not justify employment practices that have a disparate impact on protected groups.

8

Individual Employment Rights Litigation

It is increasingly apparent that collecting, maintaining, using, and disclosing employment information along with regulating employee lifestyles have the potential of affecting individual employment rights. More sophisticated and complex lifestyles make employees especially concerned that employers will excessively monitor their working time or inquire too extensively into their personal relationships.

Employee activism to enforce these individual employment rights is only now beginning. Litigation theories that are being relied on to protect individual employment rights include tort actions for:

1. Invasion of privacy;
2. Defamation;
3. False imprisonment;
4. Intentional infliction of emotional distress;
5. Negligent maintenance or disclosure of employment records;
6. Fraudulent misrepresentation;
7. Intentional interference with contractual relations; and
8. Public policy.

Contractual litigation theories revolve around violations of:

1. Employment contracts;
2. Restrictive covenants;
3. Employment handbooks and policies; and
4. Collective bargaining agreements.

PERSONAL RIGHT VIOLATIONS (TORTS)

Personal right violations or torts involve legal wrongs that are not criminal and are not based on contract. Among these are:

1. Invasion of privacy;
2. Defamation;
3. False imprisonment;
4. Intentional infliction of emotional distress;
5. Negligent maintenance of disclosure of employment records;
6. Fraudulent misrepresentation;
7. Intentional interference with contractual relations; and
8. Public policy.

These torts provide the foundation for inquiring into individual employment rights violations associated with information collection, maintenance, use, and disclosure along with employee lifestyle regulation.

Invasion of Privacy

Invasion of privacy may permit an employee to recover when an employer's actions affect matters for which the employee has a reasonable privacy expectation. It may be applicable to improper information collection, maintenance, use, and disclosure along with employee lifestyle regulation.

For invasion of privacy, the same conditional privileges are available to an employer as in a defamation action. The employer could defend by showing that its conduct was reasonably necessary to its business operation. Consent is also an important employer defense.

Current employment litigation confirms that invasion of privacy can be expected to gain wider court approval. Employer violations have been found in:

1. Employer letters regarding employee activities. [*Beaumont v. Brown*, 65 Mich. App. 455, 237 N.W.2d 501 (1975), *rev'd*, 401 Mich. 80, 257 N.W.2d 522 (1977)];
2. Removing tires from an employee's automobile while parked in the employer's lot. [*Santiesteban v. Goodyear Tire and Rubber Co.*, 306 F.2d 9 (5th Cir. 1962)];
3. Using former employee's name for advertising purposes without consent. [*Colgate-Palmolive Co. v. Tullos*, 219 F.2d 617 (5th Cir. 1955)];

4. Showing photographs of an employee's "unsightly wound" on numerous occasions at plant safety meetings. [*Lambert v. Dow Chem. Co.*, 215 So.2d 673 (La. App. 1968)];
5. Revealing confidential medical or personal information about employees. [*Bratt v. International Business Machines*, 392 Mass. 508, 467 N.E.2d 126 (1984)];
6. Using a locksmith to force entry into the trailer home of an employee who failed to report to work. [*Love v. Southern Bell Telephone*, 263 So.2d 460 (La. App. 1972)];
7. Reading employee personal mail. [*Vernars v. Young*, 539 F.2d 766 (3rd Cir. 1976)];
8. Interrogating a female employee about her sexual relationship with her husband. [*Phillips v. Smalley Maintenance Service, Inc.*, 711 F.2d 1524 (11th Cir. 1983)];
9. Interrogating an employee about dating a competing firm's employee. [*Rulon-Miller v. IBM*, 162 Cal. App.3d 241, 208 Cal. Rptr. 524 (1984)];
10. Harassing an employee for an interracial relationship. [*Moffett v. Gene B. Glick Co.*, 604 F. Supp. 229 (N.D. Ind. 1984)];
11. Inquiring into extra-marital activities. [*Slohada v. United Parcel Service*, 193 N.J. Super. 586, 475 A.2d 618 (1984), *rev'd on other grounds*, 207 N.J. Super. 149, 504 A.2d 53 (1986)];
12. Improper locker search. [*K-Mart Corporation Store No. 7441 v. Trotti*, 677 S.W.2d 632 (1984), *aff'd per curiam*, 686 S.W.2d 593 (Tex. 1985)];
13. Improper employee strip search. [*Bodewig v. K-Mart, Inc.*, 54 Or. App. 480, 635 P.2d 657 (1981)];
14. A supervisor's yelling during a workplace fight that the employee's wife had been having sexual relations with certain people. [*Keehr v. Consolidated Freightways*, 825 F.2d 133 (7th Cir. 1987)]; and
15. Termination of an employee for refusing to identify fellow drug-using employees after confidentiality had been represented. [*Paradis v. United Technologies*, 672 F. Supp. 67 (D. Conn. 1987).]

Defamation

Defamation may support an individual employment rights injury arising out of improper information collection, maintenance, use, and disclosure along with employee lifestyle regulation. It is subdivided into the torts of libel and slander. Libel essentially involves a writing while slander concerns speech. The critical finding for defamation involves "unprivileged publication to another" and fault with respect to publication. The defamatory statement's communication to one person normally suffices for publication. However, communication from one person to another within the same employment relationship where an employment-related "need to know" exists may not suffice for publication.

A recognized employer conditional privilege exists to communicate employee information. Employers are protected under this "privilege" to defame in certain circumstances. This privilege can be lost by communicating information known to be false or acting in reckless disregard concerning its truth or falsity. Negligent communications can also forfeit this privilege. It can be lost if the person communicating defamatory material does not act for the purpose of furthering the interest that the privilege protects; i.e., communicating the information for legitimate employment-related purposes. This may occur, where an employer discloses adverse information more broadly than is necessary for legitimate employment purposes.

Recent litigation may have increased recovery chances for employees asserting defamation. In *Agriss v. Roadway Exp., Inc.* 334 Pa. Super. 295, 483 A.2d 456 (1984), Agriss had been employed by Roadway Express as a truck driver. Before beginning a scheduled vacation, Agriss was handed a "warning letter." The employer refused to withdraw the warning and Agriss filed a grievance under the collective bargaining agreement.

As part of this grievance procedure, the warning letter and Agriss's protest were forwarded to the union business agent. The procedure also provided for the warning letter to be distributed to Roadway's manager of labor relations and to Agriss' personnel file.

Shortly thereafter, Agriss flew to Hawaii for a vacation. While in Hawaii, Roadway driver Joseph Verdier heard stories about the Agriss warning. He heard other drivers and a Roadway dispatcher saying that Agriss was to be terminated for looking into company mail. When Agriss returned, several drivers asked him about the warning letter. He heard the charge against him over the CB radio.

On January 11, Agriss approached the employer to discuss this further. A meeting occurred in the employer's office. The discussion became heated. It was loud enough to be heard by Roadway employees outside of this office. At one point, the employer accused Agriss with, "You read my _____ mail."

Agriss continued to receive comments and questions about the warning letter from Roadway employees and union officials. Over a year after the incident, Agriss instituted suit, claiming that Roadway had defamed him.

The employee's burden of proof in a defamation action is set out in Pennsylvania statute. The threshold question in any defamation action is whether the communication is capable of a defamatory meaning. The court must first make this determination. If the communication could be understood as defamatory, then it is for a jury to determine whether it was so understood.

The court was faced with the issue of whether Agriss' evidence was sufficient to prove that Roadway published the charge "opening company mail" in a manner that was not privileged. Pennsylvania law extends to employers an absolute privilege to publish defamatory matter in notices of employee termination.

The absolute privilege pertaining to termination notices also applied to a warning letter. Roadway had an absolute privilege to publish Agriss's warning letter to parties entitled to receive it. These were Agriss, the union business agent, and Roadway management personnel. The copy of the warning letter sent to Agriss' employee personnel file also was covered by the privilege. This formed the "protective circle" within which this defamatory communication could be published without incurring employer defamation liability.

However, while Agriss was vacationing in Hawaii the contents of this warning letter were widely disseminated by the employer to persons who were not authorized to read the letter. Joseph Verdier testified that he heard several drivers and a company dispatcher talking about the warning. Agriss testified that upon returning from Hawaii he was greeted with comments and questions about the warning from several drivers and also heard this discussed indiscriminately over the citizens band radio. Agriss testified that aside from the parties who were privileged under the grievance procedure, he had told no one else at Roadway about the charge except Ronald Brophy, a management-level employee. This was not disputed by the employer. Agriss proved that the contents of the warning letter were published by the employer in an unprivileged manner. Only a handful of possible employer sources could have originated the unprivileged publication.

Agriss argued that "circumstantial" evidence permitted the link to be made. "Circumstantial" evidence could be sufficient to prove employer publication. This paralleled other Pennsylvania decisions permitting the fact-finder to infer liability, despite the absence of direct proof linking the party held liable to wrongful or negligent acts. Based on this reasoning, Agriss was granted a retrial.

In *Raffensberger v. Moran*, 336 Pa. Super. 97, 485 A.2d 447 (1984), Joe Moran, a "relay manager" for Roadway Express, Inc., sent a telex message to terminals in seven states implying that drivers were "breakdown artists." This term was used in the trucking business to suggest that drivers are intentionally "breaking down" while on the road and thereby causing unnecessary expense to the owner in the form of delayed transit, additional wages to the drivers, and costs of paying vendors to make repairs.

Discovery disclosed that Moran had compiled his list of "artists" by reviewing employer records to determine which drivers had reported the most breakdowns of trucks and/or equipment during the first six months of 1980. The list included all drivers who had reported at least five breakdowns during this period.

Moran's telex message was found to be capable of a defamatory meaning. It was susceptible to an interpretation that the drivers were contriving equipment failures and exploiting minor malfunctions dishonestly to obtain additional compensation and injure Roadway by causing unnecessary expense. A driver with this reputation, a jury could find, could be held in low esteem by owners and drivers alike, could be subjected to ridicule by drivers and terminal managers, and could experience increased difficulty in obtaining future work.

To receive damages, however, proof of "convincing clarity" must be presented that Moran acted with "actual malice." To show actual malice, the drivers must prove that Moran's communication was made with knowledge that it was false or with reckless disregard for whether it was false.

Moran's information was based upon employer records pertaining to the frequency of breakdowns experienced by the drivers. Although he denied in depositions that he had a malicious intent, Moran conceded that his purpose was to encourage improved performance. He also conceded that the employer's records did not reveal and he did not know the reasons for the breakdowns experienced by the drivers. Under these circumstances, a jury could find that Moran's statement that the drivers were dishonestly contriving breakdowns could be made recklessly without regard for the truth. Because the existence of "actual malice" was a question of fact for a jury, a jury trial was granted.

In *Lewis v. Equitable Life Assurance Soc'y.*, 361 N.W.2d 875 (Minn. Ct. App. 1985), a group of employees were defamed by the employer's stating a false and malicious reason for terminating them while knowing the employees would pass this information on to prospective employers. Four employees claimed that they had been asked to falsify their expense account reports to reflect a lesser amount than they actually spent on a temporary assignment. They claimed that they resisted and were terminated for refusing this. Also, the reason given for their termination was "gross insubordination," so that when they later sought new jobs they had to give that as the reason for their termination.

They sued for defamation based on the treatment of their actions as gross insubordination and for breach of contract. The contract claims were based on the employee handbook. The handbook provided that, except in cases of misconduct serious enough to warrant immediate termination, no employee would be terminated without a prior warning and an opportunity to upgrade performance.

The employer lost both claims. There had been a breach of contract and a defamation, even though the defamatory statement that the claimants were terminated for "gross insubordination" had been made to prospective employers by the claimants themselves.

Based on these decisions, it is no longer clear that an employer's privilege to defame an employee during the employment relationship is absolute. Employers are susceptible to defaming an employee through information collection, maintenance, use, and disclosure along with employee lifestyle regulation. This is because of the highly charged potential in the employment relationship. Employers may now be increasingly required to assert "truth as a defense" instead of solely relying on this privilege. If this is so, employers may have to possibly meet a "just cause" standard to sustain their actions. Employers with collective bargaining agreements are already required to do this. This could considerably increase employer exposure to employees.

Employees may find it easier to reach the merits of their claims by asserting defamation. Circumstantial evidence may be relied upon by the employee to show that this absolute privilege was abused and employer negligence also forfeits it. Employers must be very careful to keep a defamatory communication within their "protected circle" to maintain the privilege. Any circumstantial knowledge of the employer's action by others outside of this "protected circle" may be sufficient to negate this privilege.

This knowledge is not required to be obtained immediately but may be learned at some point in time subsequent to the defamatory action. This could be days, weeks, months, or even years depending upon the nature of the defamatory publication. It can be allowed to fester and ripen into fruition for establishing a cause of action for defamation at a subsequent date.

Defamation claims have been sustained against employers for:

1. Unfavorable employment references. [*Geyer v. Steinbronn, et al.*, 351 Pa. Super. 536, 506 A.2d 901 (1986)];
2. Termination for lack of cooperation. [*Elbeshbeshy v. Franklin Institute*, 618 F. Supp. 170 (E.D. Pa. 1985)];
3. Informing employees not entitled to information regarding reasons for a termination. [*Sias v. General Motors Corp.*, 372 Mich, 542, 127 N.W.2d 357 (1964)];
4. Characterizing an employee as a drug user. [*Houston Belt and Terminal Railway Co. v. Wherry*, 548 S.W.2d 743 (Tex. Civ. App. 1977), *cert. deined*, 434 U.S. 962 (1977)];
5. Publicly interrogating an employee in full view of fellow employees behind a glass enclosed room and characterizing the employee as a thief. [*Norman v. General Motors*, 628 F. Supp. 702 (D. Nev. 1986)];
6. Falsely accusing an employee of having AIDS and terminating the employee. [*Little v. Bryce*, 733 S.W.2d 937 (Tex. Ct. App. 1987)]; and
7. Supervisor telling other employees that a female employee had given him a venereal disease, characterizing her as a whore, and searching her personal belongings. [*Lewis v. Oregon Beauty Supply Co.*, 302 Or. 616, 733 P.2d 430 (1987).]

False Imprisonment

False imprisonment arises in the employment context when an employer restrains the employee for purposes of search or interrogation. Individual employment rights interests are affected where a false imprisonment seeks the collection of information that is solely in the employee's possession and the employer restrains the employee's freedom by force or threat of force. This requires complete restraint of the employee's freedom by force or threat of force. The restraint may be by actual or apparent physical barriers. There is no employer liability unless the employee knows of the confinement or is harmed by it.

An employer that asserts its authority to prevent an employee from leaving a facility or denies an employee permission to leave may incur liability. It is no defense that the employee was detained during working hours. Where security guards detained an employee leaving the employer's plant because they suspected theft they yelled at the employee, "nudged and shoved him," and then confined him during interrogation. Recovery against the employer was permitted based on defamation, assault, and false imprisonment. [See *General Motors v. Piskor*, 277 Md. 165, 352 A.2d 810 (1976).] Restraining an employee in a confrontation for referral to the medical department also may give rise to this claim. See [*Strachan v. Union Oil Co.*, 768 F.2d 703 (5th Cir. 1989).]

Intentional Infliction of Emotional Distress

Intentional infliction of emotional distress involves conduct exceeding all bounds tolerated by society that is calculated to cause and does cause serious mental distress. Recovery has sometimes required showing resulting physical injury because of the difficulty in establishing genuine harm; however, this may not always be required.

Three elements must be satisfied for an employee to establish a *prima facie* case. First, the employer's conduct must be extreme and outrageous. Second, the employer must act with the intent to cause emotional distress or with substantial certainty that distress will result from its conduct. Third, severe emotional distress must result from the employer's conduct'

Successful employment applications have occurred where:

1. A security investigator made false statements in an interview of a young female clerk about cash register shortages that he had proof of her theft and threatened prosecution. [*Hall v. Macy Department Stores*, 242 Or. 131, 637 P.2d 126 (1981).]
2. An employee was terminated for filing a racial harassment charge against her employer. [*Moffet v. Gene B. Glick Co.*, 621 F. Supp. 244 (N.D. Ind. 1985).]
3. Racial slurs and accusations of theft were made. [*Contreras v. Crown Corp.*, 88 Wash.2d 735, 565 P.2d 1173 (1977).]
4. An employee was the first to be terminated as part of a plan to terminate all employees in alphabetical order until the person responsible for certain thefts was discovered. [*Agis v. Howard Johnson Co.*, 371 Mass. 140, 355 N.E.2d 315 (1976).]
5. A low level female manager was terminated for having a romantic relationship with a competitor. [*Rulon-Miller v. IBM*, 162 Cal. App.3d 241, 208 Cal. Rptr. 524 (1984).]

6. An employee submitted to a polygraph examination after termination to receive accrued wages. [*MBM Co. v. Conce*, 268 Ark. 269, 596 S.W.2d 681 (1980).]
7. Excessive employer interrogation in a windowless room occurred with threats to take the employee to jail unless a confession was signed. [*Smithson v. Nordstrom, Inc.*, 63 Or. App. 423, 664 P.2d 1119, rev. denied, 295 Or. 841, 671 P.2d 1176 (1983).]
8. A female employee refused to sleep with a foreman. [*Lucas v. Brown and Root, Inc.*, 736 F.2d 1202 (8th Cir. 1984).]
9. Verbal and written sexual advances were refused and the employer retaliated by making working conditions onerous. [*Rogers v. Lowes L'Enfant Plaza Hotel*, 526 F. Supp. 523 (D. D.C. 1981).]
10. The employer strip searched an employee in front of a customer. [*Bodewig v. K-Mart Corp.*, 54 Or. App. 480, 635 P.2d 657 (1981), rev. denied, 644 P.2d 1128 (Or. 1982).]
11. An employee refused to file false work reports and the employer retaliated. [*Milton v. Illinois Bell Tel. Co.*, 101 Ill. App.3d 75, 427 N.E.2d 829 (1981).]
12. An employer initiated a drug investigation even though it knew the employee had not committed any offense. [*Norman v. General Motors Corp.*, 628 F. Supp. 702 (D. Nev. 1986).]
13. An employer yelled, badgered, and threatened arrest to a former employee and his wife to force them to identify drug-using employees. [*Paradis v. United Technologies*, 672 F. Supp. 67 (D. Conn. 1987).]
14. There was direct observation of an employee's act of urination during an employer administered alcohol and drug test. [*Kelley v. Schlumberger Technology Corp.*, 849 F.2d 41 (1st Cir. 1988).]

Negligent Maintenance or Disclosure of Employment Records

For individual employment rights, the negligent maintenance or disclosure of employment records' tort has potential broad application. This is because individual employment rights are an integral part of information collection, maintenance, use, and disclosure. It has application at and outside the workplace.

The negligent maintenance or disclosure of employment records' tort recognized an employer duty to use due care in keeping and maintaining employment records. An employer's duty breach permits an employee to bring a cause of action where the employee is injured thereby and the breach was the proximate cause of this injury. Related to this tort is an action for negligent evaluation of performance. [See *Chamberlain v. Bissell, Inc.*, 547 F. Supp. 1067 (W.D. Mich. 1982).] Claims have been permitted where:

1. The government's rules regarding personnel files established a duty to maintain them accurately and an employer who provides services, such as giving employee references, does not act carefully. [*Quinones v. United States*, 492 F.2d 1269 (3d Cir. 1974)];
2. An employee suffered embarrassment and an adverse credit rating because the employer disclosed inaccurate information contained in the employee's personnel file. [*Bulkin v. Western Kraft East, Inc.*, 422 F. Supp. 437 (E.D. Pa. 1976)]; and
3. An employee was not hired by another employer based on derogatory information in the employee's personnel file. {*Moessmer v. United States*, 569 F. Supp. 782 (E.D. Mo. 1983), aff'd, 760 F.2d 236 (8th Cir. 1985).]

Fraudulent Misrepresentation

Individual employment rights claims may be asserted through fraudulent misrepresentation, sometimes referred to as deceit or fraud. It exists when an employer fraudulently makes a misrepresentation of fact, opinion, intention, or law for the purpose of inducing the employee to act or to refrain from action in reliance upon it. The employer would be subject to liability in deceit for pecuniary loss caused through an employee's justifiable reliance upon the misrepresentation.

Fraudulent misrepresentation could be present in any employment information collection, use, maintenance, or disclosure. The employer could misrepresent reasons for this. Where the employer was collecting information a privacy interest arose because the employer expressly promised that there would be no retaliation if misconduct by other employees was disclosed. A fraud claim was stated when the employee was terminated in violation of that representation. [*Mueller v. Union Pac. R.R.*, 220 Neb. 742, 371 N.E.2d 732 (1985).]

Likewise, a claim arose where an employer promised to buy an employee's house in Illinois if he accepted a position in California. [*Palmer v. Beverly Enterprises*, 823 F.2d 1105 (7th Cir. 1987).] When the employee attempted to enforce the employer's promise after assuming the California position, he was terminated. Recovery was permitted because the employee could not properly evaluate his alternatives based on the employer's fraudulent information. Similarly, fraudulent misrepresentation was sustained where an employer terminated an employee after the employee confided his drug addiction, allegedly in reliance on the employer's promise to provide confidential assistance and to refrain from discrimination or retaliation. [*Paradis v. United Technologies*, 672 F. Supp. 67 (D. Conn. 1987).]

Intentional Interference with Contractual Relations

Intentional interference with contractual relations is a well established tort. The burden is on the employee to establish:

1. The existence of a proper prospective contractual relationship between the employee and a third party;
2. The employer must act for the purpose of causing the specific type of harm to the employee;
3. The employer's act must be unprivileged; and
4. Actual harm must result to the employee.

Intentional interference with contractual relations has been permitted against employees where:

1. Letters from a medical staff requested a hospital board to terminate a pathologist's privileges. [*Gordon v. Lancaster Osteopathic Hosp. Ass'n.*, 340 Pa. Super. 253, 489 A.2d 1364 (1985)];
2. A supervisor's letter to a prospective employer implicated the employee in a forgery scheme and various employment infractions. [*Geyer v. Steinbronn*, 351 Pa. Super. 536, 506 A.2d 901 (1986)]; and
3. A supervisor physically and verbally intimidated a female employee after she rejected romantic advances. [*Lewis v. Oregon Beauty Supply Co.*, 302 Or. 616, 733 P.2d 430 (1987).]

Public Policy

With at-will employment's continued erosion, various states have recognized employee causes of action in circumstances that infringe on a specific public policy interest. The employer's right to terminate has been curtailed under a public policy tort when the termination violates established public policy, especially a "clear," statutorily declared policy. Other exceptions involve employee "whistle blowing;" i.e., the reporting by an employee of unlawful or improper employer conduct.

"Abusive" or "retaliatory" terminations have been prohibited when an employee refuses to accede to improper employer requests or demands.

Public policy individual employment rights can be affected when employees are terminated for: 1) refusing to violate a criminal statute; 2) exercising a statutory right; 3) complying with a statutory duty; or 4) observing the general public policy of the state. Specific examples of employee terminations, violating some form of recognized public policy include:

1. Declining to commit perjury at the employer's behest. [*Ivy v. Army Times Pub. Co.*, 428 A.2d 831 (D.C. App. 1981)];
2. Refusing to participate in an illegal pricefixing scheme. [*Tameny v. Atlantic Richfield Co.*, 27 Cal.3d 167, 164 Cal. Rptr. 839, 610 P.2d 1330 (1980)];
3. Serving on a jury. [*Nees v. Hocks*, 272 Or. 210, 536 P.2d 512 (1975)];
4. Filing workers' compensation claims. [*Frampton v. Central Ind. Gas Co.*, 260 Ind. 249, 297 N.E.2d 425 (1973)];
5. Refusing to take a lie detector test in a state prohibiting its administration. [*Perks v. Firestone Tire & Rubber Co.*, 611 F.2d 1353 (3d Cir. 1979)];
6. Performing unauthorized catheterization. [*O'Sullivan v. Mallon*, 160 N.J. Super. 416, 390 A.2d 149 (1978)];
7. Mislabeling packaged goods. [*Sheets v. Teddy's Frosted Foods, Inc.*, 179 Conn. 471, 427 A.2d 385 (1980)];
8. Avoiding commissions. [*Fortune v. National Cash Register Co.*, 373 Mass. 96, 364 N.E.2d 1251 (1977)];
9. Avoiding pension payments. [*Savodnik v. Korvettes, Inc.*, 489 F. Supp. 1010 (E.D. N.Y. 1980)]; and
10. Terminating a husband and wife after the wife rebuffed her manager's sexual advances. [*Clay v. Advanced Computer Applications*, 370 Pa. Super. 497, 536 A.2d 1375 (1988).]

CONTRACT VIOLATIONS

The modern contract theory shows the willingness:

1. To imply obligations;
2. To imply undertakings from conduct as well as from verbal expressions; and
3. To permit recovery without proof of consideration.

For individual employment rights, this is relevant in imposing contractual commitments upon employers for information collection, maintenance, use, and disclosure.

Employment Contracts

Employees and employers daily enter into employment contracts with each other that have legal consequences. Often employees and employers are not aware of this. These employment contracts may be oral, written, indefinite, for a specified term, detailed, or simple.

These contracts have particular significance. They form the employment relationship wherein the employer collects, maintains, uses, and discloses employment information along with regulating the employee's lifestyle. Certain terms, conditions, promises, representations, etc. of these contracts may form the basis for individual employment rights litigation.

Employment contracts involve the elements of *offer, acceptance,* and *consideration*. Unless all of these elements are present, there is no employment contract.

Employment contracts are formed when one party (the offeror) extends an offer that is accepted by the other party (the offeree). The offer must contain the employment contract's essential terms and conditions. To form the contract, the offeror and offeree must agree to the same terms and conditions at the same time; i.e., *mutual assent,* or *a meeting of the minds* must occur for the same understanding of what the offer is.

After the offer has been made, the offeree has the power to create a binding employment contract by accepting it or by performing the requested duties. For the offer and acceptance to become a final employment contract, consideration must be present; i.e., something must be provided for it. Consideration is that something that has been promised or given. The employee's work or promise to work will generally be adequate consideration for an employer's promise to pay a certain wage, bonus, pension plan, fringe benefit, etc. Similarly, an employer's promise to pay a salary will be adequate consideration for the employee's promise to work, to assign inventions to the employer, or not to compete with the employer.

When a written employment contract exists, employment termination before the contract's expiration generally creates liability under breach of contract principles. Normally no written employment contract exists and the employment is at-will; i.e., employment can be terminated by either the employee or employer at any time, for any or no reason, with or without notice.

To overcome the at-will employment presumption, the employee must establish:

1. A promise to employ for a particular time period or to terminate only for certain reasons or through certain procedures;
2. The enforceability of the promise because consideration was given or through a doctrine that avoids the requirement of consideration;
3. The breach of a promise; and
4. The enforceability of the contract notwithstanding the statute of frauds.

A promise may be established by a written or oral statement made directly to the employee. It can be satisfied by an employer statement contained in handbooks or personnel policies. Sometimes it can be established by proof of custom and practice upon which the employee reasonably could rely. The law may also impose this, especially where an implied covenant of good faith and fair dealing can be shown.

The employee generally has a right to recover compensation and benefits for work performed, either for breach of contract or under quasi contract principles. To establish additional damages, the employee must prove an express or implied term for the oral or written contract. This may be satisfied by express or implied employment guarantees. Where employees have been told upon hiring that they would be employed so long as the "did the job" this may create indefinite term contracts. [*Pugh v. See's Candies, Inc.*, 116 Cal. App.3d 311, 171 Cal. Rptr. 917 (1981).] It may occur through express agreement, oral or written, especially when an employer handbook or policy provides employment termination "for just cause only." [*Toussaint v. Blue Cross and Blue Shield*, 408 Mich. 579, 292 N.W.2d 880 (1980).] Handbooks and personnel policies potentially may have a much broader application. Employer liability, however, can probably be minimized where it refrains from giving assurances or promises, oral or written.

An implied-in-law covenant of good faith and fair dealing may be contained in all contracts, including employment contracts. This may exist when the totality of the relationship firmly establishes the indicia of an implied agreement that gives rise to the requirement of good faith and fair dealing. Among the factors supporting this are:

1. Extraordinary length of service;
2. Good employee performance verified by routinely receiving raises, bonuses, and promotions;
3. Employer assurances that employment would continue;
4. Employer practice of not terminating except for cause whether based on an oral or written policy; and
5. No prior warning that the employee's position was in jeopardy. [See *Cleary v. American Airlines*, 111 Cal. App. 3d 443, 168 Cal. Rptr. 722 (1980).]

Restrictive Covenants

Restrictive covenants generally involve certain affirmative employee responsibilities toward their employer during and after employment termination. These responsibilities usually involve covenants not to compete and trade secrets. They are often found in written employment contracts.

These covenants impact individual employment rights by limiting employee opportunities and curtailing use of inventions, products, information, knowledge, etc. that were developed, learned, or obtained by the employee. They restrict the geographical area where similar employment may be located. Time limitations are also included to restrict, the employee's ability to engage, use, or exercise these opportunities.

When supported by consideration ancillary to a lawful contract, and reasonable and consistent with the public interest, these covenants are enforceable. Subject matter covered by these covenants include the employee's commitment not to compete with the former employer for a specified time period within a certain geographical territory, disclosure of customer lists, information and data, disclosure of trade secrets learned during the course of employment, and granting the employer sale rights to inventions, products, and information developed during employment.

To be enforceable, a post-employment restraint must reasonably:

1. Protect a legitimate employer interest;
2. Be limited in duration and area; and
3. Be reasonable in terms of the activities prohibited.

Reasonableness of the covenant is determined by the employer interest sought to be protected. Generally, the employer's need for protection is balanced against the hardship imposed on the employee.

Brief employment may not permit a restrictive covenant's enforcement. A six month restrictive covenant barring employment for a direct competitor could not be enforced against an employee who resigned after two months of employment. [*Birmingham Television Corp. v. DeRamus*, 502 S.2d 761 (Ala. App. 1986).] The restrictive covenant must be reasonably related to a protective employer interest and cannot impose an undue employee hardship. Here the information learned by the employee during the brief two month period was insufficient to create a protective employer interest.

A restriction that is unlimited regarding geographical territory is prima facie void. Where it is shown to be necessary for the employer's protection it will be enforced. Where a buyer shows that the business purchased covers the whole nation, a restriction on the seller's right to start a similar business within the United States will be upheld. [*Hall Mfg. Co. v. Western Steel Works*, 227 F. 588 (7th Cir. 1915).] A reasonable territorial restriction was held enforceable where the employee was given exclusive selling rights in all the Catholic schools and institutions in Ohio, Michigan, Erie (Pennsylvania), and Louisville (Kentucky). The employee agreed that he would not for a period of twelve months after employment termination engage in the same kind of business as the employer, nor aid any competitor within the boundaries assigned to him under the agreement. No tendency to monopolize was shown by the restrictive covenant. [*Federal Sanitation Co. v. Frankel*, 34 Ohio App. 331, 171 N.E. 339 (1929).]

A similar result occurred where a restrictive covenant was upheld that curtailed the employee in three states (Indiana, Illinois and Kentucky). This was binding for a period of eighteen months after employment termination. Its reasonableness was considered based upon the employer's business (selling teas, coffees, and other foodstuffs) and the type of customer contact the employee would develop. [*Grand Union Tea Co. v. Walker*, 208 Ind. 245, 195 N.E. 277 (1935).]

An agreement not to disclose names or addresses of the employer's customers or solicit these customers for one year after termination of employment was not invalid for: 1) want of consideration; 2) not so vague and uncertain to be unenforceable; 3) not void as having unlawful object. The evidence supported a judgment awarding damages for, and enjoining, the use of a list of the employer's customers by a former employee. [*Gordon v. Wasserman*, 153 Cal. App.2d 328, 314 P.2d 759 (1957).]

Employers may keep secret and retain the advantages of special knowledge that they may have of:

1. Sources of supply;
2. Methods of making and selling goods;
3. Names and addresses of likely customers; and
4. Other like matters.

If this knowledge is entrusted to an employee, a promise not to disclose it or use it is enforceable. Salesmen are generally hired and paid a salary to help them build up custom, customer acquaintances, and acquiring their good will. A promise to refrain from soliciting these customers is reasonable.

Restrictive covenants may be utilized to prevent future misuse of trade secrets by employees. A trade secret can be a process or a certain *know-how* that an employer attempts to keep secret for its benefit. The process itself can be a collection of steps that are publicly known but when used in conjunction constitute a trade secret. A process for sorting customer mail has been considered a trade secret.

Where an employee covenants for some period after employment termination not to use or disclose confidential information, this will be enforced: 1) if reasonable under all the facts and circumstances; and 2) to the extent necessary to protect the employer's interests. [*Kelite Products v. Brandt*, 206 Or. 636, 294 P.2d 320 (1956).]

A clause to assign to the employer any inventions, ideas, processes, etc. made by the employee during the year following employment termination has been upheld. [*National Cash Register v. Remington Arms Co.*, 212 App. Div. 343, 209 N.Y.S. 40 (1925).] Enforcement of these restrictions are proper if the time limitation is reasonable and it is not overly restrictive in protecting the employer.

Restrictive covenants are so varied and complex that no set of procedures can completely protect the employer. However, the following should be considered in minimizing unfair competition by present and former employees:

1. When reviewing the advisability of requiring employees to sign a restrictive covenant—
   - Avoid imposing an overboard covenant on all employee without distinction,
   - Restrictive covenants are not appropriate for every employee, and extremely broad covenants may be held unenforceable as an improper trade restraint,

- Consider that a narrow covenant tailored to key employees may deter the threat of trade secret misappropriation;
2. Promulgate a written policy on confidentiality that—
   - Includes a statement on the confidential nature of certain business information,
   - Avoids broad statements that all business information is confidential, and
   - Tailors the policy to meet the needs of the business;
3. Preserve the confidentiality of critical business information by—
   - Stamping confidential documents *confidential* and keeping them in a secure place,
   - Restricting the circulation of confidential information on a need-to-know basis,
   - Not giving suppliers or customers unlimited access to trade secrets,
   - Considering written agreements protecting the business from unauthorized disclosure where access is unavoidable,
   - Restricting access to parts of the facility where trade secret information is kept, and
   - Using sign-in and sign-out logs, badges, etc.;
4. Whether information can be protected depends upon—
   - Information knowledge outside the employer's business,
   - Information knowledge among employees,
   - Employer measures to protect information secrecy,
   - Information value to the employer and competitors,
   - Efforts and money expended by the employer in developing information, and
   - Difficulty for others to acquire or duplicate the information;
5. Examples of protectible information—
   - Customer lists, and
   - Formulas, processes, techniques;
6. One step to protect secrets and confidential information includes considering a formal employment contract—
   - The employment contract usually is not necessary where an employer wants only to ensure that an employee respects proprietary information confidentiality, or to ensure that the employer will receive the benefit of any inventions the employee creates on employer time;
   - If the objective is to keep the employee from competing with the employer or working for a competitor, then an employment contract is probably necessary; and

- Noncompetition provisions are more likely to be enforceable when coupled with an agreement for continued employment than when they stand alone and restrict the employee without giving the employee assurance of continued employment or pay. [See Murphy, *Investigating, Handling, and Protecting Against Employee Theft and Dishonesty*, in Employment Problems in the Workplace 13, 35-38 (J. Kauff ed 1986).]

Employment Handbooks and Policies

Handbooks and employment policies gained importance as employers became larger. A system of rules was necessary for orderly and efficient employer functioning. Small employers can usually operate without rules. For larger employers, individualized decision making becomes impractical. Increased size multiplies the number of employment decisions that must be made beyond one person's ability to make them.

Handbooks and employment policies create this order. They standardize employee production and provide standards for employer instructions without depending on the inconsistency of individual supervisors. They usually outline:

1. Rules of expected employee behavior;
2. Disciplinary or termination procedures if those rules are violated;
3. Compensation; and
4. Benefit items regarding hours of work, overtime, lay-off, recall, health care insurance, pensions, leaves of absence, holidays, vacations, etc.

Often, they are the only place where the employer sets forth these statements. They are commonly intended to create a closer relationship between an employer and its employees. For this reason, each employer's handbooks and employment policies are not exactly alike. They reflect the employer's particular operational and management style.

Statements made in handbooks and employment policies may create binding employer commitments. Where an employee was told at the time of hiring that he would be employed as long as he did his job, this promise was supported by the handbook stating that it was the employer's policy to terminate for "just cause" only. [*Toussaint v. Blue Cross/Blue Shield of Michigan*, 408 Mich. 579, 292 N.W.2d 880 (1980).] These oral and written promises were found to be enforceable as an express or implied agreement that set forth legitimate employee expectations based on the employer's representations.

The handbook or employment policy are considered to be the offer while the employee's work is the acceptance of a unilateral contract. Consideration arises through the employee's continuation of work, although the employee is still free to leave.

By characterizing handbooks and employment policies as unilateral employment offers, the employer may still, however, unilaterally augment, modify, or even withdraw them. When an employer distributes a new handbook or employment policy, the employer makes a new offer of employment to the at-will employee. This new offer is limited to the new handbook's or employment policy's contents and becomes effective on the date it is distributed. Where these are withdrawn, the new offer becomes effective on the date that the employer notifies the employee of the withdrawal. At-will employees accept the new offer and provide consideration by continuing their employment.

Handbooks and employment policies have also been given legal recognition in determining disputes involving unemployment compensation. In cases concerning a terminated employee's right to unemployment compensation, the employer has the burden in most states of establishing that the employee was terminated for a deliberate or willful violation of an existing employer policy. Employers commonly show the existence of these policies by providing handbook's or employment policy's distribution where the rule is printed. Here, ironically, it is the employer and not the employee who maintains that the handbook or employment policy is a binding employment commitment.

Employer oral promises of continued employment can support a binding commitment. The employer may communicate an oral promise that is supported by a handbook statement providing that employment would be terminated only for cause or only after exhaustion of certain procedures. Sufficient evidence can be presented to imply a contract based on oral assurances that termination would occur for "just cause only."

Sometimes a direct oral promise can be established. Oral statements by the employer's agent can be binding. This occurred where the employee was orally assured that she was secure in her job "for the rest of her life," and "the context of her long service in a position of substantial responsibility . . . provided the critical evidentiary support for her contract claim." [*Terrio v. Millinocket Community Hospital*, 379 A.2d 135 (Me. 1977).]

Oral promises and handbooks when combined with other factors may also support the promise element. Oral agreements combined with a personnel manual, policies, and employment practices were sufficient to constitute an implied employment contract to age sixty-five. [*Schipani v. Ford Motor Co.*, 102 Mich. Ct. App. 606, 302 N.W.2d 307 (1980).] This controlled over a signed written contract stating that employment was terminable at-will.

To counter the possibility of creating binding commitments, many employers have begun using disclaimers on their applications to preserve the at-will employment relationship. The effectiveness of a disclaimer that was included on an employment application was illustrated where the employee claimed that termination after twelve years of employment was wrongful because the employer had a duty not to terminate without "just cause." [*Novosel v. Sears, Roebuck and Co.*, 495 F. Supp. 344 (E.D. Mich. 1980).]

Not all disclaimers can defeat an employee's claim. Where an employee had signed three separate employment agreements, each contained a provision stating that "the Employee's employment with the Company may be terminated by either party at any time." Despite written acknowledgement of this employment condition, the provision was silent regarding whether or not "good cause" was necessary for termination. The statement could not be interpreted as creating an agreement that the employee could be terminated for merely any reason. [*Morris v. Chem-Lawn Corp.*, 541 F. Supp. 479 (E.D. Mich. 1982).]

Many employers provide their supervisory or management personnel with policy manuals and oral guidelines to assist in hiring, disciplining, and terminating employees. The typical employee never sees these or knows of their existence. Personnel guidelines set forth in supervisory manuals are often used offensively against the employer in litigation. While most courts have not read into at-will employment agreements the full text of an employer's stated and unstated employment policies and practices accumulated over the years, several cases demonstrate a developing trend that this could occur. [*Rynar v. Ciba-Geigy Corporation*, 560 F. Supp. 619 (N.D. Ill. 1983).]

Even though personnel policy guidelines or supervisory manuals are not distributed or communicated to employees, they may not preclude a finding of offer and acceptance necessary to sustain a binding employment commitment. Policy manuals not intended for employees may be discoverable by a former employee bringing suit. Because of this, the employer should be aware that its statements and procedures could be scrutinized.

The employer's failure to comply with its own personnel policies or supervisory guidelines could have a negative impact, especially where the employer did not comply with its own termination procedures requiring notice to the employee or a series of progressive steps before termination. Substantial compliance by the employer with the requirements of its policies and procedures may provide a strong defense against the employee's claim. This affords protection to the employer in establishing a record of impartiality and consistency in handling its employees. At the same time, it better informs employees of what they may reasonably expect. The employer should also closely scrutinize personnel policies or supervisory manuals for information that is not necessarily found in the handbook. If this language is retained, the employer should seek consistent application of its terms.

Collective Bargaining Agreements

The formal signing of the collective bargaining agreement does not mean that labor relations are ended. During the course of its term, many problems will arise involving the application and interpretation of the agreement's provisions. Employer and union representatives have the responsibility of making the agreement operational through implementing its terms. The agreement establishes the labor relations framework for the parties. It sets forth employee rights and benefits, employer obligations and rights, and union obligations and responsibilities.

Union employees usually can assert claims for wrongful employer information collection, maintenance, use, and disclosure along with employee lifestyle regulation outside the work place under a breach of contract theory. Principles of federal labor law, however, dictate that these claims generally be addressed by arbitrators under the collective bargaining agreement's grievance arbitration procedure rather than by courts.

A grievance arbitration procedure is an orderly and systematic means of appealing decisions. Its two principal elements are: 1) the number of appeal steps; and 2) time limits for appeal between steps.

After the grievance arises, it becomes part of the grievance arbitration procedure through a formal filing. Depending on the agreement's procedure, it may be filed by:

1. Individual employees;
2. Groups of employees;
3. The union on behalf of an employee;

4. The union on behalf of an employee group; or
5. The union alone.

Some procedures even permit the employer to file grievances.

Usually a series of appeal steps must be instituted within specified time limits. Promptness in processing disputes may be important, depending on how the parties observe the procedure. After a grievance has been filed, failure to process it to the next appeal step may bar arbitration. Often this procedural defect will occur immediately prior to arbitration. Arbitrators may dismiss grievances when there is a failure to respect time limits. However, arbitrators have demonstrated a reluctance to bar grievances for failure to appeal within specified time limits where the employer has in the past failed to object to the union's failure to conform with time limits.

Agreements vary concerning when hearings should be held at appeal steps on grievances. Their purposes are to frame the issues, refine the evidence, discover evidence, present positions, and determine if resolutions can occur. The higher the appeal step, the more formal the hearing. This may be to the point of actually holding a miniarbitration; i.e., a hearing with witnesses and testimony.

The settlement of grievances may occur between: 1) employer and employee; 2) employer, employee, and union; or 3) employer and union. Where settlement occurs between employer and employee, the union has the right to be present. This is because the union has an interest as statutory bargaining agent in assuring that similar grievances will be treated consistently. Through this the union as co-author of the collective bargaining agreement is able to maintain enforcement of that agreement for all employees.

Once a valid agreement providing for grievance arbitration has been entered into, any controversy between the parties that is within the scope of its provisions must proceed through it to arbitration. The only instances where a court will enjoin arbitration are where:

1. There is fraud or duress in the inception of the agreement;
2. There is no *bona fide* dispute in existence between the parties;
3. The performance that is the subject of the demand is prohibited by statute; or
4. A condition precedent to arbitration under the agreement has not been met.

If the issue is solely one of the agreement's construction or interpretation, it is for the arbitrator and not the court to decide.

There is an accepted rule that where a collective bargaining agreement contains an arbitration provision, it is presumed that questions of arbitrability are for the arbitrator to decide. This presumption of arbitrability applies equally to questions of substance and procedure. In addition, it has been held that the court's function is limited to finding that a dispute does in fact exist. If a dispute exists, the arbitrator, and not the court, must examine the merits of the dispute itself.

It is only where the parties have employed language that clearly rebuts this presumption of arbitrability that the matter may be determined by the courts. The function of the court is to determine whether the parties agreed to submit specific issues to arbitration. The courts accomplish this by looking at the collective bargaining agreement's language.

Collective bargaining agreements are negotiated between employers and unions, but individual employees may bring a suit to enforce them. A suit for breach of a collective bargaining agreement arising under the National Labor Relations Act (NLRA) can be maintained in state as well as federal court. A state court, however, is required to apply federal law, and federal law requires that collectively bargained grievance and arbitration procedures be exhausted before a breach of contract claim is addressed judicially. After exhaustion of arbitral remedies, federal law requires a court hearing on a breach of contract claim to give virtually preclusive effect to the arbitration award.

The individual employee can generally not obtain a judicial adjudication of a breach of contract claim based on a collective bargaining agreement that contains a grievance arbitration clause unless a breach of the union's fair representation duly can be alleged. Under these circumstances, it is permissible for a court to hear and to determine the breach of contract claim where the union has breached its fair representation duty. [See *Vaca v. Sipes*, 386 U.S. 171 (1967).]

Assuming there has been a breach of the fair representation duty, the court has jurisdiction to hear the breach of contract claim, either before or after arbitration. This is because it would be needless to require the employee to exhaust arbitral remedies when the union is not willing to be the employee's advocate. Similarly, it would be unfair to require the employee to be bound by an arbitration award tainted by a union's misconduct.

A union is not required to pursue every grievance to arbitration. It may refuse to process a grievance or handle it in a particular manner for various reasons, but it may not do so without reason, merely at the whim of someone exercising union authority. It may refuse to process the grievance of an uncooperative employee who steadfastly neglects, fails, or refuses to provide either the union or the employer information material to a grievance. It may not refuse to process a grievance because of lack of union membership by the employee. The union is not required to investigate thoroughly and exhaustively the merits of a grievance when its initial investigation shows sufficient justification for the employer's actions. A union may withdraw or refuse to arbitrate a grievance after the grievant rejects a negotiated settlement without breaching a fair representation duty. It need not process an employee's grievance if the chances for success in arbitration are minimal. A union is only obligated to carry a meritorious grievance to the point at which further action would be fruitless. The financial impact of the arbitration cost on the union's treasury may also be considered, although there is some doubt whether a decision not to arbitrate based solely on economic considerations would not constitute a duty breach.

The fair representation duty extends beyond the collective bargaining agreement's negotiation and the handling of grievances. It has been found that the union's administration of an exclusive hiring hall, including dispatching job applicants in violation of the agreement and threatening acts of violence against those who protested, was arbitrary and capricious, and, therefore, a breach of the duty. [See *Int'l Ass'n of Ironwkrs. Local 433 (Assoc. Gen. Cont.)*, 228 N.L.R.B. 1420 (1977).] However, a union's good-faith refusal to file an unfair labor practice for a terminated employee, after it unsuccessfully arbitrated his claim, did not violate the duty. [See *Lewis v. Greyhound Lines-East*, 555 F.2d 1053 (D.C. Cir. 1977), *cert. denied*, 434 U.S. 997 (1977).] As a general rule, mere errors in union judgment are insufficient to support a claim for breach of the duty, [See *Russom v. Sears, Roebuck and Co.*, 558 F.2d 439 (8th Cir. 1977), *cert. denied*, 434 U.S. 955 (1977).] and a union's good-faith representation at an arbitration hearing moots any earlier alleged unfair representation in the grievance procedure. [See *Crenshaw v. Allied Chemical Corp.*, 387 F. Supp. 504 (E.D. Va. 1975).]

It would be anomalous to suggest that the rationale for the fair representation duty is inappropriate for the public sector. [See *Phoenixville Area School Dist.*, 8 P.P.E.R. 351 (Pa. LRB 1971).] Public sector jurisdictions have applied the fair representation duty to their collective bargaining relationships and have characterized it as involving:

1. A broad discretion in negotiating collective bargaining agreements;
2. Informing employees of their contractual right of appeal from an employer's decision;
3. Representing nonunion members of the grievance arbitration procedure; and
4. Not charging nonunion members for processing or arbitrating grievances.

Nevertheless, a union is not required to:

1. Provide assistance in matters not covered by the collective bargaining agreement;
2. Process a grievance if not requested; or
3. Arbitrate when an award exists precluding the claim.

The area in which a union is most likely to breach its fair representation duty is in refusing to process or arbitrate an individual employee's grievance. In refusing to process or arbitrate a grievance, a union must utilize various safeguards to ensure fair representation. To ensure fair representation, a union should:

1. Investigate the grievance before making a decision regarding its merits;
2. Consult with their attorney for a review of the record and evidence; and
3. Review the decision not to pursue a grievance before an internal union staff committee.

It should be noted, however, that any one of the above precautions may not be sufficient to satisfy the union's duty. A combination may be necessary depending upon the facts of the particular case. The public sector generally applies the substantive content of the fair representation duty developed in the private sector. A public sector union is obliged to represent employees in a manner that is not arbitrary, unreasonable, discriminatory, or lacking good faith. [See *McCluskey v. Commonwealth, Dept. of Transp.*, 37 Pa. Commw. 598, 391 A.2d 45 (1978).]

Index

Acquired Immune Deficiency
   Syndrome (AIDS), *see* Human
   Immunodeficiency Virus (HIV)
Advertisements, 29-30
Alcohol Abuse, 92-106
Applications, 30-34
Arrest Records, 42-43
At-Will Employment, 2-5

Bankruptcy-Debtors, 174-175
Basic Associations, 172-174
Blood Testing, 59

Camera Surveillance, 137
Collective Bargaining Agreements,
   213-217
Conflicts of Interest, 182-184
Contract Violations, 203-217
   Collective Bargaining Agree-
      ments, 213-217
   Employment Contracts, 204-206
   Employment Handbooks, 210-213
   Employment Policies, 210-213
   Restrictive Covenants, 206-210

Data Verification, 40-53
   Arrest Records, 42-43
   Credit Checks, 40-42
   Criminal Convictions, 44-47

[Data Verification]
   Fingerprinting, 47-48
   Immigration Requirements,
      49-50
   Photographs, 48-49
   References, 51-53
Debtors/Bankruptcy, 174-175
Defamation, 193-198
Dress Codes, 143-145
Drug Abuse, 92-106

Electronic Surveillance, 137-138
Employee Assistance Programs,
   91-92
Employee Manipulation, 136-137
Employment Contracts, 204-206
Employment Handbooks, 210-213
Employment Information, 16-21
   Access, 19-20
   Collection, 16-18, 121-139
   Disclosure, 20-21
   Internal Use, 18-19
   Maintenance, 18-19
Employment Policies, 210-213
Employment Privacy, 5-7
Employment Records, 73-84
   Employment, 73-79
   Medical, 79-84
False Imprisonment, 198-199

Fingerprinting, 47-48
Fraudulent Misrepresentation, 201-202

Genetic Screening, 56-59
Grooming Codes, 143-145

Handbooks, 210-213
Handwriting Analysis, 70
Health Complaints, 86-87
Hiring, 27-72
Honesty Testing, 67-70
Human Immunodeficiency Virus (HIV), 106-117

Identification Tags, 161
Immigration, 49-50
Information Collection, 16-18, 121-139
  Access, 19-20
  Collection, 16-18, 121-139
  Disclosure, 20-21
  Internal Use, 18-19
  Maintenance, 18-19
Intentional Infliction of Emotional Distress, 199-200
Intentional Interference with Contractual Relations, 202
Interviews, 34-40
Invasion of Privacy, 192-193

Judicial Responses, 14-15
Jury Duty, 141-142

Language Requirements, 164
Legislative Action, 12-14
Lifestyles, 21-22, 176-179
Literature Solicitation and Distribution, 138-139
Litigation Prevention, 22-26
Loyalty, 179-182

Medical Concerns, 85-119
Medical Records, 79-84
Medical Screening, 54-56

Monitoring, 128-132

Name Changes, 161
Negligent Hiring, 71-72
Negligent Maintenance or Disclosure of Employment Records, 200-201
Nepotism, 150-151

Off-Duty Misconduct, 184-188
  Criminal Misconduct, 186-188
  Non-Criminal Misconduct, 184-186

Performance Evaluations, 157-161
Personal Associations, 172-176
  Bankruptcy/Debtors, 174-175
  Basic Associations, 172-174
  Union Associations, 175-176
Personal Right Violations, *see* Torts
Photographs, 48-49
Physical Examinations, 85-86
Policies, 210-213
Polygraph Examinations, 64-67
Privacy, 5-7
Privacy Misconduct, 162-164
Public Policy, 202-203

Records, 73-84
  Employment, 73-79
  Medical, 79-84
Reference Checks, 51-53
Religious Accommodation, 161-162
Residency, 188-190
Restrictive Covenants, 206-210

Safety Complaints, 86-87
Searches, 121-128
Sexual Harassment, 164-167
Skill Testing, 59-64
Smoking, 88-90
Spousal Policies, 145-150
Sterilization, 118-119
Surveillance, 132-138
  Camera, 137
  Electronic, 137-138

[Surveillance]
  Employee Manipulation, 136-137
  Union Meeting, 133-134
  Workplace, 134-136

Testing, 54-70, 92-117
  Alcohol, 92-106
  Blood, 59
  Drug, 92-106
  Fingerprinting, 47-48
  Genetic, 56-59
  Honesty, 67-70
  Human Immunodeficiency Virus
    (HIV), 106-117
  Medical, 54-56
  Physical, 85-86
  Polygraph, 64-67
  Skill, 59-64
Third Party Representation, 152-157
Torts, 192-203
  Defamation, 193-198
  False Imprisonment, 198-199

[Torts]
  Fraudulent Misrepresentation,
    201-202
  Intentional Infliction of Emotional
    Distress, 199-200
  Intentional Interference with
    Contractual Relations, 202
  Invasion of Privacy, 192-193
  Negligent Maintenance or Disclosure of Employment Records,
    200-201
  Public Policy, 202-203

Union Associations, 175-176
Union Meeting Surveillance,
  133-134

Video Display Terminals, 167-169
Voting Time, 142

Whistleblowing, 143
Witness Duty, 141-142
Workplace Surveillance, 134-136

About the Author

KURT H. DECKER is a partner in the employment law group with the law firm of Stevens & Lee in Allentown, Harrisburg, Lancaster, Reading, and Valley Forge, Pennsylvania. He received a B.A. degree from Thiel College, an M.P.A. from Pennsylvania State University, his J.D. from the School of Law at Vanderbilt University, and an LL.M. in labor from the School of Law at Temple University,. He serves as an adjunct professor with the Graduate School of Industrial Relations at Saint Francis College in Loretto, Pennsylvania. Mr. Decker is the author of over 70 books and articles on employment law, including the following books published by John Wiley & Sons: *Employee Privacy Law and Practice* (1987), *Employee Privacy Forms and Procedures* (1988), *A Manager's Guide to Employee Privacy Law, Procedures, and Policies* (1989), *Drafting and Revising Employment Contracts* (1991), and *Drafting and Revising Employment Handbooks* (1991). He is co-editor of the *Journal of Individual Employment Rights* (Baywood Publishing Co., Inc.) and also serves on the editorial board for the *Journal of Collective Negotiations in the Public Sector* (Baywood Publishing Co., Inc.) Mr. Decker is a member of the American and Pennsylvania Bar Associations and their respective labor and employment law sections.